Living displacement

Manchester University Press

New Ethnographies

Series editor
Alexander Thomas T. Smith

Already published

Living displacement

The loss and making of place in Colombia

Mateja Celestina

Manchester University Press

Published by Manchester University Press
Altrincham Street, Manchester M1 7JA
www.manchesteruniversitypress.co.uk

British Library Cataloguing-in-Publication Data
A catalogue record for this book is available from the British Library

ISBN 978 1 5261 0873 9 hardback

First published 2018

Typeset by Out of House Publishing
Printed in Great Britain
by CPI Group (UK) Ltd, Croydon, CR0 4YY

To all those who are looking for their place in the world.

Contents

Figures

All images belong to the author, except for Figure 2, which is drawn by the participant and co-owned with the author.

Preface and acknowledgements

In 2011 I attended a two-day conference on 'displacement and reconciliation'. It was not one of the big alienating conferences covering an array of themes and topics. On the contrary, everyone in the room, presenters and audience, was there because they work on or have interest in the two themes. During the engaging discussions one question came up again and again: What do we mean by 'reconciliation'? It is a fair question to pose considering that reconciliation has no unitary form, that it can never be total or include everyone, and yet it is so frequently offered as an indisputable response to post-conflict processes. The query was well received among the audience, inviting a great deal of reflection. Nevertheless, I was puzzled that while the meaning of reconciliation managed to generate a reflective and critical discussion, no similar question was posed in relation to displacement – What do we mean by 'displacement'? The presenters used the expression uncritically, as if displacement were an unambiguous event, lacking the complexity of reconciliation, a unitary experience affecting millions of people in similar kinds of ways. But what would that experience be?

I wrote this book in response to the lack of critical engagements. What displacement is for those who have lived through it was the question underlying my research. With it, my aim was to put individuals in the focus, to better understand the nuances and the complexities of the phenomenon.

My sincere gratitude to all those who shared their stories with me, who invited me into their homes and allowed me to learn about their lives. Ten months might not sound much compared to a lifetime, yet it was enough that some lasting relationships and memories were formed. In Colombia, I am also very grateful to José Luis Plaza, who was my contact person when I was in the field, and who rigorously checked I was safe; to Myriam Mendez who helped me organise my fieldwork; to Flor Edilma Osorio for our conversations; to CIASE, a Colombian NGO, which provided me with a letter of institutional support; and to all those, but especially to Alberto Maldonado, who helped me organise interviews in governmental institutions which were sometimes difficult to access.

I was fortunate to receive a very engaged anonymous reviewer for Manchester University Press. Their close and critical reading of the manuscript and subsequent suggestions greatly improved the book. Any weaknesses that might have remained are of course my responsibility. I also owe thanks to the editors at Manchester University Press, for their support from the very beginning.

A special thank you to Peter Gatrell for his inspiration, numerous conversations, for sharing his knowledge, and for reading and commenting on the draft of the introduction and conclusions. I would also like to thank Jenny Peterson for her encouragement and support, and to Sarah Jenkins for reading and commenting on an early draft of Chapter 8.

I am grateful to the Centre for Trust, Peace and Social Relations at Coventry University for allowing me the space to write this book, to my colleagues, and members of the research group Migration, Displacement and Belonging for commenting on the book proposal and for their encouragement. I would also like to thank former colleagues at Humanitarian and Conflict Response Institute at the University of Manchester, where this research started.

Special thanks to my friends Saša, Fabi, Jenny, Aleks, Rubina, Sahla, aunt Sharon, Melissa, Fernanda, Alice, Birte, Gosia, Jasmin, Obi, Julija, Eva, Tjaša, Peter, Danijela, Aljoša, Nataša, Katja, Barbara, Polona, Andreja, Urška, Darja, Mateja, Veronika, Brigita, Franci and community in Sopota who have accompanied and supported me in different ways during different stages of the process.

Parts of Chapter 2 are derived in part from an article Between Trust and Distrust in Research with Participants in Conflict Context, published in the *International Journal of Social Research Methodology*, 2018 © Taylor and Francis, available online: https://www.tandfonline.com/doi/full/10.1080/13645579.2018.1 427603.

Chapter 3 has heavily drawn upon material from within: Celestina, M., 'Displacement' before Displacement: Time, Place and the Case of Rural Urabá. *Journal of Latin American Studies*, 48(2): 367–90 © Cambridge University Press 2015, reproduced with permission. Mario Martínez prepared the map of Colombia. Rob Lucas anonymised the map drawn by one of the participants, which the designers at Coventry University later turned into a black-and-white version.

Finally, my heartfelt thank you to my husband Mario Martínez, for being at my side, for always finding the right words of encouragement, for his love and support reaching beyond the writing of this book. I also have an enormous gratitude which surpasses any words to my parents Marica and Miljan Celestina, my sister Andreja and my niece Valentina for their unconditional love, support, and for always being there for me.

Abbreviations

AUC	*Autodefensas Unidas de Colombia*, United Self-Defence Forces of Colombia
CIREFCA	International Conference on Central American Refugees
CNRR	*Comisión Nacional de Reparación y Reconciliación*, National Commission for Reparations and Reconciliation
CODHES	*Consultoría para los Derechos Humanos y el Desplazamiento*, Consultancy for Human Rights and Displacement
CONPES	*Consejo Nacional de Política Económica y Social*, National Council for Economic and Social Policy
CPDIA	*Consulta Permanente sobre Desplazamiento Interno en América*, Permanent Consultation on Internal Displacement in the Americas
DAS	*Departamento Administrativo de Seguridad*, Colombian former Administrative Department of Security
ELN	*Ejército de Liberación Nacional*, National Liberation Army
EPL	*Ejército Popular de Liberación*, Popular Liberation Army
FARC	*Las Fuerzas Armadas Revolucionarias de Colombia*, The Revolutionary Armed Forces of Colombia
IASC	Inter-Agency Standing Committee
ICBF	*Instituto Colombiano de Bienestar Familiar*, Colombian Family Welfare Institute
ICRC	International Committee of the Red Cross
IDMC	Internal Displacement Monitoring Centre
IDP	Internally displaced person
Incoder	*Instituto Colombiano de Desarrollo Rural*, Colombian Institute for Rural Development
Incora	*Instituto Colombiano de la Reforma Agraria*, Colombian Institute for Agrarian Reform
NGO	non-governmental organisation
SENA	*Servicio Nacional de Aprendizaje*, National Service of Learning

Sisben	*Sistema de Selección de Beneficiarios de Programas Sociales*, System for Selecting Beneficiaries of Social Programmes
UNHCR	United Nations High Commissioner for Refugees
UP	*Unión Patriótica*, Patriotic Union
WOLA	Washington Office on Latin America

Glossary

Acción de tutela	a mechanism for the protection of fundamental rights of those who live in Colombia
Acción Social	Colombian Presidential Office for Social Affairs
aguapanela	water sweetened with *panela*, a type of non-refined sweetener, a common beverage among countryside folks
albergue	a shelter
arepas	flatbread made of ground maize
bananera	a banana plantation
bicho raro	someone who is weird, bizarre
cafeteros	coffee growers
caleta	a hiding place
campesino	a peasant
casa de familia	family home, women of disadvantaged backgrounds work in other people's homes as housekeepers
chismes	gossip
Comandos Populares	popular commandos, predecessors of the paramilitaries
compañeros	colleagues
costeños	inhabitants of the coast
cristianos	members of the Evangelical Church
Cruz Roja	Red Cross
cucarrón	a beetle
culpable	guilty
de arriba	from the top
declarantes	people declaring displacement
Desarrollo Social	Governmental Social Development Office
desplazados	internally displaced persons
duro	tough
Familias en Acción	a government welfare programme concerning health, education and nutrition
fiestero	party-like
finca	farm

Frente Popular	Popular Front
gamonales	caciques
gente	people
grupos al margen de la ley	irregular groups
guerrilleros	guerrilla members
indios	the indigenous
infiltrado	a spy/infiltrator
invierno	periods of heavy rain
jornal	a day's work, usually undertaken on someone else's farm
jornalero	a day labourer
la comunidad	a community
ley del silencio	rule of silence
limosneros	beggars
limpieza	cleansing
limpieza social	social cleansing
llanos	extensive plains
magnicidio	an assassination of important figures
mercadito	basic food stuff in diminutive
mercado	grocery
monte	uncultivated land covered with trees, shrubs, or grass; backlands
muchacho	a young man
negocio	business
obrero	a worker
orden público	law and order
panela	a type of sweetener, a brown sugarloaf
Partido Comunista	Communist Party
plaga	plague, infestation
pueblo	a town
quemarse	get burnt – an expression used in the context of losing an election
químicos	chemicals
ranchito	a house made of wood planks
raspachín	a person who harvests coca leaves
salir adelante	to get ahead
sancocho	a type of a stew
servil	a bootlicker
sicario	a hitman
subversivo	subversive
tenaz	difficult
tienda	a local shop
tierra	land
tierra caliente	hot land, referring to lands in hot climates
tierra fría	cold land, referring to lands in cold climates
urabeños	the inhabitants of Urabá

Series editor's foreword

When the *New Ethnographies* series was launched in 2011, its aim was to publish the best new ethnographic monographs that promoted interdisciplinary debate and methodological innovation in the qualitative social sciences. Manchester University Press was the logical home for such a series, given the historical role it played in securing the ethnographic legacy of the famous 'Manchester School' of anthropological and interdisciplinary ethnographic research, pioneered by Max Gluckman in the years following the Second World War.

New Ethnographies has now established an enviable critical and commercial reputation. We have published titles on a wide variety of ethnographic subjects, including English football fans, Scottish Conservatives, Chagos islanders, international seafarers, African migrants in Ireland, post-civil war Sri Lanka, Iraqi women in Denmark and the British in rural France, among others. Our list of forthcoming titles, which continues to grow, reflects some of the best scholarship based on fresh ethnographic research carried out all around the world. Our authors are both established and emerging scholars, including some of the most exciting and innovative up-and-coming ethnographers of the next generation. *New Ethnographies* continues to provide a platform for social scientists and others engaging with ethnographic methods in new and imaginative ways. We also publish the work of those grappling with the 'new' ethnographic objects to which globalisation, geopolitical instability, transnational migration and the growth of neoliberal markets have given rise in the twenty-first century. We will continue to promote interdisciplinary debate about ethnographic methods as the series grows. Most importantly, we will continue to champion ethnography as a valuable tool for apprehending a world in flux.

Alexander Thomas T. Smith
Department of Sociology, University of Warwick

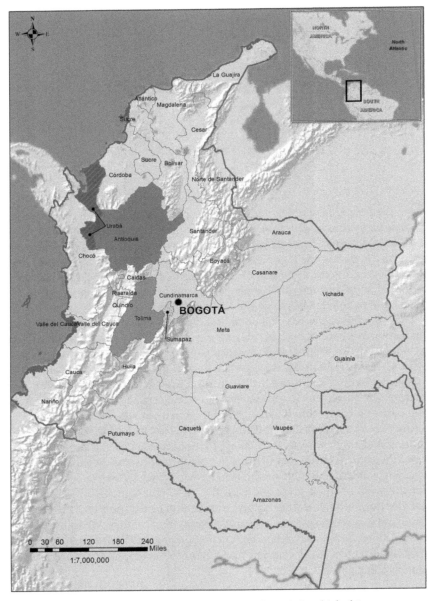

Map 1 Political map of Colombia. The map displays Colombia's thirty-two departments. The highlighted departments are the main focus of discussion. The department of Tolima and sub-region Urabá (department of Antioquia) are the areas of origin of the great majority of IDPs interviewed in this research. The Sumapaz province (department of Cundinamarca) is the area where the interviewed IDPs have resettled.

1

Introduction: reconceptualising displacement

...no one lives in the world in general. (Geertz 1996: 262)

At the end of 2016, Colombia counted more than seven million people displaced due to violence and conflict, a number which places it at the very top of the global statistics. The recurrent nature of the phenomenon, which has shaped the country's demographics, makes displacement seem a natural occurrence. A somewhat contradictory process is going on. The greater the number of the displaced, the more desensitised Colombian society seems to be towards displacement. As an employee of the International Committee of the Red Cross (ICRC) commented, the displaced asking for money at the traffic lights have become part of the common landscape. They simply are. They have become a fact. Contrary to logic, the high numbers of the displaced have contributed to their invisibility.

But who are these people? How do they experience displacement? What is displacement? What does it mean to be displaced? What does it mean to them and to millions of other internally displaced persons (IDPs) around the globe? The number of forced migrants, particularly IDPs, is on the rise. If the media and the politicians are serving us with images of numerous refugees attempting to reach western countries on dingy boats fighting off the winter currents, hiding in and under trucks, travelling on top of trains or walking hundreds of miles along rail tracks, battling with barbed wired fences or passing through environments as hostile as the desert, the number of those who stay within the borders of their own countries, who remain hidden from cameras' views, but whose plight is no less severe, is disproportionately larger. The Internal Displacement Monitoring Centre (IDMC 2017) places the number of internally displaced due to violence and conflict above forty million at the end of 2016. The prospects are so bleak that Elisabeth Colson (2003) concludes that rather than attempting to affect policymaking, scholarly research into internal displacement is done more realistically in order to inform ourselves what we are to expect if displacement affects us. Keith Basso (1996a) laments that in the age of uprooted populations holding on to places will become a privilege and a gift. And Arturo Escobar (2008) with world-weariness concludes that today's resettlement schemes and camps really are just pilot projects for the future. Displacement is indisputably a pressing issue that will continue to affect millions around the globe. It is also an issue that warrants greater and more nuanced scholarly attention.

There is a gap between displacement-producing and displacement-preventing mechanisms which is increasing and untenable (Escobar 2008). Knowing people's plight might be insufficient to convince armed actors to stop waging power over their territories, to deter the forces of modernity which are generating displacement, to encourage criminal groups to give up their activities affecting lives of so many people, or indeed to persuade respective governments to curb such processes since they themselves often have a stake in them. Nevertheless, even if we are unable to stop displacement, an engagement with the phenomenon and those who are going through the process is crucial. After all, only a better understanding of the process might help restrain displacement and address the often poor policy responses. And only a better understanding of people's experiences and attention paid to individual stories can help give back people the humanity they have lost through being grouped together and categorised as IDPs.

This book is an attempt to reveal the complexities of displacement processes. As Doña Flor and Martina, two of the research participants, pointed out, it is difficult to fully grasp the process if you have not lived through it yourself. Even if you do, displacement is so individualised that the meanings given to it differ. No two experiences are the same. The displaced might share certain similarities and aspects with others, but very personal circumstances such as one's social role, the point in one's life when displacement occurred, or one's biography generally speaking make displacement a highly personalised experience. Explaining displacement might therefore seem an impossible task for the scholar.

Nevertheless, without undermining this diversity, there is a way to discuss the long nights, the fear, to interpret the loss, the hope, the anger, the disillusionment, the difficulties with forming attachment to a new place, the negotiation of relationships among the displaced and their 'hosts', grappling with the new identity, agency and the seeming impossibility to leave the past behind. It is possible to think of a general framework which allows for differences, contextualises displacement and which helps bring people's experiences closer to our understanding. I propose to do so through conceptualising displacement as a process of loss and subsequent making of place. Displacement is not only about loss, trauma and struggle, but also about agency, getting to terms with the situation and an attempt to move on in life. Both the loss and the making of place are its essential and indivisible components (Celestina 2016; Turton 2005). In this introduction I make a theoretical case for thinking about displacement through such an approach. But before doing that I introduce the country where I listened to people's stories of displacement – Colombia.

Conflict and displacement in Colombia

When I first travelled to Colombia in 2009, I was arriving in an unknown territory. Having read widely about conflict, violence, displacement, disappearances, recruitment of minors, sexual abuses and human rights abuses in general, I was surprised that at the Bogotá airport, apart from greater than usual presence of armed officers, conflict seemed as something belonging to a different place. The two months I spent in the country at the time left an impression that the country, and Bogotá itself for that matter, are living a number of different realities. While some regions are involved in fully fledged conflict, others are enjoying relative peace. While some Colombians are struggling to survive and make a living, others are leading luxurious lives. While some are attempting to heal the wounds of violence and conflict, for others these are a distant reality which they do not and wish not to engage with. These impressions only deepened during my ten-month stay in Colombia in 2011 and 2012, when I was gathering the narratives on which the material in this book is based. Between my first, second and third visit, the number of internally displaced steadily rose. A Colombian non-governmental organisation (NGO) CODHES, *La Consultoría para los Derechos Humanos y el Desplazamiento* (Consultancy for Human Rights and Displacement) recorded 286,389 new cases of displacement in 2009, 280,041 in 2010, 259,146 new cases in 2011 and 261,050 in 2012 (CODHES 2013).[1]

For over a century a number of diverse actors have been trying to realise their opposing interests, aiming to get control over Colombian territory and its people. A chapter in a book would not be sufficient to describe and analyse the twenty-five national civil wars and about sixty regional wars Colombia experienced since its independence from Spain in 1810 (Ruiz *et al.* 2006) or to cover the numerous regional particularities of the conflict since almost every region is a story to itself. Other scholars (see for instance Hylton 2006; Palacios 2006; Pearce 1990; Sánchez and Meertens 2001) have in detail covered major historical events which have shaped the country. Here, I only briefly discuss the reasons and the actors involved in displacement at the national level.

Displacement is not a new issue in Colombia. Conflict and violence have accompanied much of the country's history and have persistently affected civilian population. Displacement was present in the nineteenth-century civil wars, the War of a Thousand Days (1899–1903) and, in more recent history, the first major displacement took place during the period known as *La Violencia*, which started in 1948, with the assassination of Jorge Eliécer Gaitán, a Liberal party leader.[2] *La Violencia* is usually thought of as a clash between the Liberal and Conservative parties for political dominance. Nevertheless, socio-economic circumstances, including persistently unresolved land question, should not be ignored. Rather than categorising it as war, Palacios (2006: 138) describes *La Violencia* 'as some twenty years of crime and impunity facilitated by political sectarianism' (see Figure 1). One of the consequences was extensive displacement; estimates say that up to two million people were displaced (Roldán 2002).

Conflict and tensions did not end with *La Violencia*. Social inequalities and discontent gave birth to various guerrilla groups in 1960s.[3] The most important were the largest guerrilla group *Las Fuerzas Armadas Revolucionarias de Colombia* (The Revolutionary Armed Forces of Colombia); the FARC, which has recently undergone demobilisation under the administration of Juan Manuel Santos; *Ejército de Liberación Nacional* (National Liberation Army); the ELN, which is still

Figure 1 The view from the natural bridge close to Porvenir, where truckloads of corpses were allegedly thrown into the River Sumapaz during *La Violencia*.

active at the time of writing of this book but in process of peace negotiations; and *Ejército Popular de Liberación* (Popular Liberation Army), the EPL, which gained importance mainly in Urabá, and which demobilised in 1991. The guerrillas gained support among the peasantry, since small-scale peasants were under constant harassment from the big landowners who enjoyed military support. Nevertheless, some of that support has been lost since then, partly due to guerrillas' involvement in drug trade and in part since some, including some of the interviewees for this book, believe the guerrillas no longer follow the initial political principles.[4]

The fighting between the guerrillas and the military gained new dimensions when a new actor entered the stage – the paramilitaries. The paramilitaries were financed by landowners who wished to cleanse regions of guerrillas and their supporters. They joined under an umbrella organisation *Autodefensas Unidas de Colombia* (United Self-Defence Forces of Colombia), AUC.[5] The paramilitaries collaborated with the military and often did their 'dirty work'. They are accountable for some of the greatest atrocities committed in the country and they were also the armed actor that generated most of displacement. Among others they contributed to greater land concentration or 'counter-reform' (Machado 2004). They drove people off their lands and enabled drug traders to buy large plots of land.

AUC demobilised during Álvaro Uribe Vélez' administration (2002–10).[6] The demobilisation was unsuccessful and new neo-paramilitary groups have emerged. Their structure is unclear but a visible link to the drug trade exists. They operate like private armies and use the same practices as the demobilised AUC, but unlike the latter they do not unite. They have territorial disputes among themselves, form temporary alliances with criminal groups and the guerrillas for the purposes of the drug trade. Since the number of registered IDPs in 2008 (380,863) was almost as high as at the height of conflict in 2002, the increase in the number of the displaced was linked to the existence of these drug-related emergent groups (Meertens 2010: S152).

In recent years in particular, there has been a stronger link between official national development projects, conflict and population exodus. Power, road and rural infrastructure projects coincide with the areas where armed conflict is most prevalent. In these areas there has been evidence of (neo)paramilitary involvement in displacement. Displacement has been present especially in regions where development projects are designed around the mono-cultivation of the African palm, where the lands 'have to be "prepared" – emptied – for the entrance of capital-induced development' (Oslender 2007: 759), which might otherwise lead to local resistance.[7]

Displacement in Colombia has therefore been generated from more than one source. Like conflict and violence it has been shaping the population, and the cultural and political mosaic of the country. The same as with conflict, the pattern of uprooting differs from region to region. Perhaps unsurprisingly those most affected by displacement come from the disadvantaged parts of the country's society, where state protection is not a priority. These are *campesinos* (peasants), Afro-Colombians and the indigenous;[8] people who, as Daniel Pécaut (2001) so adequately puts it, have never fully enjoyed their citizenship rights and for whom displacement is not a simple circumstance but is almost always lived as a permanent social condition.

The great majority of the displaced are in urban centres. They usually stay on the fringes of the cities, where they mix with the urban poor population. Therefore, while the areas they move to lie within cities, they are at the same time outside the cities in social, economic and physical terms (Salazar *et al.* 2008). Most displaced people come from a rural background and are not accustomed to urban life. This increases their alienation as well as the residents' anxiety about the displaced's impact on the city. The displaced are not welcome because the poor hosts and local governments see them as a burden for the public utilities and limited job market (Jaramillo *et al.* 2004; Salazar *et al.* 2008), since they increase poverty belts in urban suburbs (Osorio Perez 2000) and since their presence drives up property prices (Vidal López *et al.* 2011). Due to such problems and higher numbers, urban IDPs have received more academic attention.

In this book, in contrast, I explore the rural context. Not paying attention to those in the rural areas risks maintaining *campesinos* in an inferior position compared to urban inhabitants. Keeping them at the periphery of interest and concern reflects the historical position of smallholders and arguably also the countryside in Colombia. Lack of studies into rural lives and attempts at resettlement gives a false impression that those resettled into the rural environment do not face challenges in adaptation in the same way as the displaced in urban settings; in short, a *campesino* is believed to be a *campesino* everywhere, a general feature of urban bias towards the peasantry. Furthermore, in the advent of the current land restitution process, exploration of place-making in the countryside is pertinent. Estimates say that 8.3 million hectares of land have been appropriated (Grupo de memoria histórica 2013: 76). A better understanding of place-making practices, be it at a new location or an old one, is crucial for a constructive approach that goes beyond the mere land allocation. Finally, the countryside and land issues have been at the core of the conflict. It thus makes sense to explore conflict and displacement from the countryside perspective.

I examine the trajectories of loss and making of place of displaced people who resettled in two small hamlets in Cundinamarca, in the locality of Sumapaz. Respecting people's anonymity and due to honest fear some expressed that they might still be followed, I changed my interviewees' names and named the two hamlets as Esperanza and Porvenir. Those who are trying to create a new home in Esperanza came from Urabá, whereas the displaced who are now in Porvenir came from different parts of the country, but predominately from neighbouring Tolima. Both hamlets are in relative proximity of Bogotá: Esperanza just over two hours and Porvenir around four hours by a combination of buses, *busetas* and walking. While the readers cannot find the two hamlets on the map, they can imagine Esperanza as a hamlet in *tierra fría* (cold land). The bus connection to the village leaves you at an altitude of around 2,200 metres, after which there is a good forty minute relatively steep descent towards the hamlet's scattered houses. It sometimes takes hours for the sun to reach and warm the soil of the *fincas* (farms) further up the slope. Porvenir, on the other hand, lies at an altitude of around 1,600 metres with a moderate climate warm enough for coffee cultivation, and an array of fruit trees including occasional banana and plantain trees.

Esperanza and Porvenir may appear hamlets just like any other; however, a closer look reveals a negotiation of place greater than in villages where there are no displaced people. It is where new relationships are not forged to the degree they could be, where some relationships have even been lost, and where everyone involved, the displaced and the non-displaced, claim the right to belong; a right which might exist on paper but does not always materialise. Below I examine the concept of place to give a meaning to these negotiations and to provide a lens through which we can better interpret people's displacement experiences.

Displacement and place

Displacement is often considered as a phenomenon with time boundaries. As Brigitte Sørensen (1997: 146) states, the main narrative 'demarcates displacement as a historically limited experience running from uprooting to integration'. The international Guiding Principles on Internal Displacement and respective national legislations speak of the displaced as people who have left their areas of origin and this act of leaving becomes the starting point of displacement. At the same time, return, resettlement and local integration are considered the so-called 'durable solutions' (IASC 2010) to displacement. As the word 'solutions' itself entails, the three allude to an end state, to termination. The limited timeframe reflects institutions' view and does not necessarily reflect people's experiences. Displacement is not just about movement of leaving and settling in a place. It is much more. Displacement is 'uniquely political' (Bakewell 2011: 17). It tears apart the social fabric. It destroys collective identities since it destroys symbolic and social worlds of individuals (Bello 2001). It dismantles social organisation, fragments communities, and it presents the loss of natural and man-made capital (Cernea 1997: 1575). It can also incite strong psychological responses. If we think of displacement as having these consequences, considering it as a historically limited experience becomes impossible.

At the same time, the sole focus on loss of relationships, capital, the self and other types of loss, can be misleading. It can unfairly present the displaced as lacking agency, skills or ability to recover. The displaced not only experience the pain of leaving their places of origin behind, of broken relationships and tarnished identities; they also attempt to form renewed belonging to new or old place(s). Despite challenges and uncertainties they plan and think of the future. The displaced are therefore victims and agents at the same time. They might lose social relationships but this does not prevent them from forming new ones. They might have lost capital, but they might also be able to recover it. They might have lost the sense of self, but they did not necessarily lose it permanently. One way of capturing and also contextualising the interplay between victimhood, loss, struggle, resistance, agency and (re)making of self is through analysing displacement and individuals' experiences through the prism of place.

In the past few decades the importance of place has been undermined. Research and discussions have emphasised globalisation, travel and diaspora, and stressed mobility as source of identity. However, the romanticisation of mobility is inappropriate in the context of those who have been forced to move. For some displaced people 'the ability to not move may appear as a luxury denied them' (Ballinger 2012: 391). It is also 'foolish' to expect forced migrants and other unprivileged populations to embrace a notion of 'dispersed belonging' (Stefansson 2004: 185). Steff Jansen rightly finds 'rootless fantasies … cruelly naive to those violently expelled from "their" places' (Jansen 2009: 44). Places indeed matter, especially for those who have been forced to move, who have lost their local attachments and who are looking for a new place to settle down to continue with their lives. Nevertheless, rather than assuming that being grounded means being fixed and that being mobile means being detached (Ahmed et al. 2003: 1), place attachments – an affective bond between an individual and a specific place, and detachments – need to be examined analytically.

To fully appreciate the importance of place and its suitability for the examination of displacement experiences it is necessary to understand what constitutes a place. The concept of place is attractive due to its seeming simplicity as it forms part of a basic vocabulary. Nevertheless, it is the frequency of use and familiarity of the term that obstructs a more developed comprehension of what place is (Cresswell 2004). Places are not territorialised units rather relationship between people and their territory. Tuan (1977) and Relph (1976) were among first prominent human geographers that stressed this relationship and who emphasised individual's emotional attachment to place. Places touch most intimate aspects of our lives, our sense of self, and our sense of being at ease (or not) with where we are. The appreciation of place is therefore a highly subjective manner. Nevertheless, this subjective recognition is under the influence of objective factors. The broader context impacts the manner in which we relate to places and how we experience them. Places are not simply inactive physical locations or 'inert containers. They are politicized, culturally relative, historically specific, local and multiple constructions' (Rodman 1992: 641). They are contested and struggled over.

One of the most all-encompassing frameworks for the understanding of place which captures both its objective and subjective features is that proposed by John Agnew (1987: 5–6). Agnew defines three aspects of place: locale, location and sense of place. Locale refers 'to the structured "microsociological" content of place'. It is the setting for social interaction where the everyday life unfolds. Location, is place as located in the geographical space, which also represents 'the impact of "macro-order" in a place'. This impact for instance, is seen through the influence that governmental policies have on uneven economic development, or segregation of social groups. Finally, there is the sense of place which denotes subjective emotions and affection to place. It manifests itself through place attachment (or lack of it), and sentiments of (non)belonging. Agnew's framework captures the very micro, personal level of place that is embedded in the broader political, social, historical and economic context. As I argue, displacement is a multifaceted process reaching all aspects of people's lives; as such it requires a complex and comprehensive analysis including both personal feelings as well as objective circumstances.

In this book I take Agnew's three aspects of place as the general framework of analysis. I consider how features of location such as the positioning of a place on the world map, the specific climate belt within which it lies, the availability of natural resources or soil fertility in the region, the place's geostrategic position, its situatedness on the periphery or in the centre of the country, the infrastructure and development afforded to the location, market forces, and the unresolved land question influence the locale, the setting for everyday interaction. Within these everyday settings I pay particular attention to physical and social landscapes. That is to people's engagements with the natural, built environment including land cultivation, and to relationships between the displaced and their 'hosts', and among the displaced. Besides the influence of the location and locale on people's sense of place, I explore people's cognitive landscapes, consisting of emotions and memorialised images people brought with them.

In addition to these features I also explore the consequences of categorisation of people as *desplazados* (Spanish for IDP). Rather than looking at the categorisation as replacing people's identities, I use Brubaker and Cooper's (2000) framework of external identification, internal identification or self-understanding and groupness to demonstrate how categorisation cuts across the three aspects of place. I look at how the external identification undertaken by the government affects location through segregation of social groups. This segregation, the external identification of people as *desplazados* undertaken by the receiving populations, as well as assumed groupness of the displaced, has repercussions for the social relations at the everyday settings.

Finally, all the enumerated factors combined with the displaced's self-understanding influence the sense of place and displacement. What becomes clear is that the three aspects of place cannot be considered in isolation, but are interconnected. As Agnew so compellingly states, 'local social worlds of place (locale) *cannot* be understood apart from the *objective* macro-order of location and the *subjective* territorial identity of sense of place. They are all related' (Agnew 1987: 28, emphases in the original).

Places are relational. It is their relationality that makes them dynamic. They present a 'throwntogetherness' (Massey 2005) of people, things, powers and interests which need to be negotiated. As Doreen Massey puts it, places get their specific characters 'out of a particular constellation of relations, articulated together at a particular locus' (Massey 1993: 66). They are not enclosed spaces but rather get their meanings through interaction. Places are constructed on relationships between places. The very local is what it is due to the influences of other places, including at the global level. Without 'fetishized insistence' on this kind of global relationality at the expense of 'in-place lived experiences' and recognition that places get their uniqueness also from the particularities they possess (Oslender 2016b: 34), relationality between at least two places cannot be ignored in the analysis of displacement.[9] These are the place of origin and the place where place-making endeavours are in process. These places are relational through continued contacts and relationships with those who stayed behind, through cultural and other practices that the displaced continue realising in the new place, and through the sole process of memory construction of life in the place of origin and its influence on current place-making efforts. The local place can be affected by the global in many ways but it still has its own idiosyncrasies. Places are also constructed out of relationships within places. They consist of social landscapes, arising from relations and interactions among people. Relationality is visible at an even smaller level – through (non)belonging sensed through significant others. How those close to us experience a place, shapes the place as we perceive it.

Place, when understood in its complex terms, is particularly fit for studying displacement. Like displacement, place means different things to different individuals. It draws attention to personal and communal experiences as well as examining the political context. It is an effective tool to study experiences of people who are relatively powerless (Cresswell 2004: 83). It allows us to portray those who are usually absent from analysis as 'fully present' (Feld and Basso 1996: 5). Besides, its suitability for the analysis of displacement arises through its temporal character. Places are processual and always in the making. As such, place can challenge the assumptions that displacement is a historically demarcated experience beginning with the flight of people and ending upon their resettlement, return or integration.

The processual nature of place is especially noticeable after physical relocation, when people settle in a new location and need time to learn to live in and with a place and to develop a sense of place. If place-making takes time, there might also be different temporalities when it comes to the loss of place. Not everyone necessarily leaves their areas of origin instantly. They might be confined to the place (Kelly 2009), resist occupation (Todd 2010) or simply persist hoping that things would eventually calm down. For these people, the loss of place is not necessarily abrupt; the unmaking of place can unwind gradually. Conflict and violence can lead to 'lifescape reconfiguration', to the changes made to place and people's practices; due to such reconfiguration people may be 'displaced in place' (Lubkemann 2008). That is, they may be displaced, without having actually migrated. Stephen Lubkemann makes an imperative case for considering those who stay trapped in conflict. Nevertheless the lifescape reconfiguration pertains not only to those who stay, but also affects those who persist in the area of origin for substantial time and only eventually move. Their displacement entails not only the unmaking of a known place but also consists of attempts at (re)making it at a new location. The sense of temporality of places therefore manages to capture these processes, while the previously mentioned relational character of places provides the ground for examining the link between them. As I argue in this book, to get a grasp of displacement we need to examine both the loss and making of place, as well as the relationship between the two processes. Such an approach challenges the perspective of thinking of displacement in statistics, as a number of people moving from location A to location B, brings to the fore personal narratives, and also stresses the political in displacement – a phenomenon that is too often considered in merely humanitarian terms.

Outline of the book

This introductory chapter challenged the often uncritical understanding of dis-placement. It proposed to think, analyse and conceptualise displacement through the lens of place, examining both the processes of loss and making of place. Through this lens I explore the terror, resistance, break-up of social relations, journeys, the struggle and the process of endowing places with meaning. Chapter 2 discusses the difficulties of traversing landscapes of (dis)trust when working with conflict-affected populations. Coming from the proposition that trust entails elements of vulnerability and risk (Hardin 1992; Mayer et al. 1995), the chapter identifies some of people's vulnerabilities. It demonstrates that trust is dynamic and that it can co-exist with distrust. The chapter additionally introduces some of the protagonists of the book with whom I negotiated trust.

Chapter 3 focuses on the process of loss of place. I ask the question when displacement starts in order to draw attention to people's lives before they physic-ally relocate. I examine displacement experiences of urabeños (the inhabitants of Urabá) since their persistence in the region despite widespread violence specific-ally marked their displacement.[10] I concentrate on paramilitary terror and violence which unravelled on the ground. The analysis of terror produced at the very local level is often overshadowed in state discourses (Oslender 2008). Yet it highlights the adverse conditions people caught in conflict experience, whether they relocate or not. The chapter shows how violence and terror changed the microsociological content of place through the impact they had on people's social, physical and cognitive landscapes. It demonstrates how the transformation of place brought upon by violence altered the sense of place and set off the displacement process before people actually migrated.

Chapter 4 reinforces the argument of processual nature of displacement. It looks at the route taken by the displaced travelled in order to point out that people's journeys form an essential element of their displacement. Journeys are coupled with insecurity of not knowing where to go, of fear of being caught, and they also provide the first setting for the transformation of family roles. The analysis of the journey is crucial because it provides an insight into how people managed to secure the land for resettlement. The latter is not a mirror of effective policy but rather reflects years of IDPs' struggle, sacrifice and persistence. The two hamlets, however, are not necessarily the final point of the journey. The chapter discusses how policy that is supposed to help the displaced keeps them in place but can also compel them out of their places. It can, in short, 'displace' them again.

Chapter 5 is one of the three chapters that examine the consequences of categorisation of people as *desplazados*. Categorisation is one of the macro-forces that most prominently shape people's places after physical relocation owing to the effect it has on people's social world. The chapter focuses on external categorisation undertaken by the government. It provides a short background on how the category *desplazado* came into existence and then looks at the bureaucratic, decontextualised approach to categorisation. It shows that becoming a *desplazado* is not necessarily a process mediated by conflict, but is largely directed by bureaucracy.

One of the influences on people's place-making is their self-understanding as *desplazados*, which is at the core of Chapter 6. Even though being labelled as a *desplazado/a* is 'a mark of the beast', a deeply negatively felt othering, a great number of the displaced persistently recourse to it more than a decade after physical relocation. The chapter examines why this is the case. I move away from the usual focus on instrumental use of the category to explore its non-instrumental, symbolic uses. The chapter argues that the symbolism behind self-categorisation and self-understanding alludes to its long-lasting use. The deeply individualised self-understanding confirms just how heterogeneous the displaced are.

The supposed groupness of the displaced is the focus of Chapter 7, which undermines the idealised notion of 'displaced communities' and challenges it in a number of ways. The chapter examines the measures the displaced take to differentiate themselves from other displaced. They create 'displacement hierarchies', which they base on the level of suffering, the degree of severity of their displacement, but also on a hierarchy of moral behaviour. The differences among the displaced affect their social interaction and social landscapes, while the loss of the community also leads to renewed sense of displacement.

Chapter 8 continues with its focus on social landscapes. The displaced were resettled to a place which had already been meaningful for other people; they thus need to negotiate their place with those who are already there. In Chapter 8 I examine the social interactions between the displaced and their non-displaced receiving population, some of whom are landless peasants. Years of sharing the same place have not erased social boundaries between people. The displaced's prioritised treatment in policy coupled with absence of visible destitution has contributed to deep divides between the two populations. Deepening this divide even further is also the receiving population's belief that the displaced have brought displacement upon themselves. The chapter looks at the driving force behind such beliefs and analyses how the thinking that the hosts are sharing space with potential liars, guerrillas and thieves affects place-making of everyone involved.

Even though the displaced may have land – the base to build on – this is insufficient for the sense of belonging. Besides having to negotiate their social landscapes, they also need to deal with the challenges of forming land attachment. This is what I discuss in Chapter 9. Physical nature of places has received little attention in studies of place attachment (Lewicka 2011). And yet, the material dependence, 'the potential of a particular setting to satisfy the needs and goals of an individual', is one of the main contributors to place-making (Cross 2015: 513; Raymond *et al.* 2010). Even though the displaced are all peasants, they have faced a number of challenges trying to tame the land. In this chapter I explore how the continuation or disruption of old cultivation practices shapes place attachment. The chapter also shows that whether the physical landscape is perceived as hospitable or hostile also depends on an individual's family role and the extent to which the land allows them to meet that role.

Chapter 10 deals with cognitive landscapes. It shows that while people left behind a physical place, the social and cognitive aspects of the old place live on. The memories – which result in two main emotions; nostalgia and fear – influence the present place-making endeavours. The chapter looks at how the dissatisfaction with the current state of affairs has given way to retrospect place-belonging. It argues that while nostalgia is not static or complete, and can even help people survive, it nevertheless stands in the way of greater appreciation of place of resettlement. Rather than decreasing with years, nostalgia can grow. Fear, on the other hand, has been decreasing. Through time, greater caution, lack of tranquillity, vigilance and restraint have replaced the initial strong reactions to sounds or suspicious sights. Nevertheless, the sustained uneasiness continues affecting people's interactions and sense of place. The chapter demonstrates that witnessing and living in a place endowed with violence leaves consequences for post-migration lives, linking past to present.

Since one of the early chapters addressed the question of when displacement starts, the concluding chapter questions the 'end' of displacement. In so doing it stresses the need to listen to the displaced, their views, concerns and wishes. The chapter also re-emphasises the necessity of a longer time frame when studying displacement.

Taken together, the chapters bring individuals' displacement experiences to the fore. I work from the premise that what displacement entails is insufficiently understood. This is particularly true in relation to temporality of the phenomenon. The focus is too often placed on either the life before physical relocation and even more so on the life after physical relocation. Such an approach breaks up the two time periods which are undoubtedly interlinked. Before setting off to the core of the book, it is worth mentioning two more things. The first is that while in the book I problematise categorisation, I nevertheless use the category IDP or *desplazado/a* in the book. On the one hand, in order to challenge it, it is impossible not to use it. On the other, it reflects the vocabulary the displaced and non-displaced villagers of Esperanza and Porvenir use. Second, I aim to present the displaced as ordinary human beings who happen to be displaced, with their strengths but also their flaws. Idealising them, presenting them as 'pure and inno-cent' would only add to the already distorted beliefs of who is a deserving and who a non-deserving victim. Therefore, while I recognise that the displaced are undoubtedly indisputable victims, I also treat them as people.

Notes

1 There is discrepancy in terms of numbers of the displaced recorded between CODHES and the government. The government statistics includes only the numbers of those whose displacement status has been confirmed, whereas CODHES has no such requirement. The two entities use different methodologies and have started recording the number of the displaced at distinct times. CODHES keeps a register of people from 1985 onwards, whereas the government from 2000 onwards. For a more detailed discussion on the two entities' 'war over numbers', please refer to Oslender (2016a).
2 Gaitán promised to unite subordinate groups in Colombia regardless of their class, race and their region of origin. He managed to gain a lot of popular support and was due to run for presidential elections in 1950.
3 Liberal guerrilla groups formed already during *La Violencia*. A US-sponsored counter-insurgency strategy known as *Plan Lazo* (plan lasso) was designed with the aim to iso-late the liberal guerrillas from their supporters. In 1964 *Plan Lazo* failed drastically when *Operación Marquetalia* (operation sovereignty) was launched (Hylton 2006: 56). In response to the bombing carried out in this mission, peasants from different inde-pendent republics formed mobile guerrilla groups. The guerrilla leaders organised them-selves into *Bolque Sur* (Southern block) in order to design a new agrarian programme. The FARC was born during their second conference.
4 The FARC first opposed the cultivation of coca but then gave in under pressure from the farmers, who could not find any other comparably lucrative crops (García de la Torre and Aramburo Siegert 2011). Despite the initial resistance, coca later became important for the operation of the FARC.
5 Paramilitary groups existed already during *La Violencia*. These were *chulavitas*, the police aligned with the Conservatives, and *pajaros* (birds). The aim of both groups was to oppose the liberal guerrillas of the time. The paramilitary groups' intervention formed part of the civic-military programme enshrined in law. These 'not-quite-official counter-insurgency forces' already then carried out dirty acts instead of the military (Palacios 2006: 190).
6 Uribe's administration passed *Ley de Justicia y Paz*, the Justice and Peace Law, which gave the paramilitaries near impunity. At the time that the law was passed, the parami-litaries controlled the Congress. According to two paramilitary leaders, Mancuso and José Vicente Castaño, this control amounted to 35 per cent of seats in the Congress (Hylton 2006: 114).

7   The African palm, which has an important role in the Colombian national development plan, was promoted as an alternative to coca cultivation under Plan Colombia.

8   There have long been no statistics that would consider people's ethnicity and currently different organisations cite different percentages. In these estimations, the share of Afro-Colombians displaced by violence varies between 10 and 37 per cent (Oslender 2016a).

9   There may be more such places of influence especially when people's journeys include stops where they spend a substantial amount of time. Additionally there is also the centre-periphery influence.

10 Due to security issues I did not travel to Urabá. Since I was unable to interview anyone who stayed behind, I decided to retract their perspectives through the lens of those who had moved.

2

Traversing the landscapes of (dis)trust

Juanita, my local gatekeeper in Porvenir, took me to Doña Flor's house in order to introduce me to her, so that I could explain my presence in the hamlet and invite her to participate in the research. I went through the usual ethics script about her rights, issues of anonymity and confidentiality and said I would be back in a couple of days to see what her decision was. Upon my return Doña Flor was in the kitchen, where she spent most of her days, preparing lunch for a handful of *jornaleros* (day labourers) working on her and her husband's well-kept *finca*, planted with hundreds of coffee bushes. I recited my ethics scrip again, as I habitually did when I asked for people's confirmation if they wished to take part. Doña Flor, who had already taken her decision, wiped her hands on her apron, her eyes narrowed slightly and perhaps without really expecting an answer, she asked: 'And how can I know you won't be telling others what we discuss?' A fair question. The only guarantee she had was my word. A word from someone she had barely met. What worked in my favour was that I was introduced to her by someone who she has a good relationship with. Nevertheless, in the given research context, any precaution on behalf of participants seems sensible and can be easily justified.

Conflict and post-conflict contexts are extremely challenging environments to undertake research in. On the one hand they present a potential risk to physical safety to participants and researchers; on the other, they are characterised by an atmosphere of suspicion, uncertainty and distrust. Conflict reaches the very micro-level of people's lives and greatly affects social fabric, whose reconstruction can take generations. The wariness of the atmosphere impacts all kinds of relationships including those between the researcher and participants. Participants in conflict and post-conflict environments are fearful, guarded and can deliberately distort information (Chakravarty 2012: 252). Carolyn Nordstrom even warns that '[e]veryone has a story, complete with vested interests, and all the stories collide into contentious assemblages of partial truths, political fictions, personal foibles, military propaganda, and cultural lore' (Nordstrom 1995: 139). Participants can also distrust the objectives behind the research.

No fieldwork process is perfect and without challenges but it is also not 'fatally flawed' (Magolda 2000: 210). My time in Porvenir and Esperanza was marked by a number of different challenges. Some were of emotional character. I felt powerlessness in the face of participants' situations. Even though I was clear about my lack of power, I felt and still feel a sense of guilt that I have moved on in life while the fate of my participants has not changed. Some of the stories I heard had an impact on me for which I had not been prepared. I also struggled because of my feeling of entrapment in local disparities, putting every effort into making sure I did not hurt anyone's feelings. Other challenges were ethical. What should I do when one of the participants beat up her son with a hosepipe? How do I distinguish 'sensitive' questions from 'non-sensitive' ones? What can or can I not write about? Can I write about unequal power relations and clientelistic behaviour among the displaced?[1] Yet other challenges were related to trust. Do people trust me? Are they telling me the 'whole' story? Are they telling the truth? And also, do I trust them?

There is a unanimous agreement among scholars that trust forms an essential aspect of research process, especially in research with conflict-affected and other marginalised populations (Bosk 2004; Hynes 2003; Lammers 2007). Yet my time in the two hamlets demonstrated that trust should not be treated as a binary, where trust has been either generated or not. Rather, trust is complex, dynamic; it exists at many levels and can co-exist with distrust. This chapter aims to give the reader the sense of circumstances under which I took data collection with particular reference to landscapes of (dis)trust. I first give some background about my access to the two hamlets and data collection process. I then examine some vulnerabilities of participants which made the generation of trust more challenging. After reflecting on my own distrust, I make a case for a dynamic, compartmentalised and non-linear understanding of trust. Finally, I introduce some of the protagonists with whom I was traversing the landscapes of (dis)trust.

My time in the two villages

The initial access to the two hamlets was made possible by Sonia, a psychologist and an NGO worker, who had been running 'gender workshops' for 'displaced' and 'vulnerable women' once a month for the previous three years. The 'vulnerable' were the local, non-displaced women in the two hamlets.[2] I explained to them what the purpose of my research was and offered to help them farm and teach their children English in exchange for information. To verify I was telling the truth and that I really was from the countryside as I claimed, Anita, a local asked me how maize is cultivated. I luckily passed the test and the women accepted my request to stay in the two villages and made arrangements as per my accommodation. In Esperanza they jointly decided I would be circulating different homes and spend a few days with each family, the displaced and non-displaced, and in Porvenir they decided I would stay in Don Eduardo and Doña María's house and visit the rest during the day. Such arrangements enabled me a close look at people's personal lives, but each also brought its challenges. In Esperanza I sometimes felt there was a sense of 'jealousy' or disappointment if I spent more days with a certain family, and on a couple of occasions I was probed about it. In Porvenir, in contrast, the fact that I stayed with Don Eduardo and Doña María gave an impression that my side in local disparities had been decided. In other words, my housing arrangements contributed to people's relational vulnerability, which I discuss below.

I carried out fieldwork in two parts – six months in 2011 and four additional months in 2012. My research participants were diverse. I worked both with the displaced and the non-displaced receiving populations with different regional, cultural, socio-economic and political backgrounds.[3] Apart from a few non-displaced who migrated to Esperanza and Porvenir after getting married, or moved there from Bogotá, the rest were long-term residents of the two hamlets. With one exception, the displaced in Esperanza were originally from Urabá, a sub-region of the department of Antioquia. In 2012 there was also a recently arrived family, who reached the hamlet from Bajo Cauca Antioqueño. In Porvenir the great majority of the displaced were originally from Tolima, both north and south of the department. There was also a family that fled Cauca, another from Valle, and one individual who came from Huila.

During my time in the two hamlets, as promised, I helped people cultivate land and was helping their children with English and, despite my limited knowledge, any other school subject they asked me to assist them with. Besides the wish to better understand people's lives and stories, the main reason for my active participation in people's day-to-day activities was to give something back to people for their hospitality, acceptance and information. At the same time, the decision was also a practical one. *Campesinos* do not have much time to spare – time, when we would talk, was one of the concerns women raised when I asked for permission to stay with them. Most of the conversations were thus carried out while we were picking blackberries, tree tomatoes and coffee. When we were pruning, planting and when we were plucking chicken; when we were preparing food, at the table, on our way to the shop, and before going to bed. These work-along interviews, while it was impossible to record them, were helpful in many ways.[4]

Farming helped me break the ice in the initial months of my stay in the two hamlets. Unaccustomed to working with a machete, especially not for hours at a time, I got blisters all over my hands. The 'local intelligence' worked faster than my movement and for a few weeks whenever I joined a new family to help them work, they would greet me and open the conversation laughingly asking me about my blisters. My farming anecdotes, including my complete lack of skill in milking cows, were also helpful in showing that even though I came from a European university, and I had greater educational background than my research participants, they possessed knowledge I did not. I was therefore not necessarily perceived as a person in a more powerful position since I was learning from them.

Due to their character, the conversations took place in people's natural environment. They helped me experience the place where the participants lived better as well as the tasks they normally perform. They also proved helpful for recruitment since I would meet other people in the field or on the road who would be interested in my presence. Ultimately, by assisting people with their everyday chores, I was able to generate rapport with some participants. I was regularly labelled as *juiciosa* (in Colombian context hard-working and responsible) and someone who showed she 'cares' by her efforts. In some cases my farming resulted in people's greater appreciation of my presence and helped with the generation of trust. Yet in others, this was not necessarily the case.

Trust and people's vulnerabilities

Trust entails elements of vulnerability and risk. It concerns the 'willingness of a party to be vulnerable to the actions of another party' (Mayer *et al.* 1995: 712). The research participants in both hamlets were vulnerable to different degrees and in a number of ways, which was reflected in their levels of trust. Their willingness to take the risk and make themselves vulnerable could at worst be fatal. Had they misplaced their trust, they might be in danger of retaliation from respective armed actors. They could be vulnerable to criminalisation by the state if their potential involvement in coca cultivation or potential support to the guerrilla groups, by choice or force, would become known. They were vulnerable emotionally. The research can bring back painful memories, some of which they perhaps prefer to forget. Additionally, research can unexpectedly touch upon a current sensitive issue.

Working with people affected by conflict there is a danger of 'conflict fetish' (Goodhand 2000: 15), an assumption that conflict is the only point of reference in their lives, whereas during and in the aftermath of conflict people continue facing some of the everyday problems that they might be facing in times of peace. Avoidance of questions related directly to displacement does not necessarily remove emotional vulnerability. Once the displaced have put their experiences 'into a framework of meaning' and have moved forward in life (Loizos 2002: 44), they may find issues that they are facing currently and which are not directly related to displacement, more 'sensitive'. Since everyone I spoke to left their homes at least seven and at most fifteen years before, it was not uncommon to see some women more affected and emotionally vulnerable when they were speaking about their teenage daughters' pregnancies, or their husband's unfaithfulness, rather than when they were recounting their experiences of displacement.

Finally, there is also relational vulnerability, which refers to different webs of relationships. So-called 'local communities' are not exempt from internal tensions and disparities, even less so in conflict and post-conflict environments.

When researchers enter the community they, at the same time, enter the community's 'political fabric' (Cohen 2000). I was working with people displaced by armed groups at the distinct side of the political spectrum and with the non-displaced who feel they compete with the displaced for government's attention. Grounds for tensions were plenty and real due to which my aiming at supposed 'neutrality' was often challenged and did not necessarily pay off.[5] The non-displaced were not accustomed of receiving scholarly attention, and greeted my interest in their lives. Nevertheless, since they also live in anything but favourable circumstances, but are largely ignored, I was asked twice up-front to state who I thought lived in worse conditions – themselves or the displaced. Some were expecting I would take sides. So did some displaced. Not in relation to their non-displaced neighbours but in connection to other displaced people.

Political disparities among the displaced were particularly felt in Porvenir, where it was publicly known that some families due to their distinct displacement background and political preferences did not get on. Whenever I left Doña María's house in the morning to visit those living further up the slope, like Linda and Carlos, Doña María disapprovingly asked me 'And this? Why?'. Upon my return she would ask me if and what they gave me to eat, and about the couple's working habits. At Linda and Carlos', in contrast, I needed to continuously emphasise that even though I was staying with Don Eduardo, who was a candidate for a town councillor at the local elections, I had no political preferences and even if I did, I was not able to vote. While everyone mentioned spoke to me and shared information, I would have probably generated greater trust and even richer narratives had I only spoken to one of the two families. At the same time, working with everyone enabled me a view into different sides of the story. It helped me realise the extent to which the disparities affected people's attempts at place-making, which was ultimately also what my research was about.

I managed to attain higher degrees of trust with those on the political left, in particular with some of the displaced *urabeños*. One of them was Martina, a woman in her late forties, who was an active member of *Partido Comunista* (Communist Party) and *Unión Patriótica* (Patriotic Union – UP – a left-wing political party which was born as a result of peace negotiations between the government and the FARC in 1985, and was supported by *Partido Comunista*). She said she could see that like her I 'had socialist ideals'. Knowing I was working with a diverse group of participants, I did not make my political sympathies known. However, I also did not downplay Martina's statement. Had I done so I might have risked causing distrust since Martina could see me as someone who is not being her true self. My relationship with her developed to the extent that she 'overexposed' herself. I stopped her on two occasions reminding her I was there as a researcher. She was telling me what could be politically very sensitive information which contained names of those who were persecuted due to their participation in the UP. As Liisa Malkki (1995) and Alan Feldman (1991) both rightly state, to demonstrate trustworthiness we need to show that there are things we do not want to know.

With Martina, her father Don Andrés and their party colleague Fabio, I managed to generate 'identification-based trust' based on empathy, understanding of one's stance and shared values (Lewicki and Bunker 1996). These individuals also became key in explaining both conflict and displacement in Urabá, as well as the existing tensions in social relations in Esperanza. At the same time, closer relationships with the enumerated participants and some members of their families inadvertently meant that I did not manage to generate the same degree of confidence and trust with some other villagers. As mentioned, the two hamlets are not inhabited by a homogenous group of people. On the contrary, the interests, beliefs and values are numerous and even conflicting. Claiming that everyone opened up would be downplaying these complexities. It would also give a lower profile to my presence in the two hamlets – researcher's presence can make people more vulnerable in their relations. If people are seen to trust the researcher with important information, this may result in mistrust from within the community. Particularly where some tensions already exist.

(Dis)trusting researcher

The participants were not the only ones who distrusted. So did I. I learnt to distrust or be cautious in conveying some of my political opinions, especially with people I did not know that well. I additionally found myself particularly cautious in my interviews with governmental representatives. There is no doubt that assistance to the displaced has improved through years. Nevertheless, I initially took a rather defensive posture when I visited the headquarters of *Acción Social*, the Colombian Presidential Office for Social Affairs, and Incoder, *Instituto Colombiano de Desarrollo Rural*, the Colombian Institute for Rural Development. The former used to be in charge of provision of assistance to the displaced under the previous legislation, and the latter manages the land programme under which the displaced included in this research got land for resettlement. The aptness of my posture was confirmed when I came in touch with some officials who had little empathy for the displaced's situation. Nevertheless, I was also pleasantly surprised at the self-criticism high-ranking officials in respective organisations conveyed. This instilled me with some hope and also helped me to decouple individuals from their respective organisations.

A level of distrust was also present in my conversations with some of the research participants. When I came across inconsistencies in stories, for instance the amount of land that one family lost, I put a greater question mark to some other information they had given. Since reputation and information we get about people can lead us 'to approach the relationship attuned to trust or to suspicion' (Lewicki 2006: 99) I additionally found myself less trustful towards those that a number of the interviewees, displaced and non-displaced, complained about. I suspected, probably rightfully so, there was more to their stories than what they had told me. Perhaps if I had probed them directly about some of the matters that were the subject of complaints, they would have defended themselves. But I raised no such questions not to break my promise of confidentiality. Had I posed the questions, they might be able to identify the person who made the comment, which could further exacerbate social relationships among the people.

The multiple layers and non-linearity of trust

I soon realised that rather than asking myself whether people trust me or not and whether I trust them or not, because the answer would never be a straightforward one, it is more appropriate to ask to what extent, in what dimension the trust exists and what it is influenced by. In many respects, trust in research environment shares similarities to trust in non-research contexts. If we reflect on everyday relationships we have with our friends, family members and colleagues, what becomes clear is that relationships are multi-layered. There might be a few people with whom we share everything, or almost everything, but more often than not, we reveal and in turn get to know only certain aspects of people's lives in both our personal and professional lives. Segmented relationships are the rule rather than an exception (Lewicki *et al.* 1998: 444).

Relationships that are born out of research are in many respects similar; we are likely to form a very tight-knit trust relationship with certain individuals, but the number of these tends to be small. The large majority will be people who might be comfortable speaking about certain aspects of their experiences but not others. They might be happy to narrate objective facts, which others may confirm, such as for instance who were the actors responsible for displacement. But they might not be so willing to share their opinions, parts of their stories or anything that they believe might present them in a less positive light. In other words, trust and distrust can co-exist.

Trust also does not necessarily grow with time. Frequent are references that the longer the time spent in the field, the more rapport and trust researchers are able to build (Mazurana *et al.* 2013; Miller 2004). Some of the participants' narratives indeed became more detailed and complex as time passed during my fieldwork. It was principally during the second visit to the field, when I returned to the two villages as I had promised, that I collected some of the richest data; be it about participants' displacement experiences, political engagements or their private lives. But such evolution of a trusting relationship was not the case with everyone, which puts the simple formula of more time equals more trust under question.

There are three elements implicit in a number of trust definitions (Lewicki 2006: 94): a person's trust of another depends on their predisposition to trust, the history of the relationship, and situational parameters. Situational parameters play an essential role in the trust generation process, especially in sensitive contexts. Alterations in political climate, for instance, can bring about a re-evaluation of one's trustworthiness (Mayer *et al.* 1995: 727). In politically sensitive contexts, being seen or associated with the 'wrong' person can inhibit progression of the trust relationship or take you a step back in what has already been achieved. As mentioned, it is possible that my closer relationship with certain individuals curtailed the levels of trust with others. Trust is dynamic, fluid and situational. Once it is gained it is not necessarily there to stay. Rather than trust per se, extended time in the field helps us acquire a certain amount of local knowledge which helps us develop a sense of what is credible (Fujii 2010: 240).

Therefore Dean and Whyte (1958: 38) emphasise that rather than asking ourselves 'How do I know if the informant is telling the truth' researchers should focus on what participants' statements reveal about their feelings and perceptions, and what they tell us about the actual environment. 'Partial truths' (Chakravarty 2012), 'shades of lies' (Fujii 2010) and silences (Poland and Pederson 1998) can reveal a great deal about the situation people live in, involving everything from personal sentiments, such as feelings of shame, to the impact of conflict and people's response to displacement and loss. Trust as well as distrust thus form part of any research context, and both need consideration.

Some of the protagonists of (dis)trust landscapes

As mentioned, I managed to establish different levels of trust and rapport with research participants. Here there are brief stories of some of them, whose narratives will be appearing throughout the book.

Martina

Martina is a strong woman in her late forties. She is a person of principles and someone who fearlessly stands up for what she believes in. She is a mother of five, one of whom, Alejandra, she adopted after her own mother disappeared. Martina has a distinguished loud laugh which tends to accompany stories she tells, even when these speak of disillusionments, challenges and incredulous things that she has been through. Such an attitude was not something she was necessarily born with. 'We had to learn how to laugh to be able to cope,' Martina replied when I asked how come that she, her husband Miguel, and her brother Alejandro laugh, when recounting sometimes horrific memories. Despite her occasional laughter, displacement has affected her to unimaginable proportions. Alejandra, her daughter, reflects: 'It's only now, the last couple of years that she is like this. That she is better. She was very embittered before. All she thought and spoke about was Urabá.'

Urabá was Martina's beloved *tierra* (land), her place of origin, where she was born and raised, where she was active in politics, promoting and nurturing leftist political causes, where she had her *finca* and where she was planning to grow old. 'I dreamt there. I was dreaming of having a big house. Big enough that each of my children would have a place to stay when they'd come and visit. Each with their own room ... I can never love a place again.'

Her love for Urabá was such that displacement affected her more than the death of her first husband, which she witnessed.

> I married young, when I was fifteen, and I widowed young, when I was twenty-one. After I gave birth to Camilo [her eldest son], my husband joined *faruchos* [an expression used for the guerrillas, the FARC]. He thought I'd be visiting him but because I didn't, I didn't want him to join, he dropped out. They offered him to be a *pistolero* (gunman, militia) to work for them from the outside. They once sent him to a *finca*. He was supposed to give orders only but because of how things played out, he had to enter the *finca* and people there recognised him. I knew they'd be after him. We moved. We went to live in his mother's hamlet. One morning he got up early because he had some medical exams for his work. He was a driver. He got home at about nine in the morning and went to his room to read – he loved reading. He asked me to bring him breakfast and then I went outside to wash clothes. I saw a man who was supposedly his friend but who was with *Comandos Populares* (popular commandos, predecessors of the paramilitaries). I went to my husband and he told me to let him in. The man asked him whether he'd lend him his gun because he had a job to do that day. My husband agreed. I called

him outside. As if I had foreseen everything I told him 'You'll be killed with your own gun.' He simply shrugged his shoulders. I don't know whether he was bored of his life or what. I don't know. He had a Colt 45 under his pillow and fifty bullets. He gave him a loaded gun and sixteen bullets. The man left. That evening my husband asked me if I wanted to go and bathe in a fountain. It was hot so I agreed. When we were there I saw four men approaching. I told him to look. He had our son in his arms, he put him down and sent him to me. One of the men came close and I saw he had a gun. They told me I was screaming like crazy. I don't remember … He shot him twice and I started running. The other three men came closer and shot him seventeen more times. […] I saw who killed my husband and I felt I was persecuted all the time. I left the village. Still my husband's death did not hit me as much as displacement.

This happened in 1986 and Martina went to Irra, a mining town in the department of Risaralda. She returned to Urabá after six months because she was pregnant with her second child. She never intended to leave for a long time and she does not consider these six months outside of Urabá as displacement. But little did she know she would go back to Irra ten years later, with greater fear, and with little prospects of return.

Back in Urabá she started working on *bananeras* (banana plantations) to make a living. She joined *Partido Comunista*, and started participating in workers' strikes trying to secure better working conditions, defending the workers from exploitative banana companies. She got married again, to Miguel, her current husband. In the presence of the guerrillas, the area was still relatively calm, and workers found some protection in the armed group. With the arrival of the paramilitaries, the atmosphere changed.

> Later on, towards 1990s paramilitary groups came. They called a public meeting and in the meeting they said that anyone who had been there for more than ten years needed to vacate the land. I said I wasn't going. I said: 'They can kill me and the land will remain in my children's hands.' At the time I thought it worked like that. That … I don't know. That they'd kill you and leave the rest in peace. The week after the meeting they killed five villagers in the manner only they know … if you know what I mean. To raise fear among us.

Political participation was becoming increasingly difficult, including the labour union movement.

> There was a meeting of the labour union which I never liked attending. It was held in Apartadó and they sent for me. I got there at around eleven. They told us to go to the coliseum but I didn't want to go. I left. Some people got killed and the military locked people in the coliseum and kept them there for two months. My cousin and her daughter were there. I took them milk once, but they wouldn't allow me to pass. That day the military thought they'd kill me on my way home but I took a different route.

After years of struggle, sleeping outside of the house, and defending the territory, Martina started planning her escape. 'I really got scared once they started killing my *compañeros* (colleagues) … One never gets used to seeing people killed. Especially if they are people one knows, one's friends […] I wanted to die when I had to leave but I fought. One needs to fight, look for new places.' She rented a truck and once again left for Irra this time with her children, her mother, her sister and her cousin and their respective children, believing she was only going for a few months until things calmed down. Contrary to her expectations, the situation in Urabá got worse and other family members joined them.

Life was difficult in Irra, economically speaking but also in terms of safety. 'In *Partido Comunista* we received training of survival. What to do if someone attacks you, how to read people to know if they are dangerous or not, how to sustain pain. This was a prevention strategy in case we got caught. This training helped me survive in Irra.' Martina and the rest left Irra and began looking for a new place. They eventually ended up in Esperanza, the village of resettlement, and have been there for over ten years. Martina, however, has never managed to settle.

> When we came here, I worked, worked … We came here and it was *duro* (tough). The coexistence with the people from the community and outside it. We started to work. I might be the woman who worked the most. But when each got what they have, it was more difficult to stay still [not to move]. Here they'd say: 'We'll get things for everyone,' but it wasn't so. It was for two or three families and this is what I find most depressing.

Martina and her family moved to Venezuela, save for Camilo, her eldest son and Alejandra, her adopted daughter, but then returned to Esperanza, in order not to lose the *finca* they managed to secure. She is trying to overcome the challenges she faces cultivating the barren land, and unfavourable social relations within and outside the displaced 'community', which no longer lives up to its name.

Don Andrés

Martina's leftist inclinations and the sense of social justice, which she shares with her brother Alejandro, can be largely attributed to their father Don Andrés. Don Andrés has always fought for the left-wing cause. Because of his political activism, which was not in line with the government's anti-communist doctrine, Don Andrés was under the government's radar. In 1979 he was sent to prison.

> I wasn't eating for ten days. I didn't drink. They made me walk in full sunshine. I was hallucinating. They wanted me to talk, but the only thing I'd say is give instructions to my wife or son on what needed to be done. The ninth day they wanted to send me to *monte* (uncultivated land covered with trees, shrubs or grass) but I couldn't walk. Beans they gave me. To feed me … They said I was a guerrilla commander. They said on the radio they caught the top commander. But those who knew me said '*Pobre campesino* (poor peasant), he has a family.' In the United States they said 'Yes, they got one [a guerrilla]!' And me? I was

tortured. I lost everything. Then, after being in prison for eighteen months they said 'Oh, no, it wasn't him,' but I lost everything. To make so many false accusations, all the things they did [to me], and me without any guilt. And then they come and tell me I was not guilty of anything after they had already finished with me. It made me destitute.

Imprisonment did not change his stance and stop him fighting for what he believed in. He was a local junta leader and a member of the *Unión Patriótica*. He was a well-respected man, who took pride in his defence of those with less power.

An owner of ten *bananeras* came to speak to me and soon after his arrival a poor person came. I said 'Excuse me, *doctor*, you do politics this way [he demonstrates a top-down approach], but here we do it this way [he again uses his arms, to demonstrate a ground-up approach].'[6] I attended to the poor man first. He came to look for advice, help, because he had no work. In the end I asked the rich guy to give him a job. The poor guy lives in Bogotá now and he still sends me greetings […] There was also a woman who was fired without any reason after having worked five or six years on a *bananera*. She went to complain to the labour union but they said there was nothing they could do. They had already sold themselves. I confronted the president [of the union]: 'Who are you protecting? The rich or the workers?' I managed to get three million pesos [approximately £770] compensation for the woman.

Don Andrés was respected to the degree that he would confront the guerrillas if he felt that was necessary. 'I would talk to them not to kill certain people. You can't achieve change by killing. You need to change those who are alive,' he explains his philosophy. Despite danger he offered a hiding place to the persecuted members of *Unión Patriótica* and continued his resistance to the changing landscape of Urabá. Don Andrés was first angry at his wife Doña Olivia and Martina when they left, since he believed they should have stayed and resisted. Two months later he followed them realising he was in danger. Like his daughter, Don Andrés has equally not adapted to the life in Esperanza. Leadership and political engagements are a matter of the past, old age has caught up with him and his economic situation cannot compare to the one he had in Urabá.

I lost my cattle, I had everything, my place there. Everything. To lose it like this. My yoke of oxen, my cattle, poultry, my big house. I had everything. I had a car … and now with *una ayudita* (help, assistance in diminutive), and *un mercadito* (basic foodstuffs in diminutive) which on top of it is … [does not finish the thought]. This puts me in a bad mood. Before I was buying good *mercado* (grocery). I was working. It was on my land.

Fabio

Urabá with its political atmosphere has greatly shaped the biography of a number of individuals including Fabio who came to Urabá from the neighbouring department of Cordoba. He was fourteen and was looking for work. Soon after his arrival he started with political participation which took a prominent role in his life. He was first youth in *Partido Comunista* and later one of the initial members of the *Unión Patriótica*, which surged with the support of the *Partido Comunista*. He spent three to four months in Cuba for political training and he was an active labour unionist for twenty years. He speaks of the unfavourable position of the left in Colombia but also stresses the banana industry's influence on the conflict.

> So this is what happened. Because of this, because one claimed one's rights as a worker, one logically became a target, let's say a military target. Because the Colombian military, the paramilitaries, banana companies, which supported them and which financed them, like Chiquita Brand, Uniban, and the owners of banana companies themselves were the promotors of this *magnicidio* (assassination of important figures) that was expanding through the zone. It didn't fit their interests that the labour union continued living in the region. They were looking for ways to exterminate the labour union, to manage things their own way, and have workers they wanted.

Due to his political engagements Fabio spent two years sleeping outside of the house – a survival strategy he adopted.

> I didn't leave because I thought things would calm down … It was about power over territory. Who can dominate most … They eliminated people. From 1984 till 1996, when I left, you could see dead people every day [...] Urabá is a rich zone. There are many personal interests involved on behalf of businessmen and foreign countries. At least the United States has its eye on this region. The richness of the region hasn't even started to be exploited yet. We were only exploiting bananas and plantains, but the richness in minerals that it has, hasn't started to be exploited yet. They haven't done it because of the violence itself [...] They [the paramilitaries] are assassins. That's what I call them. What can one do if one has children? One leaves.

Fabio left Urabá first and his wife Fernanda followed him some months later when the situation in Urabá got even more complicated. They joined the displaced who had already been in Irra. 'In Irra they didn't like *desplazados*. They said it gave them bad image.' Additionally, people were sent from Urabá after them, due to which they had to leave. When they ended up in Esperanza, the sense of people disliking them persisted.

> Bad things [such as thefts] happened, and people would say it was us. There was an investigation which showed it wasn't us but people still say '*estos desplazados*' (these displaced). We tried to show we are not who they think we are. We've been more honest than people from here. There are people who are angry … This was a dead hamlet. We raised people's spirit.

Like other displaced in Esperanza, Fabio feels affected by less than welcoming attitude of the locals. Additionally, working on his land does not always cover all of his needs. 'There is work on the farm but I also often need to look for *jornal* (a day's work on a different farm) because I need money.' Unlike most of the displaced, he is considering staying in Esperanza despite the challenges.

Doña Beatriz and Juan

Like Martina, Don Andrés and Fabio the couple comes from Urabá, unlike them, they were not members of the UP. Doña Beatriz, even though she describes life in Urabá as *sabrosa* (tasty), was hit by the loss of numerous family members. The military killed her first husband.

> The day my husband was killed, seven *guerrilleros* (guerrilla members) and eighteen soldiers were killed. In the news they only mentioned the number of the guerrillas. They wouldn't mention any deaths that the military suffered. It wasn't convenient for the government to admit they were losing. This was in 1988. I was twenty-nine and I was left alone with seven children. My husband worked for the same company for four years but he had no insurance. When he died, I got twenty-two thousand pesos [approximately £6]. I went to his boss and said I deserved work to feed my children. My husband worked there and he was killed there. They gave me work.

With the paramilitaries' presence, violence in Urabá got worse. 'See someone killed, and don't say anything,' Doña Beatriz describes the situation. Juan, her current husband, adds:

> *Autodefensas* came and said they were protecting *campesinos*. The military robbed whatever they could, without asking permission. They'd say, 'You don't charge the guerrilla for water and yucca, you'd charge us?' We said, 'we sell, we don't give. It's our work.' So it started. There were a lot of *infiltrados* (spies/inflitrators); they gave money for intelligence. If you gave water, the word would come out, they'd say you were a collaborator. The group, whichever, puts one in conflict. You are in the middle.

The paramilitaries killed Doña Beatriz' father and disappeared her sister and her mother. All on the same day. 'They buried them somewhere like animals.' After this harrowing event Doña Beatriz left Urabá.

> They [the paramilitaries] should be called 'locusts' not paramilitaries. They don't know that they hurt more those who remain alive than those who die. You kill the parents and what do the children do? They join the guerrilla. I left because of my children. There they would come and take the young. They'd take you to join them. I didn't want that to happen to my children. They drug them. They have to be drugged to be doing such things.

She and her children left Urabá by bus, with the assistance of *Cruz Roja* (Red Cross). Juan stayed in Urabá for another month. She first went to a town where her aunt lived, but due to the difficult economic and security situation she joined the rest in Irra. Juan could not find work and violence seemed to follow them – Doña Beatriz got shot in her arm. Don Andrés, who had already left Irra and reached their current municipality, invited Doña Beatriz and Juan to join him and his family. Together with the rest of the displaced they lived in a landfill for two years and persistently fought to secure a plot in Esperanza. 'We decided to fight for a *finca*. But how would we get one. Here there were people with money, good *fincas*. Who's going to give it to us? We decided to start knocking on doors,' explains Juan.

Juan, together with Pedro, Don Andrés' son, became an IDP leader. He is also the vice president of the local junta. His political engagements at one point became the main source of income. Namely, Doña Beatriz and Juan stopped cultivating the land because it gave bad returns. Like the rest, they complain over the poor soil but also over poor relations with the non-displaced.

> It's been a difficult process. People are suspicious. When we came here we bought some land from a pilot but people said we invaded the land. They gave it to us on October 12. People would ask who we were and wouldn't believe we were the owners but we had a copy from the register. *Esa gente* (these people) … We suggested a meeting, where we showed the papers. People looked at us in a strange manner, but they withdrew. 'Everything clear.' Some believed it some not […] People don't appreciate what we did for them.

While Juan admits they are relatively speaking in a better position than other displaced and some poor non-displaced, he, Doña Beatriz and their daughter moved to Bogotá, hoping to improve their status.

Don Eduardo

Don Eduardo is a hard-working man in his sixties. He is married to Doña María, and together they have ten children. He is an IDP leader and was voted a town councillor for the second time in a row. His leadership and political roles are not new to him. He was the president of the local junta in the village in Tolima where he comes from. Doña María believes it was on account of his political engagements that he was threatened.

Like Don Andrés, Fabio and Martina, Don Eduardo is on the left side of the political spectrum. Besides his role as a junta leader, he was part of the coffee growers' committee and he participated in the biggest coffee growers' protest which took place in 1995 in Líbano.[7]

> In mid-1993 a *plaga* (plague, infestation) called '*broca*' [caused by coffee berry borer] attacked coffee.[8] A *cucarrón* (beetle) attacked coffee and coffee didn't serve for anything. It was lost. *Cafeteros* (coffee growers) didn't have money to eat, nor to pay back the loan. We worked with credits from Bancafe, Caja Agraria[9] … No one chose coffee since it didn't have any value. It was *café podrido* (bad, rotting coffee).

They started with judicial debt collection. Because people found themselves in such a terrible situation – everyone lived off coffee – the guild of coffee growers was born. We united and organised a protest in the park of Líbano. I saw no other alternative but to protest to see if the government is going to pay attention to us. I was there for sixty-eight or sixty-nine days. We asked for more finance opportunities and new credits to be able to work. We wanted to knock down coffee and start with new crops. Yucca, plantain … Coffee? Why would we still think of it? We didn't see a solution. We didn't know the illness. Two years later we started to co-exist with the *plaga* … We demanded that the debt of small and middle-sized producers is written off. We experienced many difficulties. The time spent, the deaths … before we could triumph. A law was passed under which small and middle-sized farmers received a decrease in their debt and opportunities for new finance. However, after having achieved all this, the repression of the guild of coffee growers began. They said we were *subversivos* (subversive) because we were demanding our rights from the government. This led to mass displacement. The government said we were protesting due to the power of armed groups but we were explaining our case and demanding our rights. It wasn't that we didn't want to pay, we didn't have anything to pay with. The displacement of leaders in the north of Tolima began. Everyone had their hands tied.

In Tolima, the committee of coffee growers did a lot of work on municipal departments, such as building roads, viaducts and electrical infrastructure.

I got in trouble due to political jealousy. In 1997 they put me to prison. It was a political persecution. At that time they followed the policy of 'el juez sin rostro' (faceless judge).[10] In those times they weren't looking for evidence. I spent two years in prison. I met people who had spent five years there without ever being sentenced. I returned to the same territory but it was no longer possible to continue there. The armed groups began threatening.

Doña María and Don Eduardo left their village in 1999. They first went to Chía, a town in Cundinamarca, where they spent two years and then managed to be included in the land programme and secured a *finca* in Porvenir. He continues working in coffee cultivation but in a lot harsher conditions than in Tolima, since his *finca* is situated on a rocky terrain. He and his daughter Juanita are both IDP leaders in the hamlet. Nevertheless, some displaced in Porvenir who are of different political convictions, recurrently put the legitimacy of his title under question.

Linda and Carlos

Linda and Carlos, both in their early forties, are from the south of Tolima. They have four children, two of whom are school-going and live with them in Porvenir. They prefer Porvenir to their village of origin. Linda explains: 'We lived in a very remote place, without electricity. The houses weren't as beautiful as they are in Porvenir. They weren't built in stone and didn't have a bathroom.' Besides the greater comfort they find in Porvenir, they describe Tolima as very dangerous.

They'd kill people they didn't know. If a stranger came and asked about anything, like for example, which bus to take, no one would tell them since they were afraid they would be seen with the stranger and accused of something. One would be afraid to go to town, because they'd say one is a spy ... If one was a thief, one was a thief. If one was a spy, one was a spy, but they would also kill innocent people.

Unlike Don Eduardo, who left owing to the paramilitaries, the couple left their village due to guerrilla activity.

It was the guerrillas who managed the place and one had to live according to their laws. They weren't in the hamlet but they had four or five militias in each village. We didn't always know who was and who wasn't a militia. If one had a problem with somebody, they would tell the militia and they would tell the guerrillas who managed the problem. It was terrible.

Carlos believes the guerrillas lost support because of the militias.

They gave power to a few people and these people would kill you for any kind of problem or if they heard something over a beer. Things got out of hand. A commander could forgive you but if you had a problem with the villagers, they'd arrange it with the militia to get you out. This is displacement by a third party and it happens a lot. The people themselves throw you out assisted by the militia.

Linda and Carlos cultivated coffee and bred cattle. They both miss vast spaces they had in Tolima, which enabled them to work both with crops and with animals. Nevertheless, Linda explains, they were expected to share part of their earnings. Coupled with the threat of recruitment, the circumstances were sufficiently insecure that they decided to leave the village.

They demanded that at each harvest we give them one and a half or two million pesos [approximately £385–515] but we were saving to pay for my daughter's education [...] They would come and take the youth. Half of my daughter's class went with the guerrillas. Half died and we don't know what happened to the other half. I always lived in fear they would take any of my children.

They came straight to Porvenir, where Carlos' brother secured a plot and invited them to join him. Generally speaking they are happy in the hamlet. Carlos explains: 'It's not paradise, but it's nice. The soil is fertile and there's tranquillity.'

What follows is an interpretation of stories, opinions, feelings, past and current circumstances the above-mentioned and their neighbours live in. The narratives are based on people's experiences but also memories of those experiences. Memories are not static; they change with time and different events give a new twist and weigh to different points in people's lives. Remembering can therefore be a contentious process. The stories we tell others and ourselves about our lives and experiences are not 'necessarily accurate, nor they should be; they are, however, mostly congruent with one's self knowledge, life themes, or sense of self' (Barclay and DeCooke

1988: 92). The book is therefore a recollection of events and feelings participants felt at the time of fieldwork. Some memories and conveying of experiences are more constant than others, whereas some others might be truer for the specific period of time within which the research took place.

Notes

1 I decided to write about clientalism and internal disparities since they bear burden on some individuals' place-making to the extent that they are re-living the loss of relationships and displacement they underwent in the place of origin. As Springwood and King (2001: 406, emphasis in the original) note, '[t]he ethical field of consideration becomes ambiguous … when some informants are exploiting or harming *other* informants'.

2 The term 'local' is here not taken at face value. How long does one need to be at a certain place to be considered local (Massey 2005) and who defines what local is (Clifford 1997)? While I acknowledge this critique, I use the term since it reflects the non-displaced's own sentiments when they refer to themselves 'we, people from here', to differentiate them-selves from the displaced. The latter despite the relatively long period of time spent in the two villages, still seem not to fall within the category of being 'from here'. The term 'a local' will be used interchangeably with the terms 'non-displaced', 'long-term residents', 'hosts' and 'receiving population'.

3 Even though I entered the hamlets through the 'gender' group, I was working with people beyond the group. In part to reduce any potential bias that may occur when recruiting people who belong to the same organisation or group, and on the other, because the number of the displaced women participating in the gender workshops was continuously decreasing.

4 The majority of the conversations were not recorded – partly due to the nature of field-work, and partly because of the potential sensitivity of information. Therefore some of the quotes used in the book are not ad verbatim. They nevertheless capture the essence of the idea, coupled with detailed description of the context.

5 It is difficult if not even impossible to stay neutral in a ground that is not neutral (Cohen 2000). While I agree that the research context at times requires the researcher to take sides and express their political stance, in this research, it was the context that made this impossible. I was working with too many different kinds of groups of people. I sided with all of them in relation to the breach of their rights, and/or the government's failure to recognise the plight of the poor, but I did not take sides when it came to armed actors.

6 'Doctor' is the common way of addressing people with high education or assuming high positioned posts in Colombia.

7 The protest started in February 1995. It was first a local protest which soon got regional dimensions. It started with eight thousand *cafeteros*, but at its peak, it reached the partici-pation of fourteen thousand *cafeteros* (Bautista Bautista 2012).

8 '*Broca*' is caused by a beetle, the coffee borer, which inserts itself into the plant. The damage it causes expresses itself in various ways. Small fruits can fall off, coffee can lose in weight, and it also affects the quality of coffee.

9 *Bancafe* is a Colombian bank, previously known as *Banco Cafetero*, whose largest share-holder was the National Federation of Coffee Growers in Colombia. *Caja Agraria* was a financial body dedicated to supporting the agriculture and livestock sector of the economy. After its liquidation, it was replaced by *Banco Agrario*.

10 Faceless justice in Colombia was first invented in order to protect judges from retaliation of drug lords. It helped judges keep their anonymity and thus made the passing of sentences safer. Nevertheless, it started to be used also in other cases; for instance against labour union leaders, under invented motives linking the latter with narcoterrorism. The system offers no guarantees to the accused person, chances of defence are minimal, and it violates the principle of presumption of innocence, meaning that one is considered innocent unless proven the contrary (Bergquist *et al.* 2001).

3

Displacement as an unwinding process

Speaking of displacement, Alejandra remembers the disappearance of her mother at the end of the 1980s. Only one of her mother's shoes, a sandal, was found at the entrance of the house – all other traces were lost. Alejandra, who is now in her early thirties, was nine years old when her mother vanished. Her mother's friend, Martina, took her in but she treated her differently to her own four children. As a result Alejandra feels she never had childhood. She dreams of going back to Urabá, but not so much to the place itself, but back in time to the days when her mother was still alive. She is dismissive of the reparations for displacement. Money, she says, can never repay her loss: 'Money doesn't bring one back. I don't care about the *finca* in Urabá. I want them to give me my mother back, alive or her bones.' Not knowing what her mother's fate was and spending a childhood without her is what Alejandra associates with displacement. The emphasis she places on the disappearance of her mother shows that for her displacement began as a result of this harrowing episode, as opposed to 1996 when she, along with some other people interviewed for this research left Urabá – her region of origin.

When does the 'clock' of displacement start? If displacement is effectively about loss of place, this loss needs to be analysed. Is it abrupt, a result of flight, or does it unwind gradually? Circumstances surrounding violence differ, and often dictate people's (im)mobilities. The onset of violence can in certain cases trigger almost an instant movement of people. In others, it can curtail it, resulting in confinement of those trapped amid it. But there are also examples where people decide to stay, organise themselves, resist and leave only after other means have been tested out. Such was the case with the interviewees who came from Urabá. They shaped 'terrains of resistance' (Routledge 1993), defending their place from the paramilitaries and from the threatening expansion of capital-thirsty *bananeras*. Alongside their bravery and resistance, however, they were also experiencing and witnessing violence, loss of loved ones, displacement of their colleagues, friends and neighbours, and curtailment of territory where they would be able to move with relative ease.

Numerous narratives depicting life in the place of origin, the changes people underwent adapting to life in conflict, and persistent alterations to the usual ways of being, set the clock of displacement further back in time before relocation, when people were still in their respective villages, to the time when they were 'displaced in place' (Lubkemann 2008) where home no longer fulfilled its role of a shelter (hooks 1991). Persisting in the region during the height of violence, *urabeños* witnessed and lived the transformation of a familiar and loved place into an unknown one. For some, it turned into a place beyond recognition.

In this chapter I examine how violence changed the manner in which people sensed the place. How terror and violence changed the way in which the place was 'known, imagined, yearned for, held, remembered. Voiced, lived, contested, and struggled over' (Feld and Basso 1996: 10), to the point that it became alien. This was also what set off the displacement process. To give the reader a sense of the region, and introduce the macro-impacts of location (Agnew 1987), I first look at some economic, social and political factors that influenced the making and unmaking of Urabá. I present the context within which people's subjective experiences of place, their biographies and the conflict developed. I then discuss some of the reasons why people persisted in the region despite violence before I turn to the analysis of Urabá of displacement. I explore how conflict and violence transformed people's social, physical and cognitive landscapes. Physical landscapes refer to the natural and built environment, social landscapes to the transformation in people's relationships, and cognitive landscapes refer to the alteration of sensing the place. The residents' estrangement from place and alienation in affection launched the process of displacement prior to people's departure from Urabá.

Urabá: a territory of exclusion, resistance and dispute

Urabá is a sub-region of the department of Antioquia in the north-western part of Colombia, bordering the Caribbean ocean. Colombian scholar Carlos Miguel Ortiz Sarmiento (2007: 44) describes it as a place of adventure, escape, luck and money but also of danger, violence and death. It can be divided into three zones: the north, the south, and the central region or the banana axis, which is the focus of this discussion. This is the area from which the interviewees came and it is also the part of Urabá, which saw the most violence. It is estimated that 80 per cent of all violent acts committed in Urabá took place in the central region (García de la Torre and Aramburo Siegert 2011: 315).

Conflict has not been foreign to Urabá. During *La Violencia* local people's resentment towards the government and its neglect of the local population surfaced. Violence, which extended beyond Liberal-Conservative conflict, was so widespread that the armed forces considered Urabá the third most violent area in the country in 1951; consequently it was put under military control (Roldán 2002).

The administrative centre of Antioquia, Medellín, wished to 'antioquianise' and homogenise what they saw as the 'uncivil' population of Urabá through increased colonisation of the region (Steiner 1994). Though the attempts to increase immigration were initially unsuccessful, colonisation of the region was a constant, albeit slow, process. It was only after the *carretera al mar*, the road to the sea connecting Medellín with the coastal town of Necoclí was constructed that a noticeable increase in migration took place. The road denoted the introduction of capitalist modernity to the region (Roldán 1998), since it opened the way to the banana companies, which arrived in the 1960s.

The banana industry was inserted into Urabá without the resolution of the existent conflicts; even though it became an important part of the Colombian economy, it initially resembled plundering as the process was not regulated by the state (Uribe 1992). The working conditions were poor with long working hours, lack of hygiene and unfair treatment. Fabio, who was an active unionist, describes the time before labour union movement as the second period of slavery. 'If you didn't do what you were told, you were fired.' Unionism changed this. Accompanied by numerous strikes, the workers negotiated eight-hour workdays and greater job security, limited subcontracting, better wages and improvements in health and education (Carroll 2011: 87). 'The workers were very well organised,' explains Martina. 'We would be on strike for ten, twenty days during which time nothing moved, not even buses! We went on strike for two months once. We only picked the bananas we ate ... We protested for better work conditions, more security, and better payment.' These achievements in political, work and personal spheres still nourish IDPs' nostalgia and the dream of the place left behind; they were also one of the reasons why it was difficult to leave the region in the face of violence.

Unionism was not successful from the very beginning. The workers' initial lack of progress in negotiating their rights opened avenues for the guerrillas to form a relationship with the repressed *bananera* workers (Carroll 2011: 62–5). Martina has nice memories of the early years of the guerrilla presence, more specifically of the FARC. 'I remember I heard about them for the first time in 1977. They did too many good things. They were all very educated. They started organising people to demand things from the government, services. The countryside was completely abandoned by the state.' Besides supporting the peasants' land struggle, the two main guerrilla groups operating in the area, the FARC and EPL got increasingly involved in the labour union movement and they each stood behind a different labour union.[1] These two unions did not collaborate but were in opposition to each other, in a 'labour union war' (Suárez 2007). A war not even people understood. Fabio laments:

> Labour union movements fought for territory. No one could cross the line. People could not go and work on a *bananera* which was under a different labour union movement. The labour union they were members of would not allow them to ... *Partido Comunista* was born out of political necessity, first on the national level. The labour unions were born out of workers' necessity. *Partido Comunista* helped orient the labour union movement. Some lived peacefully, others not. Not even we could understand it. Why did we turn into enemies if we were fighting for the same cause? Peasants, workers ... and enemies?

The opposition became intertwined with armed confrontations and the conflict between political actors over institutional control. The social actors, members of labour unions and peasant organisations were politicised and the circumstances, including ever more severe violence, were such that María Teresa Uribe (1992) holds that it was almost impossible to remain neutral.

The two guerrilla groups entered into peace negotiations with the Belisario Betancur government after 1984. As a result, they both founded new electoral parties. The EPL formed *Frente Popular* (Popular Front) and the FARC formed a leftist political party, *Unión Patriótica* (UP). UP emerged as a third electoral power (alongside the two traditional parties, the Conservatives and the Liberals) and achieved substantial success. 'It was open to whichever political class or religious group, be it conservatives, liberals, communists. The name comes from their openness – "union", explains Fabio. After unsuccessful peace talks in 1987, the UP announced a split with the FARC. Nevertheless, in the minds of the people, they have continued to be associated with the guerrilla group (Giraldo 2001). An association those affected disapprove of. Martina says: 'The party was political. The *Unión Patriótica* was following the guerrilla fight but a non-armed one. Difference should be made between the guerrillas and their sympathisers. They are not one and the same thing. One thing is to support the ideals, another thing is to fight.'

Despite the successes in labour movements and in politics, the left was unable to firmly secure its position vis-à-vis the economic elites (Carroll 2011). One reason for this was the lack of unity of the left. The EPL demobilised in 1991 and the FARC, wanting to get control over the territory previously controlled by EPL, declared the demobilised EPL members and their supporters to be military targets. Consequently, many former EPL *guerrilleros* and their sympathisers became tolerant towards the paramilitaries who entered from the north and started disputing territory with the FARC. The second reason was the stronger elite, which further militarised the region. Believing that the left could be defeated by repressive violence, the elite turned to the use of its paramilitary apparatus. The collaboration of the paramilitaries with the state has since then been widely recognised, as has the banana industry's partial funding of paramilitary activities.[2] Don Fernando, who worked on *bananeras* for twenty-five years is convinced that the *bananeras* wanted to get rid of old workers so that they would not have to pay them their pension.

> They brought them [the paramilitaries] to end with trade unions. Banana companies have a lot to do with displacement. Trade unionists supported workers. They'd be forcing companies to pay what was just and that's where they finished with the people. They didn't end with labour unions but with old workers so that they wouldn't retire, that they'd get bored and travel to other parts of the country. Frighten them so that they'd leave.

The overall goal of the paramilitaries, to reign over the territory, was in part achieved specifically through land appropriation. Since many peasants did not possess land titles and were not protected by the state, Urabá was highly susceptible to paramilitary expansion (García de la Torre and Aramburo Siegert 2011). Alongside greater land appropriation, the arrival of the paramilitaries marked the time when 'threats and assassinations of UP leaders began in earnest' (Chomsky 2008: 195). The extermination of UP leaders and members through massacres, homicides, disappearances and threats made their political participation impossible. Over three thousand UP members are thought to have been assassinated in Colombia and some made to disappear. In 1997 the UP renounced their electoral participation; this coincided with the time when those interviewed for this research left the region.

In a history as complex as that of Urabá, it would be difficult to determine one single reason why people were forced off their lands. The interviewees or their family members were UP and Communist Party members, and/or worked on banana plantations, and/or were labour union members, and/or had a piece of land which was in the way of expansion of the banana industry. While displacement was related among other reasons to 'political cleansing' directed at UP supporters, economic factors were also at work. The reasons were cumulative and undoubtedly interlinked.

Persistence in the region despite violence

Despite violence people considered their options and decided to stay for a substantial number of years after the arrival of the paramilitaries. They aimed to resist the attack on their place. Sometimes they persisted because the guerrillas did not want their sympathisers to leave the area. The latter were told not to abandon their *fincas* but to resist and collaborate with each other in order not to lose the land. Such a strategy of non-abandonment is not uncommon with the guerrillas who give people what they perceive as 'the right orientation' (Giraldo *et al.* 1997: 159). Even after some *fincas* had been abandoned, the guerrillas sought volunteers who would temporarily settle on the properties of those who had fled. Martina stayed for a number of years because as she says, 'One is fighting, struggling for things to return to normality.' Nevertheless, she was also thinking of leaving. 'I was thinking of leaving long before. At least two years before. The guerrilla would keep me back, saying that I had to stay and resist,' explains Martina. The guerrillas did not want her to leave Urabá as she 'knew a lot', and letting her go could present a risk.

There were also other reasons which contributed to the decision not to leave. Adrián, Martina's brother explains: 'We stayed because we thought it would soon finish. We thought we'd be left alone because we had nothing to do with the conflict. We were innocent. But they started killing innocent people so we left.' Some decided not to leave because they did not want to lose their *fincas*; agrarian problems and unequal land distribution is, as in many other countries of Latin America, part of the historical trajectory of Colombia.[3] Land was and still is, when its quality is good, considered invaluable, especially for peasants. Ownership of a plot was possibly the most visible result or fruit of people's work and struggle. The prospects of getting a new *finca* elsewhere, based on previous experiences, appeared remote. Juan, a former *bananera* worker in his mid-forties and now an IDP leader, who had hated leaving his *finca* behind, and who stayed at the *finca* for another month after his wife had left, recalls acquaintances saying to him: 'You can get new land, but not a new life. What is worth more?' They tried to convince him to leave Urabá and to realise that even though land is precious, its value needs to be put in perspective.

For others, it was not only their individual properties that were at stake, but the broader structural problems of inequality which they, as supporters of the left, needed to stave off. This persistence to stay influenced by their political stance reflects the region's historical culture of resistance. Leaving the region meant giving in and very possibly giving up their fight and achievements as the networks of support and infrastructure would be lost. In the end, support networks were nevertheless lost, or at least greatly curtailed, despite persistence in the region.

Urabá of displacement: the changing taste of a place

In contexts of ongoing violence, armed groups succumb to practices which make them memorable through time and space. What is often inhumane treatment of their victims is not only an expression of power over the opposing group(s) and possible rage against the target, but it is also used as means of exercising control over the population. People are expected to act in line with the group's expectations; if not, they might be facing the same fate as the victims before them. Both the guerrillas and the paramilitaries were responsible for killings and massacres in the region. Nevertheless, I here focus on paramilitary violence, since paramilitaries were responsible for the displacement of the displaced who are now in Esperanza.

The paramilitaries came to Urabá with the objective to clear it of guerrilla sympathisers, explains Doña Beatriz.

> In those times paramilitaries would come to meetings and say 'we are *autodefensa campesina* (peasants' self-defence group) and we come to clean anything related to the guerrilla'. They promised 500,000 pesos [approximately £128] to anyone who would report cases of sympathisers plus the land of the person who was reported and whom they would kill if this person had a *finca*. They'd break into houses, break roofs, windows, doors, take TVs, refrigerators and give them to their friends. I beg God not to have any contact with these people ever again.

Allegations of one's involvement with the guerrillas were frequent Juan remembers.

> We might have been calmer at night [after having slept in town] but when we returned to the *finca*, always early in the morning … they would detain you on the road. It didn't matter in which car you travelled, they would stop you. If one went by bus or a private car. Or by bicycle, because it is *llanos* (extensive plains) so one would go by bike. They would stop you. They would ask you where you were going knowing that they had seen you a number of times before. 'Where are you going?' 'I'm going to the lot where I'm working'. So they would ask you, 'How is the *ambiente* (mood, atmosphere), how are the people you have meetings with?' Psychologically they are entering into your mind that you are meeting with the guerrillas. 'What guerrilla? One doesn't meet them.' That is when they would say, 'No, you don't meet the guerrillas but you are their informer.' This inflicts one with a psychosis.

The paramilitaries launched their mission of clearing the territory of guerrillas and their sympathisers through the 'sowing of terror', Fabio observes. One way of inflicting terror was through the number of people they killed. As a result of the level and persistence of the violence, the killing of one or two individuals was no longer noteworthy. Felipe, a *bananera* worker in his late forties, reflects on the situation saying: 'There had to be a massacre of fifteen people to attract attention. In Urabá one would wake up with ten, fifteen people dead every day.' Don Fernando confirms:

> Life wasn't worth a peso in 1996/97 in Urabá. There'd be thirty, forty workers on a truck, they'd stop them, made them get off and 'bang, bang, bang'. They came to sow fear … They put funeral services near the hospital in Apartadó. It was a lucrative business. They'd come [to the place of the event] before the family did.

Besides the number of casualties the paramilitaries maintained the levels of terror through performative acts of violence (Schröder and Schmidt 2001), through the manner they killed the people as well as through the display of victims' bodies. Martina describes the practices employed by the paramilitaries as 'sadistic'. It was like 'a rat hunt. They'd say they would make people sing'. Before the paramilitaries killed their victims they often tortured them, pulled their nails and skin off and beat them. In some cases they would cut their bodies with a chain saw or even quarter people alive. The physical results of violence were occasionally put up on display. The physical place saw transformation though the appearance of dead bodies. Corpses would be occasionally hung on trees, Mónica a widow in her early forties remembers. Or they would be left lying around 'like any old animal. They wouldn't collect them,' recalls Doña Isabel, a highly religious woman in her sixties. 'There was a lot of violence. All my friends who stayed there, they all died. Innocent people. Even those who didn't have anything and who claimed they were "clean" got killed.'

Sometimes the terror of paramilitary activities was amplified through encounters where the scent of death was closely felt. Miguel, Martina's husband, had a number of such happenstances; from getting off the bus just in front of a man who was shot, being made to lie in the sand face down, one of the manners in which the paramilitaries killed, to feeling someone else's blood running down his leg. The terror was further spread by rumours regarding paramilitary acts. From a football match where a villager's head replaced the ball, to a gang rape of a teenage girl, whose limbs were cut off and the torso left for her father to find. Through all these activities and circumstances paramilitaries were turning physical geographies into 'landscapes of fear' (Oslender 2008).

Terror was thus not exercised only on those who were killed but also on 'indirect' victims. On those who witnessed it, heard about it or were affected by it through their relationship with the victim. Fear is a powerful means to regulate everyday life and terror represented deliberate policy. The fear influenced the perception of the place as well as its use. People were more aware of their position in the physical landscape. Heidegger (1977) argued that one becomes aware of places during moments of reflection; that is when lived relationships are most fully felt and experienced. In such moments the physical landscape 'becomes wedded to the landscape of the mind' (Basso 1996b: 55). In the presence of violence, people became over aware of geographical space; moments of reflection were numerous and not without consequences. Even everyday chores entailed greater thought and planning. Individuals adjusted their behaviour, and payed increased attention to the use of physical space, which was experienced as completely territorialised, with no neutral grounds to place a foot on.

The mapping of Urabá

Martina drew a map which among others depicts the territorial division of the place (see Figure 2).[4] Social cartography in Colombia is often used with black and indigenous populations helping them advance their land claims. Produced cartography is based on people's knowledge related to the use of local resources and it helps recuperate local memory. Maps help identify the threat of displacement and development projects and they suggest alternatives to managing territorial conflicts (Montoya Arango *et al.* 2014: 196). They also help communities demonstrate their historic and cultural presence on the territory (Vélez Torres *et al.* 2012).

The map Martina made is not without its flaws since cognitive or mental maps can be quite different from reality. They are 'incomplete, distorted, schematised and augmented' (Downs and Stea 2011: 315). Placing the *carretera al mar* in the centre of the map makes the two territories, the one on the left which people say was under the control of the paramilitaries, and the one on the right under the guerrilla control look as if they were of the same size. The straight lines denoting rivers which are separated by more or less the same distance are an additional sign of distortion. If drawn by a different individual, the places marked on the map, its composition, and the scale used would look different – mental maps are highly subjective.

Nevertheless, the map is suggestive for various reasons. Even though the distances and proportions depicted are not accurate, the map shows the social context which is mute in the 'official' maps (Sletto 2009). The map is a sketch of the way in which its author saw and lived in Urabá. As such, the map depicts how violence and conflict have influenced interviewees' use of space, their movement and perception of danger. It shows people's behaviour in relation to place. It marks out the areas that were considered relatively safe from those considered unsafe. It visualises part of the conflict – more exactly, what the objective of territorial expansion was – and finally, it is an example of relational and interconnected character of physical, social and cognitive landscapes.

Some hold that the places that are included in mental maps are those that, for one reason or another, are meaningful in people's lives; and that areas, which the individual does not find significant, are not entered on a map (Madaleno 2010; Smiley 2013). However, mental maps affected by conflict challenge such perceptions. Past and present cannot be separated one from another and this insep-arability is reflected in mental maps. There might be places that are significant but

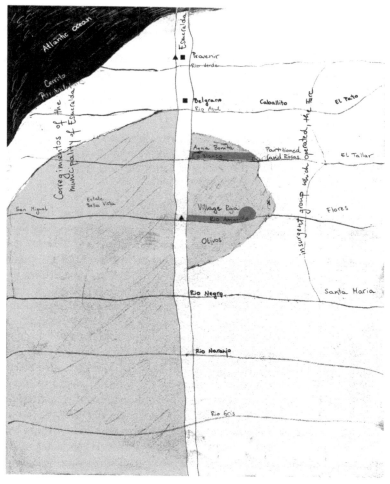

Figure 2 An anonymised map depicting conflict and displacement at the place of origin. Drawn by participant and reproduced with her kind permission.

people may wish to erase and forget them. Others might be meaningful and very present in people's minds but are not transferred to the paper as a sign of cautiousness, due to insecurities about what the consequences of drawing a particular place might be. The map cannot be separated from the politically sensitive context in which it is drawn.

What is missing from people's maps might be equally important as what is present. In the given map one absence is particularly telling and it shows a visible intersection between physical and cognitive landscapes. Among the features and places that are missing is Martina's father's *finca*, even though it is present in her mind. While drawing the map, Martina pointed to it, explaining that it was a place near *el monte* which served as a hiding place for a number of people who were being threatened or as a stop on their way out of the region. It also served as Martina's refuge.

Once, after she joined her political colleagues at a meeting which she left early, five out of seven attendees were killed. A few days later, they killed the remaining attendee and she knew she wasn't safe.

> I didn't sleep or eat for five days. I then decided to go to my father's *finca*. When I got there, there were already another fourteen members of *Unión Patriótica* there. The location of the *finca* was such that we would know two hours before-hand if anyone was coming. People would report anything suspicious, using a horse to carry the news. I stayed there for a month and a half.

Despite its importance, the *finca* did not make it on the map. Even though Esperanza is miles away from Urabá, there is no guarantee of protection. Someone has already been sent from Urabá looking for her father and Martina and her family fear they might come again. The place left behind might be geographically distant, but it is not distant in people's minds. Neither do people believe that the geographical distance can protect them from violence and retaliation, especially when the same armed actors are still active even if under a different name and composition. The *finca*'s absence on the map speaks of Martina's preoccupation of protecting her father, since they both believe the danger still exists.

The map predominately depicts Urabá of displacement but it also contains elements of nostalgic Urabá. There is the Rio Amarillo, where those who did not have money to go to the sea or to nicer rivers south of Rio Negro would go for picnics. On the river banks 'there were kiosks with drinks and cigarettes, pots to cook food and children would bathe in the river. It was *muy chévere* (fantastic)'. The map also contains childhood memories; it pictures *finca* Flores where Martina would get eggs from when she was a child. It shows the first plot where she lived, in Rosas, where people obtained land as a result of a subdivision of a big property which was taken away from a big landowner. It also shows a *finca* which she bought in village Roja. The drawing of numerous rivers brought back memories. 'Fishing fascinates me. I dream of living near a river even if it has bream this big [she puts her hands together to demonstrate the smallness of the fish], just to feel how it bites.' But alongside these pleasant memories and depictions, the main focus of the map is on conflict and territorial control.

After sketching out the road and rivers, the first hamlet that Martina drew was Olivos. 'The only one I remember well because it was spoken about a lot,' she says. A massacre of thirty-two people happened there she remembers, hence the name stayed ingrained in her memory. She drew *finca* Bella Vista where she worked for six years and San Miguel by the sea, from where people would dispatch the plantain and bananas. The light and dark grey areas explain the land problems. The light grey areas were *bananeras* and the dark grey *plataneras* (plantain plantations). The latter stood in the way of the expansion of the *bananeras* and these were the terri-tories that people were defending. The map also marks the armed actors' presence.

The triangles and the square are military bases and a police station respectively. Cerrito, a large palm tree plantation denotes the entrance point of the paramilitaries to the zone and the line on the right represents the beginning of *el monte* where the FARC operated from.

Miguel explains that the guerrilla and the paramilitaries each controlled a different portion of geographical territory; those living in these territories were assumed or expected to give support to the respective armed group. Due to the association of people with distinct non-state armed actors, moving between these two territories became challenging and even dangerous. It, however, had to be done. Some people, for instance, worked on a side of the road different from the one where they lived. To reduce the risk of crossing, Martina occasionally used a pulley running above the road to get to work. Similarly, entry to the territory controlled by the paramilitaries was needed to ship plantains from people's farms. When the situation got 'complicated', as people tend to describe it, they would send a car with the crops to the embarkation point rather than go there themselves.

Practices of the use of space likewise altered when people remained on the 'right' territory. Martina remembers that she would not get off the bus or get out of a car near her house but would ask the driver to stop before or after her house and continue on foot. Believing that she might be followed, she did not want to give away where she lived. For the same reason and also to avoid possible ambush, she made sure that she changed the route she took on a regular basis. Due to such alterations, the familiarity, which is in normal circumstances generated through the everyday use of space and repetitive movement through it, was gradually decreasing. Even when people used the same routes, their perception of them changed as they sensed danger. These are all important experiences of estrangement.

Social landscapes and the rule of silence

Alterations to physical and social environments were additionally expressed through absences. 'There used to be houses on *bananeras* but they pulled them down due to conflicts and killings. Workers moved to town and travelled to *bananeras* by buses organised by *bananeras*,' explains Martina. The empty houses and abandoned *fincas* left behind by those who had relocated, been killed or had simply disappeared changed the landscape. Places saw less activity, with fewer people engaging in work with animals and crops. The area was becoming increasingly desolate.

Paramilitaries occasionally replace the displaced population. They also brought new people to Urabá. Fabio confirms that the *bananeras* in collaboration with the paramilitaries wanted to get rid of old workers. 'We produced bananas, plantain … companies started to interfere. They wanted to finish with the old workers to place their own. … They brought a lot of people to work from the interior of the country and also a lot of foreigners,' he explains. While this might stop the process of desolation, it does not stop the increased estrangement of the place. The physical landscapes, the 'landscapes of fear', are interwoven with social landscapes. The visible absence of people means loss of support networks – be it at the family, friendship, ideological or work level. Even if people are replaced, the 'replacees' are strangers. The meaning and value of a place are gradually lost. Through the absence of familiar faces and the presence of unfamiliar ones, one becomes estranged from one's own place.

Social landscapes and relationships were affected not only through absences and replacements but also through communication between the old residents and among those who stayed. In order to protect themselves people often resorted to complete or partial silence. They followed (and they still do) *la ley del silencio* or rule of silence. As Linda Green (2004: 189) so aptly states, silence is a 'powerful mechanism of control enforced through fear'. The presence of multiple actors operating in Colombia is a frequent cause of mistrust. It is not always clear whom one can trust. Speaking out might mean risking being killed or being forced to leave. On the one hand, this is due to the dynamics by which the parties to conflict frequently change in power and thus create confusion in people's lives. On the other, even members of the same family may support different armed groups. Where uncertainty reigns, few people are considered potential friends. The war in Colombia has generated 'a state of ambiguity' where friends and neighbours have lost their usual connotation of cognitive proximity (Castillejo Cuéllar 2000: 264). Friends are considered hard to find or a false concept. Martín believes there is no such thing as a friend. 'One doesn't talk about things to anyone. One is alone. Those who are supposedly your friends end up killing you,' he concludes.

The high scale of violence served for settling personal accounts. When people reported on guerrilla collaborators, the paramilitaries did not look for the truth behind these reports. If someone 'had a problem' or did not like a certain individual, they could invent reports about guerrilla collaborators. They similarly did not always check if they had the right person. Felipe was one of those detained because of this.

> I was once detained for four days because they mistook me for someone else. I had a silver tooth and the man they were looking for also had one. After this happened, I had the silvering removed. Too many innocent people were killed because they wouldn't check if they got the person they were looking for. If someone had the same shirt, they would kill the person and only then check their identity.

The indiscriminate killing got to the point where people were afraid of people. Doña Isabel explains: 'During those times they'd kill you if you had an argument with your neighbour, or didn't like somebody. You could have them killed. We become afraid of people like one is afraid of tigers.'[5] Anyone was a potential risk to one's safety as even *chismes* (gossip) could get you killed. With a decreasing number of acquaintances and greater levels of terror, *la ley del silencio* was increasingly applied. Phrases 'see what you like, hear what you like but don't tell anything', 'see someone killed, shut your mouth', 'if you see and speak, you die', 'if you see and speak, you never speak again' describe the prevailing attitudes. People are social beings and feeling comfortable somewhere is also achieved through those with whom we feel at home; silence, however, creates the opposite effect. Silence sustained and emphasised social distance, even though people were physically close.

While the silence might have saved lives, it came at a price. One of the consequences was that many crimes went unreported. The version you were told about what had happened was the one you had to accept, explains Martín. 'They kill people, you look away, they say why it happened and that's accepted as a reason.' If the act affects you directly, you not only question your position in the society where you receive no protection from the dysfunctional mechanisms of justice, but your relationship to those who have possibly witnessed the act and are afraid to speak out, changes. Rather than taking your side and resisting the demands of silence, they give in to the established structure; this has a negative impact on the relationship.

Another consequence of silence is that many people get buried as unidentified persons. While some were unidentified simply because they were migratory workers and had no relatives in the region, as was occasionally the case with workers on *bananeras*, others did not recover their relatives' bodies due to fear. People practised *la ley del silencio* in relation to civilians but also public figures. Many *urabeños* never really managed to establish a constructive relationship with the state (Ortiz Sarmiento 2007; Uribe 1992), and after the arrival of the paramilitaries this was even less possible or desirable. Martina remembers only one occasion when a woman who denounced the military for the death of her brother was not killed.

> No one prosecuted there. People were passed as N.N. [*nomen nescio*, Latin for 'no name'] because of the fear people had. If you denounce, they know where one is. I know of one case that was denounced. A guy started running when he saw the military, such was the fear people had of the military. They shot him. They dressed him in military clothes and said he was a *subversivo*. But in his case they first killed him and then put on the clothes so the clothes they put on, were not damaged and his sister won the case.

In general, silence led to estrangement with those who were still alive and present, but also with those who had died. By not being able to claim or recover bodies, people were forced to deny their feelings and to demonstrate indifference. The dead, who had names and faces and were part of people's personal histories, became 'unknown' or 'unidentified' strangers.

Cognitive transformation of place

Certain locations, even if they were not greatly modified physically, underwent cognitive transformation. One such was the *bananeras*. The change affected both the possibilities for exercising workers' rights as well as the relationship which had been previously formed with the plantations. Working conditions on these *bananeras* had not been favourable but, as seen above, workers actively resisted the established system by organising into labour unions and taking strike action. Activism and the defence of workers' rights formed an important part of what Urabá represented for the interviewees.

The strikes and acts of resistance became more dangerous after the arrival of the paramilitaries, which made labour union activism progressively more difficult. Martina recalls that not many people organised when 'inquietude' settled in. Place is about what one does there since '[p]ersonal biographies, social identities and a biography of place are intimately connected' (Tilley 1994: 27). The inability to continue exercising the place-bound activities which formed part of people's biographies affected the way they related to the place. Urabá was no longer experienced as enabling individuals to voice their concerns through protests or strike actions.

Despite the necessity to continuously negotiate conditions of work, employment on the *bananeras* offered relative financial security. The relationship with the plantations thus played an important part in people's lives; plantations reached individuals' private spaces through the means of provision for the family. Unfortunately, *bananeras* gradually acquired a different connotation. Owing to their importance in the lives of the inhabitants of the banana axis, they were chosen as a suitable location for massacres, partly because of the labour union movement and different political affiliations of the unions, but also because these were populated spaces.

Some of the massacres happened in the vicinity of the interviewees' homes, others on the *bananeras* where they worked. Miguel recounts twenty-eight people being assassinated within six months on the *bananera* where he worked; Martina, who started working on the same plantation some time later, remembers twenty-two deaths. Both Miguel and Martina were present on certain occasions when the paramilitaries came and they remember hiding and/or fleeing from them. The latter reflects:

> We knew they came to kill we just didn't know who. In the warehouse where we had cardboard we would dig out holes where we would hide and cover ourselves with boxes. People are foolish. Even though we knew they came to kill, we would start running and hid only after we had heard the first shot.

The relative frequency of violent acts committed on *bananeras*, be it on the ones where the interviewees worked or on more remote ones, created the sense that any *bananera* could be next. Going to work thus generated a degree of uneasiness. Greater attention was paid to the location itself, as well as to anyone present. Although these plantations had previously represented places where one earned a living, they increasingly became places of potential threat.

While *bananeras* were perceived as particularly dangerous in the morning, the situation was quite the opposite when it came to people's houses. The perception of houses – specifically among those politically active – likewise changed; houses came to be seen as unsafe, especially during the night. 'As soon as it got dark people were killed. Bang bang bang. [she pauses] We were afraid of darkness,' affirms Doña Isabel. 'These people came during the day to check how to enter to then come at night and attack *campesinos*, those who were living on the plot,' says Juan, explaining how the military and the paramilitaries were often one and the same people. He continues:

> We had a psychosis, working during the day and at night there was no tranquil-
> lity. When the night came, terror came. Why? Because they entered the plots and
> killed one or two persons so that we would gain fear and that we would leave …
> We went to the *pueblo* (town) [during the night] to be a bit calmer.

Many began sleeping outside their houses. 'It was most nerve-racking. One wouldn't wake up in the house but in the *monte*. They would come to look for you [in the house] at whichever hour of the night,' recounts Fabio. Some, like Juan, would spend the night in town and return in the morning to work. Others remained in the vicinity of the house, just not inside. Martina had three *caletas* (a hiding place) outside her house on her *platanera*. She deliberately did not cut the lawn there as it served as a hiding place. She and her five children used these *caletas* to sleep, while her husband slept at a different location. Every morning when they came back home they would spend some time checking if anyone was in or near the house. They slept in the house only two or three nights a week. These nightly relocations, a form of everyday displacement, were not necessarily a short-term practice. Fabio slept outside the house for nearly two years.

Even if people continued sleeping in the house they did not feel safe. 'One did not sleep as deeply there as people here [in Esperanza] sleep,' comments Martín, explaining the high state of alert people were in.

> Here people go to bed and sleep like the dead. There one slept like this [he mimics
> one eye opened]. One develops the ability to hear the slightest noise. I sleep more
> peacefully here but things never go away. One is always alert. It is like your first
> love. You might be doing something different and all of a sudden you remember
> that person. It's there all the time.

Some had their doors blocked, others their beds raised. Beds were placed on bricks so that they allowed for sufficient room for people to use as a hiding place. Alejandra has her bed raised even now in the area of resettlement, where she feels no imminent threat. 'I have this habit from Urabá,' she explains. 'We'd use stones and bricks to raise the bed so that we could hide when the shooting started.' Martina learnt to sleep standing up.

> I slept like you are now: on foot, with a bag and boots. One Saturday I came home
> at about 5.30 in the afternoon and they started shooting, throwing bombs as if it
> were the end of the world. It lasted all night. I grabbed my two children, ran and
> jumped into a shaft with water. I held my daughter against my breast and my son
> in my arm. The girl only had her underwear on so I took off my blouse which
> was all wet but the collar and I wrapped her in it. I thought we walked, how to
> say, like from here to the municipality [about an hour's walk] but in the morning

> I realised we were only about 600 metres from the house. I was so tired I thought
> we walked far but we didn't.

Displacement was therefore no longer a phenomenon occurring only in Urabá, as a region, but was encroaching upon the home and the bed. It was affecting people's places of intimacy and creating a sense of displacement in their own homes. *Bananeras* and houses, two important features of the physical and cognitive landscape, were no longer perceived as before. The physical landscape underwent a cognitive change. What had previously represented financial security (banana plantations) and shelter (people's houses), became places of risk, of potential threat.

Finally, perhaps the most telling example of a change in the perception of a place is the modification of one's plans. Sense of place is not only affected by the present but is influenced by past memories and thoughts of the future. The same memories of past lives that might have kept people there when they still believed that the conflict would not last long, were also the memories that served as a point of comparison with what Urabá used to be like, how it had changed and what it was becoming. The plans to pass the land on to their children, as many had hoped, made less and less sense as Urabá was no longer seen as a desirable or indeed possible place to grow old. The discussions and thinking about the future changed too as is evident from Martina's example.

> We were a group of seven friends, five men and two women. Three are still alive
> but separated. One lives on help, which I disapprove of. With the other three par-
> ticularly, we would dream of getting old together. We would be joking, talking
> about what we would look like once we were old and who was going to bring
> medicine to whom. Later on, when things started getting ugly, we started talking
> how we should have ourselves killed in case we got caught. If not, we knew they
> would torture us to give out information because we became military targets.
> Two got killed. I was told not to go to the funeral but I did anyways. The third one
> stayed alive for about a year after we had left Urabá. They killed him too. They
> wanted to take him away [to torture him] but he made them shoot him in the way
> we discussed. I thought I would go crazy. I was thinking of committing suicide.

Torture is a form of social death, which kills people's identity and spirit (Robben 2014); being shot on the spot was therefore a preferred option. The political colleagues no longer referred to a distant future of experiencing old age in Urabá but instead to an imminent and hostile future.

All of these changes, despite the fact that people had not moved physically and might have still been living in their respective houses, transformed their places substantially. The place they had once known, the one they had created in response to often disadvantageous social, economic and political factors, was no longer the same and could not be considered suitable for the future. Their processes of displacement, the substantial change in their ways of being, the transformation of the familiar into the unfamiliar, therefore started before they actually left the region.

Notes

1 The FARC and EPL established their presence in Urabá in the second half of the 1960s. However, the first record of guerrilla presence reaches back to 1950 and the period of *La Violencia*. The governor of Antioquia sent a military official on an expedition to assess the region's 'subversive' presence. The latter reported a lack of authority from Antioquia, a lack of civilisation, and the immoral character of the inhabitants. As a response, the governor declared Urabá a militarised zone and handed its management over to the military (Roldan 1998).

2 See for instance (CCJ 2010; García de la Torre and Aramburo Siegert 2011; Hylton 2006).

3 For history of land struggle in Colombia see for instance (LeGrand 1988; Machado 1998, 2004).

4 Place names on the map have been anonymised and the map has been converted into black and white for the ease of representation in this book. The distances and shapes are the same as in the original.

5 Tiger is an expression used for jaguars, which form part of Urabá's fauna; an animal instilled awe and fear among inhabitants, hence the comparison.

4

The road to Porvenir and Esperanza: the struggle for land

After coming back from the field, Don Fernando, a displaced man in his sixties, and I sat outside his temporary accommodation enjoying the last rays of the day's sun. 'Have you heard of the landfill story?' Don Fernando asks me, sitting on a bench with his back leaning against the house. He had arrived in Esperanza three years before. 'Yes, I have,' I reply to his question, realising once again the story's importance. The landfill story is a story of the groups' arrival to Esperanza. I heard it during my very first short visit to the village and a number of individuals referred to it on different occasions after that. It has become some kind of signature story of the group, a 'group myth' (BenEzer 2002); it speaks of people's humiliation, rejection and struggle, but at the same time also of their resistance, persistence and strength. Its strong presence, even among some of those who have never lived on the landfill, such as for instance Don Fernando, alludes to the fact that the journey people have travelled bears great importance and that it has marked their lives. The importance of the journey is such, Gadi BenEzer and Roger Zetter (2015: 299) hold, that it could be the most significant process of 'becoming' or 'being' a forced migrant, in this case a *desplazado*.

The displaced never 'simply arrive' at a certain location (Oslender 2008: 88). Uncritical assumptions exist that journeys are linear, straightforward undertakings during which people move from the place of origin to the place of settlement. Policymakers, NGOs, media and academics tend to use arrows to depict these journeys, which only reinforces the mistaken perceptions that journeys are straight passages (Mainwaring and Brigden 2016: 247). But the arrows and assumptions do not capture the emotions, the fear, the separation from loved ones, the distinct length of journeys, the various stops a journey may contain, and the living conditions during each separate fragment of the journey. They do not capture the insecurities, uncertainties and risks people may experience on their way.

To highlight the non-linearity of trajectories, and the importance of the journey, this chapter looks at the route that people undertook to get to Esperanza and Porvenir. A closer look shows that journeys are social processes which have marked people's experiences and shaped who they are. Examination also alludes to the difficulties of negotiating settlement, including the power dimensions interfering with the process. I trace some of the routes that brought the displaced to

Esperanza and Porvenir. These experiences show the difficulties many were facing on route, the transformations that the journeys have brought about at the personal, family and community levels, and the great struggle it took to negotiate land in the two hamlets. The last part of the chapter examines the role policy has in keeping people in place or compelling them out of their place. It shows that the unequal power relations which were involved in the negotiation of plots continue shaping the journeys and consequently displacement experiences.

The first fragments of the journey to Esperanza

Despite violence, threats and death, the decision to leave is not an easy one to take. It entails leaving behind the product of years of hard work, cradle of memories, a place where essential life events such as marriage or birth of children have taken place, and sometimes it means also giving up political fight and resistance. When she was still in Urabá Martina remembers watching TV where they would show stories of 'abandonment' of homes. In those times, she recounts, no one spoke of 'displacement'. The images of people portrayed on the screen seemed a distant and impossible reality to her. 'I was a regionalist. I was born and raised in Urabá. I never thought I'd leave the region.' After years of being caught in violence Martina finally decided to leave for her children's sake but also in search of her own safety.

> You know what it's like there. If one isn't working or active, they start looking at you with suspicion. I got less involved with the party [Communist Party] and knew it would be better to leave. My sister left first. They [the paramilitaries] sent someone to her house. Supposedly he was meant to kill her, but he told her that she had been behaving well, that she was a good person, and that she should leave. He also told her that if she told anyone, they would come after her. She sold the cattle and left.

Important considerations arise which might be detrimental to people's security but also to the way their future life develops. Where to, when, and how? *Campesinos* do not tend to know many places beyond their respective villages, and even less beyond the region. The nature of their life and work, the associated costs, and potential remoteness of the villages, make travelling a rare undertaking. Martina for instance knew only one place outside the region – Irra, a small poor mining town in the department of Risaralda where she had spent six months years before, soon after her first husband had been killed. The 'where to' in her case was therefore relatively straightforward. The decision of the place was made even easier through knowing she had someone who could receive her upon her arrival. Her brother-in-law's mother lived in the town. Martina had some time to plan, to decide when and by what means they were going to travel, what was possible and not keeping in mind the circumstances.

> We were organising everything for two weeks. We didn't tell anyone. I was afraid to tell my father. Not because I was afraid he'd do anything to me but you know what he's like, he speaks a lot. I was afraid he would tell someone we were

planning to leave and that the word would come out. We decided we would leave on a Friday, June 28, at four in the afternoon. From where we lived it was about an hour to the military control point, which we had to pass. They had a changing of the guards between 5 and 7 p.m. so we wanted to pass during that time. We hired a truck and on the Thursday before we were supposed to travel I passed by my mother's house to let her know. She said she wanted to come with me. The priest had told her he'd had a vision and that she was in danger. He thought she'd better leave. At least they [the priests] serve for something [she laughs]! We then went to look for my father. He was angry. He told me a new *frente* (front) was coming and that things would change, that I should stay, that they needed people. He also told me I was destroying the family. I said I was only going for six months. I needed to breathe. I was no longer alive.

The careful planning nevertheless did not manage to remove the uncertainties such a journey presents. Even less so when the plans started going astray and the secrecy of the escape, which was essential for Martina, was under threat.

On Friday morning they told me that the truck we had hired broke down and that we needed to wait until Saturday afternoon. I was afraid and said it had to be in the morning. It would have been too long to wait until afternoon. By that time, someone might have learnt about our plans. In the end we left on Saturday morning. It was me with my five children, my sister with four children, my cousin with five children, Miguel [her husband] who returned to Urabá, and my mother with her youngest daughter. My brother-in-law, who received death threats, travelled in a separate car in case we got stopped. I took almost nothing since I thought I'd be back in six months. We put mattresses in the back of the truck and the children, my mum and Miguel were lying down in the back. They were there to calm the children. We, the three women, sat crammed in the front. The seats were separated by an engine, so one was sitting on the engine. We left the truck uncovered, so that one could see what was inside [not to raise suspicion]. If they stopped us, we would say that we were going on a short holiday. They didn't check us. We went *dandole* (giving it some, very fast). We got to Irra at three in the morning. We spent the first night in the house of my brother-in-law's mum. We put the mattresses on the floor and slept there. The following day Miguel got down to work and went looking for a place to rent. He then returned back to Urabá to rent out our *finca* and joined us a month later.

Martina was certain she would be back in Urabá by December the same year or January at the latest, when school started. That is why when her husband suggested they sold the cattle, she disagreed. 'We rented the *finca* out to someone for 200,000 pesos [approximately £51] a month. Imagine! We got 1.5 million pesos [approximately £385] a week from plantain we cultivated! But we said it's better to rent it out cheaply and have someone there than leave it empty.' Her plans to return were put in doubt when the paramilitaries came to her *finca* and took the cows. Among the cows, there was also one which was stubborn; 'they probably couldn't get her onto the cart,' Martina supposes, so 'they burnt her. They burnt her.' Remembering the moment when she realised there was no turning back and that she had probably left the region she held so dearly forever, her voice is still coloured with anger, sadness and disbelief.

Martina and her mother's decision to leave separated the family, not only physically but at first also emotionally. For Martina's father Don Andrés, a strong supporter of the left and an important political figure, staying was a political stance he took. Angry at the women's decision, he prohibited his sons from calling their mother. A week after the women's departure the paramilitaries broke into the house and took a photo in which he featured. They tore it in two and took the half with Don Andrés. It was a clear sign he was in danger. He and his son started looking for ways to join the women. The guerrillas helped them to leave, but it was difficult. They spent a month in the *monte*, trying to cross through the forests and rivers, but could not find a way out since everything was closed off. They went home and back in the *monte* again. It was only three months later that they managed to leave, which they spent in hiding or keeping low profile. They flew to Medellín[1] and took a bus from there to Irra.

Martina and her children were the first of the group of the displaced who are now in Esperanza to leave. Others that followed left either individually or as families, facing many of the same considerations. How to travel and who and what to take? Fabio decided it was safer for him to travel alone, even if it meant months of separation.

> I left on December 3, 1996. I left at night by bus. My wife and the children went to live with my wife's mother. I followed those who had already left and spent the first couple of nights at Martina's place. I then went to live with a relative. My wife would come and see me and go back to Urabá saying it was safe until one day the paramilitaries killed her father and disappeared her mother and sister. She then joined me. It was seven months later. The Red Cross bought her the ticket.

This particular massacre prompted not only Fernanda, Fabio's wife, but also her sister Doña Beatriz and her children to leave. This time with no planning. Like those before them, they were uncertain as to where to go. Juan, Doña Beatriz' husband, remembers the situation, explaining:

> At that moment there was a massacre of family members. They killed three of my wife's family members. It was July 17. Because they had already told us to empty the zone they said, 'since you don't want to leave, we'll kill one.' They made one *señor* get off [the bus], my father-in-law of 75 years, who was sick and was carrying medicine. They said he was carrying medicine for the guerrillas. That's why they killed him. In this moment they disappeared one of the sisters. We managed to collect my father-in-law, we buried him, but as for the sister and my mother-in-law we still don't know if they are alive or dead. With this massacre we had to leave […] That day [the day of the massacre] I was at the *finca*, working with my wife's oldest son. At 8 o'clock someone told him to leave because the *paras* were coming to get him. We said, 'No, we have nothing to do with anyone.' Then another one came saying the same. They were coming. We left on our bicycles. We saw a house in flames – they killed the wife and children of a *compañero*, who was an informant

of the guerrillas ... We went from the *finca* to *pueblo* to ask *Defensoria del Pueblo* (the Ombudsman's Office) and the Red Cross for protection. They helped us, they got us out of there. They paid for the tickets, because they wouldn't allow us to take anything we had. We had to leave everything. The Red Cross in Apartadó asked us 'Where are you going?' 'Well, where are we going?' We buried my father-in-law but we had to leave without knowing where to. When I was very young, perhaps I went to Medellín once, but I didn't know any places from here to there. When we had to leave, we left with only our clothes on and some clothes in a small suitcase and that was it. We left cattle, chicken, tools ... because you know you've got every-thing in a house ... and well that is when we left.'

Juan stayed for another month looking after the *finca*, and the bus took the rest to Pereira, the capital of the department of Risaralda. Doña Beatriz had an aunt living in a small town nearby. When she reached her aunt's town, she still did not know where she was going.

> I knew my aunt liked to play lottery so I asked the man selling lottery slips if he knew her. He said it might be the same *señora* that had bought tickets from him and he pointed in the direction in which the woman lived. While I was looking for my aunt, I saw how somebody got killed. I thought 'Dear God, here there's also violence.' But I couldn't go back. I had no money. I was afraid. Someone got killed and I was a stranger in the town. Imagine! I was afraid to ask anything.

When she found her aunt she wanted to work to *salir adelante*, get ahead, but would not get work at first since she needed a letter of recommendation. She was without work for two months. 'I felt bad because my aunt was also poor and my children would go to bed without dinner.' She decided to go to the mayor's office but 'they did not know what displacement was, they said they didn't have dis-placement there'. She went to *Instituto Colombiano de Bienestar Familiar* (ICBF), Colombian Family Welfare Institute, and got a box of *panela* (type of sweetener, a brown sugarloaf) and a bag of flour a month. The Red Cross gave her blankets and pots. 'I remember we were sitting at the door of the house and could smell food on the street. My children said they were hungry. We didn't even have a plantain.'

Pedro, Don Andrés' son, who is married to Doña Beatriz's daughter invited them to join the families in Irra. Even though for many Irra was the first place of arrival, it was never meant as the final destination. The town's main income was mining, which the displaced were not familiar with. Work was difficult to find and it did not give much return. 'Sometimes we had one thousand pesos [approxi-mately £0.26], sometimes five thousand [approximately £1.20], at other times nothing,' explains Martina, who worked in an old people's home for seven months but received no payment. They gave her food to take home and allowed her to leave for a couple of hours in the morning, when she engaged in mining.

> I'd get up at four in the morning and leave breakfast and lunch ready, go to the old people's home, ask for permission to leave at ten and go to work in a mine for an hour. We were a group of four; one would dig and I would collect whatever he managed to dig. I then went back to old people's home and they would be

washing the sand and looking for gold. It was very unstable. Sometimes we'd only get two thousand pesos [approximately £0.65] a day. One of the group died in an accident so we stopped going.

Camilo, Martina's son, describes the period in Irra as 'We weren't starving but only just surviving.' He was affected by his mother's decision to leave him with the grandmother while she went to look for work elsewhere. 'I was all alone. I felt embarrassed when the school wouldn't allow me to take part in classes because nobody paid for me,' he explains. In Irra, at this intermittent stop, family relationships were modified. On the one hand, some family members were separated, whereas, on the other, family roles shifted. Don Andrés could not find work, hence his son Alejandro, who was fifteen at the time, took up dangerous work in a mine to help with family finances. This experience of the journey has marked him forever, since he feels he lost his childhood. Juan was also out of job at one point, which resulted in Doña Beatriz becoming the main breadwinner. She had two jobs picking oranges which paid eighteen thousand pesos [approximately £4.60] a week. When the employer realised Juan and her son were helping her, he fired her. Due to such circumstances, due to 'lack of land', and 'little entry of money', Irra was seen as a place 'in passing'.

Economic security was not the only issue that was affecting people. They might have left Urabá and its conflict behind, but 'violence followed us,' Doña Beatriz concludes. Part of the insecurity and lack of comfort arose from the experience of violence itself. Juan reflects, 'What does one do when one gets from there? One comes with fear, comes *psicosiado* (paranoid, distressed), one doesn't talk to people. One sees police, the military and one is afraid.' The other part was the actual violence. Doña Beatriz was accidentally shot in the arm.

> One of my acquaintances suggested I could help sell fruit and that she could help me get work. She organised a meeting for 7 o'clock at night. When I arrived, there was no one there so I went to a shop nearby to wait. I started talking to the owner. It was December 14. Then at one moment someone shot the owner and the bullet hit my arm. One doesn't feel the pain at first. I looked at the owner and she fell on me. I ran away. People later said the woman was a drug dealer … At the same time there were also rumours that the paramilitaries were performing *limpieza social* (social cleansing) and were getting rid of the displaced. I was frightened. I couldn't take it anymore.

With the rumours on the one hand that the displaced were linked to the paramilitaries, and on the other that there would be social cleansing, the remaining of the total ten families who were still in Irra, decided to leave. 'We suffered two displacements,' Juan assesses. This time they did not have to leave in hiding and with less of a rush, nevertheless some of the same questions remained.

> One of the families said, 'Ok, I'm leaving, I'm leaving. Let's go somewhere else, let's go to Bogotá.' We said, 'Yes, let's go but where in Bogotá if we don't know the *pueblo*, we don't know anything, but no, we can't stay here. They already told us we need to leave, let's leave.' We left, from this *pueblito* (little town) we went to

the bus terminal in Pereira. We had to beg to be able to travel until here [current municipality]. We didn't get to Bogotá because one of the families which had left before, told us there is a department called Cundinamarca. And we 'Um…' [shrugs his shoulders] We didn't know anything about it, and ok, agreed. This family was making way, a path for the rest of us to be able to leave one by one, to be able to get here. We arrived at the municipality in 1998, some in 1999, 2000 also in 2002.

The first one to leave Irra was Alejandra, Martina's adopted daughter. Alejandra remembers that because of the lack of money her parents took her out of school, saying the other four children had preference. She left home and found work in *casa de familia* (as a housekeeper in the family home) in Manizales, a city nearby, and she would send some money back to Irra. After speaking to a friend she decided to find herself a partner. 'When I was in Urabá, my plan was to stay single, have no children. But after all this I said, 'Why don't I find myself a husband?' I didn't marry out of love. I married out of necessity. I learnt to love my husband only after I gave birth to my first son.' Alejandra got married and went to live in Prado, Tolima. She asked Martina to come and help her out; she was pregnant but she lost the child upon birth. Martina left with her daughters, leaving Camilo behind. They stayed in Prado for a month. They started asking around if they could get work anywhere and someone offered them work close to the current municipality. Both Alejandra and Martina eventually got work on a chicken farm. Martina's husband found some occasional work in construction and since his salary was not sufficient to cover the expenses, she also left to look for work and would return home only every eight days.

> We had a psychologist visiting the house asking us why we were leaving the children home alone. It was the most humiliating thing that had happened to me. I told her I wanted to give my children education and that Miguel's salary wasn't enough. She promised me to arrange something and both of us [she and her husband] were offered work to look after chicken. It was freezing there. We wouldn't sleep! The psychologist came to see how we were doing and she gave us blankets. We stayed there for five years. It was the best period after we had left Urabá. We left the *finca* because the rest of the group invited us to join them, saying they got land.

While Martina and her family were working on a chicken farm and found at least a temporary place, the rest of the group were paving their way to the land they have today.

Not everyone passed through Irra. Doña Isabel and her husband Don Jorge, who are both orthodontists, set off on their own journey. A completely unplanned one. Don Jorge was being observed since he was accused of being a guerrilla dentist. 'One doesn't ask who one is and where one lives if one fixes their teeth,' explains Doña Isabel in their defence and continues:

> We left in 1998. I don't remember the year but my husband does. I remember the day. It was a Saturday. We were to go to a cult [religious meeting of *cristianos*,

members of the Evangelical Church]. I looked outside and saw a military car pass full of soldiers. I said they had to be going to Turbo, the municipality. There were two paths leading to our house, the central one and one from the back, from around the corner. We were late so we used the central one and left on bikes, without realising the military was coming to ours, from the back. Our son, he was eight at the time, came on a bicycle behind us to tell us that some masked men came looking for his father. It was the time when people were disappeared. They would put them on trucks, kill them and bury them somewhere … The day before his niece invited him to go with her to Buenaventura to work there. He said he would think about it but as it happened he left the same day. He didn't even go home! Oh, I was afraid so much. I was alone with my three children for three months. We wouldn't leave the house. They thought he'd be back and I felt I was persecuted on every step. In those three months I would see the para-militaries near the house every day […] Three months later I went to see him in Buenaventura. Luckily I took my children with me because he wanted to see them. When I was there, they told me they were looking for me. I didn't go back. I left everything. I only took four or five items of clothing. We lost everything but luckily not the most important thing – nothing happened to our family.

After leaving Urabá Don Jorge and Doña Isabel travelled a lot for work. They were in Cali, Nariño, back in Cali. Then Pedro, who is Don Jorge's nephew, called them and invited them to come to Cundinamarca, where the displaced were negotiating land.

The landfill story

Martina sent bus tickets to her mother Doña Olivia, to be able to join the rest in Cundinamarca. On arriving at their current municipality, a local offered her a house in *obra negra*, a house under construction, 'without utilities, without doors, without anything'. Fernanda, Fabio's wife, remembers they slept on the floor, but that they had to persist if they wanted to find land.

> I was eight months pregnant. I had to sleep on the floor. I had to wash clothes in the river with water up to here [points to her waist]. I didn't feel my son for three days because of the cold. We came from *tierra caliente* (hot land). It was a night-mare to come here. We were to go to Bogotá to an *albergue* (a shelter provided by the government) but what would we do there? Ask for money at the traffic lights, sleep with men, women, children? We had to find a *finca*.

The man was an official working at the municipality. He offered the house to Doña Olivia, who said there were six of them, but the entire group of about forty at the time, moved into the house. The man also helped the displaced find temporary work. Doña Olivia found this part of the journey the most difficult. 'We were humiliated for everything, water, electricity. We depended on others.' After a bit more than a year, the man asked the displaced to give him back his house. He gave in to the pressure of his family who believed that the displaced would invade his property, since they started growing vegetables on the plot. Not knowing what to do, the displaced went to the municipality and asked for a meeting with the mayor. To do so they had to pass through the *Secretaría de Gobierno* (Secretary of Government). The latter, Juan explains, did not want the displaced to stay in the municipality.

> The Secretary of Government said this phrase: that if she wanted she could have us collected in a dump truck and dumped in Soacha. We said, 'No,' and she said, '*Uy*, the municipality got full of bad people.' And one of us said, '*Doctora*, we are *desplazados*, we don't have education, but with all due respect I ask you one thing. Why do you want to dump us like animals? Respect us, because we also deserve respect. You work here in the municipality, you need to give us a hand. What you have to say is, 'I can help you with this, but I can't promise you this, because I don't have it,' but you can't throw us out like animals. Do me a favour, if this isn't Colombia, show me the map, if Cundinamarca doesn't belong to Colombia, we'll leave, but for now we are staying and we need a meeting with the mayor.'

Various attempts to get a meeting with the mayor did not work out, therefore the displaced visited the local priest who helped them access him. The priest and the mayor visited the displaced in the unfinished house where they were staying and both were surprised by the amount of people who lived there. They brought them some food and clothes, and the mayor helped link the displaced with the *Red de Solidaridad Social* (Social Solidarity Network).[2] The displaced negotiated a permission to move onto a landfill site with the mayor where they stayed for almost two years. The mayor expressed concern over the number of youth in the group and delinquency. To address these concerns the displaced signed an agreement on coexistence in which they outlined the rules of behaviour, including the responsibility for any people that members of the community invited and a commitment to keep children and youth away from trouble. They set up houses made of plastic and cardboard. The dwellers of the landfill later managed to get electricity which Juan proudly labels as a clear demonstration of their capabilities.

Their stay at the landfill site attracted attention; they became of interest to the public who came to look at them as if they 'were animals'. The displaced sent a photo of the landfill to the *Red de Solidaridad*. Juan explains, 'Steam was escaping, gases were escaping. We didn't know. We had itches, children started to get sick and *claro* (obviously) when these people came [from the *Red*] they said, "You live on a time bomb. This is a landfill, it develops gases, it can explode or sink".' The displaced used this fact to exert pressure and negotiate with Incora (*Instituto Colombiano de la Reforma Agraria*) the then Colombian Institute for Agrarian Reform to obtain access to land in Cundinamarca.

This was no easy engagement. They were among the first to be recognised as *desplazados*, and they often had to explain to local government representatives what the concept meant. They studied Law 387, concerning displacement, to equip themselves with knowledge of their rights as IDPs. The long process required a great degree of persistence. 'Being displaced we had a drive,' explains Juan. Sometimes men would work and women would go to Bogotá to visit the

Figure 3 The landfill where the displaced lived. Rubbish, like bottles, is seen close under the surface. This is one of the reasons it was described as a 'time bomb'.

necessary institutions; at other times the roles would be reversed. Both women and men often had to wait for the entire day to receive assistance from governmental officials. 'Three women would go to Bogotá to ask for rights. They left at 3 or 4 a.m. and got back at 9 p.m. … The officials don't respect *campesinos'* time,' observes Fabio, reflecting on the long waits, often to no avail. In 2002 they finally managed to obtain the *fincas* where some of them still live today. The government processed their request as one made by *campesinos* rather than *desplazados* and therefore subsidised only 70 per cent of the purchase, while they had to provide 30 per cent by themselves. 'What did we do?' asks Juan.

> Living on the landfill, we met and well 'You, what do you have *de lo mejorcito* (of the best available)?' 'Ah, I have these shoes, what precious objects do you have?' Some people managed to bring gold, a chicken, a hen, a pig, a calf, what do you have to sell? We had to sell all this to give money to the man [who was selling the land]. I don't know how we did it, it's a God's thing, *mi diosito* (God in diminutive form) helped us, but we collected eight million pesos [approximately £2,050], including coins of fifty pesos I remember. But the man said it wasn't enough that he wanted everything.

The displaced were about three million pesos [approximately £768] short for which they needed to take out a loan in the agrarian bank. Since they were not able to get a loan for land, they lied, saying it was for productive projects. A year and a half after, when they were supposed to pay some interest, the planning officer visited them and realised that the displaced had not undertaken any projects on the land. They nearly lost their plots since they were caught on a lie, but also because they had no means to repay the loan. An NGO saved them with another loan which they used to repay the agrarian one; they were still repaying the debt in 2011.

Listening to these stories, it came as no surprise that Alejandra concludes the land 'cost us blood'. The precarious life in the mining town of Risaralda, the time spent living on the landfill, the days when they endured hunger, the persistent fight to access land, the sale of their personal possessions, and their work to pay off the debt, all present an important history of their struggle for land acquisition and form an essential part of the journey and displacement experiences.

A different kind of struggle

The journey and the process of land acquisition was similarly not an easy matter for those displaced who are now in Porvenir. Since they come from different parts of the country, their routes and stories in most cases came together only after they had reached the current village. Some of them, including Cesar, were involved in a struggle for their piece of land as arduous as the displaced in Esperanza. It required a great amount of persistence as well as organisation. Cesar, who is originally from Valle, was nineteen years old when there was a confrontation between the guerrillas and the paramilitaries near his *finca*. He and his family escaped to town that night and he returned the following day together with his brother.

> There were two *guerrilleras* (female guerrillas) at the *finca*. They told us not to worry, that we shouldn't be afraid. They spent the night there and I got involved with one of them so I became an assistant. I was once asked to do a *mercado* for the guerrilla and on the way back I met the military. I was very afraid but I continued. A few days after, upon returning home from town I realised the military had burnt down everything – my house, *cultivos* (crops), they killed the cattle, chicken. The military at the time was worse than now.

Cesar went to town, told people what had happened and they helped him. He stayed living in town and worked on his father's *finca*. He left the town in 1999 when his cousin was killed and since he was still believed to collaborate with the guerrillas he was afraid the same thing would happen to him. Together with his wife and two children they took a bus to Soacha, because one of his brothers lived there but he did not know where. 'I didn't know how to find my way around Bogotá and I didn't find my brother. He found me later on.' In Soacha, the police picked the family up and took them to an *albergue*, where they received food and accommodation for a month. Cesar started selling sweets on the street to provide for the family. One morning in December 1999, he heard about the occupation of the ICRC headquarters on the radio. He walked the entire morning to reach ICRC premises and one of the spokespersons invited him to join the protestors. 'He asked me if I had family and told me to bring them along.'

Occupation of public spaces and offices providing services has been an important strategy for the displaced to confront the state and demand their rights. The initial number of those who started the occupation at ICRC was small. The word soon spread and Cesar assesses there were 1,200 people present at one point. At the beginning of January the following year, the police surrounded and closed off the area, registered the occupiers and began to control the entrances and exits into the premises. Only those registered were allowed to protest; those who left the grounds had to return on the same day or were not allowed to re-enter. As a result of this restricted movement, some of the occupiers declared themselves 'prisoners of their own occupation' (Agier 2001: 96), or as Cesar concludes reflecting on the situation more generally, 'Our rights were being breached on the territory of an organisation which promotes human rights.'

In January 2000, the government started negotiating with the occupiers, granted them some assistance such as a three-month rent but the displaced called for long-term measures. 'We demanded land, housing, health and education.' The government broke off negotiations two weeks later and raised suspicions that not everyone had actually been displaced – that a number of them were involved in coca cultivation and/or had links with the guerrillas. Cesar who is convinced that it is impossible to get anything from the government through non-confrontational means explains some 'crucified' themselves in order to achieve what the group of protestors demanded. The crucified had themselves nailed to wooden poles in an act of symbolism. After months and even years of not being listened to, when the government in its position of power had not done anything to address people's rights and demands, the act of crucifixion was aimed at gaining people's support. It served to show the rest that the displaced were right in demanding their rights, that what they were fighting for made sense. Crucifixion was not only a strategy of gaining attention; for the protestors it also had emotional bearing.

Things started moving after images of hungry children were transmitted to the public. Cesar remembers the occupiers held a journalist of TV Caracol, one of Colombia's most important private national television networks, for a couple of days and made him film children making noise with pots saying they were hungry. The protestors detained the journalist because the TV station did them harm by reporting that half of the people who were protesting were in reality not displaced. 'There truly was not enough food,' Cesar adds as a sort of an apology for detaining the journalist. 'My wife would be asking for money at traffic lights to make ends meet and only in the evening return to *Cruz Roja.*' The image of hungry children and hungry IDPs was sent out and crossed the borders of Colombia. 'We got fifty toilets, more food and people from 112 countries came to see us,' he adds with a sense of pride and achievement. The international pressure, people's activism and the effect the occupation had on ICRC's work in the country – ICRC partially suspended its activities in Colombia during that period (El Tiempo 2000) – led to a writ of protection of fundamental rights (*Acción de tutela*) T-1635 of 2000.[3] The latter was initiated by the Colombian Ombudsman against Social Solidarity Network. The Constitutional Court ruled that people's rights as defined in the Colombian constitution had been affected, and demanded that the government provided resettlement for the displaced, whose numbers were in a couple of hundreds, within a maximum of thirty days (ICRC unknown).

As a result of the Court's ruling, some of the occupiers of ICRC were assigned the *fincas* in Porvenir. Roberto remembers that only five families were initially due to be resettled there. However, Incora decided that the plot as a whole was big enough to support the resettlement of fourteen families and the land was thus partitioned to smaller lots. The designation of land did not solve the issues the displaced were facing. The *fincas* in Porvenir had already been involved in a process of negotiation with Incora, having been originally earmarked for landless peasants from the area, not for the displaced. The Court's decision obliged the government to look for a quick solution for IDPs and consequently the landless *campesinos* lost out.

The sudden change in plans and the lack of consultation with either the locals or the landless peasants who were supposed to have been the new inhabitants of the *fincas* provoked a strong reaction. The locals, who were not keen on having *desplazados* as their neighbours and who were additionally angry at the development of events, 'displaced' the IDPs. Under the pretence of being guerrillas, they threatened the displaced. The latter looked for temporary shelter in the nearby city, Fusagasugá (or Fusa as locally known). The mayors of the municipality where Porvenir is based and of a neighbouring municipality paid for the displaceds' accommodation in Fusa. Don Sergio, a non-displaced resident, believes that some of the IDPs had links with the guerrillas and used their connections to verify the true nature of the threats. When these proved to be false the displaced returned to Porvenir but this time accompanied by the police. They showed the locals official papers confirming that they had a legal right to be there. The landless peasants were consequently assigned plots in a different hamlet in the same municipality, which are allegedly of lower quality. The relationship with the non-displaced was therefore marked from the very start – not only for those who got there first, but also for any subsequent IDPs who moved to the hamlet.

Not everyone in Porvenir had occupied the ICRC headquarters. Some, like Daniel, an evangelical priest in his late forties, got the opportunity to be allocated land after the estate had been divided into more than five plots. But before then, he and his family underwent a number of insecurities.

> We left Tolima because I feared they would recruit my children. I have six boys and three girls. Children no longer join voluntarily. They are taken by force more and more. My cousin's daughter joined when she was thirteen. She escaped after three months and they killed her … We went to Saocha first and since we didn't know what to do there or where to go we turned around and started walking back towards Tolima. There were eleven of us and we were walking for two days. We stopped in Fusa because my wife got injured and couldn't walk anymore. We lived under a bridge for four months.

Under the bridge they met Angelica, Roberto and their seven children who also left Tolima due to similar concerns. 'We received a *boletín* (newsletter, notice). I don't know how to read so I don't know what [exactly] it said, but it said that parents are expected to hand their children over to the guerrillas,' explains Angelica. Since two of their sons were ten and eleven years old at the time, the couple were afraid they might be potential targets of recruitment. They only took clothes and money for a month's rent. Angelica also managed to save some photos. They returned later to collect their things but they were gone. Roberto continues:

> We left Ataco at night and arrived to Fusa at one or two in the morning. I still don't know why Fusa. We just took the bus. We had no family there. We slept in the park under plastic covering. We stayed there for a week, when *Red de Solidaridad* noticed us and gave us subsidy for three months' rent after which we were on the street again.

Angelica confirms they lived like that, in a plastic hut, for a year and then two or three more years in Porvenir. In Fusa they lived on handouts. A bakery would give them bread that was left over from the previous day and hot chocolate for breakfast. Someone gave them a child's bed. Roberto explains he was not able to find work. 'I couldn't get work because I was *desplazado* and people think one is a thief and I don't know what else.' When the land in Porvenir was partitioned, they were invited to participate in the programme. Their current neighbours Doña María and Don Eduardo also got their chance.

Doña María and Don Eduardo left their village in Tolima in 1999. Don Eduardo was the president of the local junta, which Doña María believes was the reason why he was receiving threats. They no longer slept at night. 'We had a pedigree dog whose ears were so long that they would always touch the food before it started to eat. We kept the dog in our bedroom at night so that it would warn us if they were coming,' Doña María remembers. Don Eduardo started sleeping outside the house, returning home in the morning. When they decided to leave, they left the *finca* at night and spent the night in town, in Líbano. In the morning they took a bus to Chía, a city in Cundinamarca, where Don Eduardo's friend lived. Doña María explains:

> We only took clothes and blankets since we knew it would be cold in Chía. I asked my daughter to store our photos and we later brought a small fridge we had in Tolima. We also took a small radio and we left the big one to the children. […] We only took the youngest daughter, the rest stayed behind … *Uy no*, it is difficult to be separated. Before we all lived together. We stayed in Chía for four months. I barely left the house. I wouldn't, no … [does not conclude the thought]. The mare, the *macho* (the horse), pigs, chicken, the dog … we left everything.

After four months in Chía, the three went to Soacha, south of Bogotá, to live with Doña María's brother. Doña María was selling *arepas* (flatbread made of ground maize) to get by. It was enough to buy them food but it was '*duro*'. She suffers from headaches and insists that she developed them during that time because of all the smoke and heat from *arepas* (see Figure 4). Don Eduardo worked in construction. His colleague told him of the land in Porvenir and he managed to be included as one of the fourteen families which got access to land. Doña María describes their initial time in Porvenir:

Figure 4 Preparation of *arepas* in Doña María's current kitchen.

> We lived in a house made of cardboard, plastic and plantain leaves. After I got
> ill, Eduardo asked for a room in this house [the house where they are now living,
> which had been at the property before their arrival]. We were sharing it with
> other people. Uh no, there were some lazy people here. They wouldn't work, eat,
> all they did was smoke. I gave food to three *muchachos* (young men) because
> I couldn't see them like that.

She adds, 'When we arrived, here there was plantain everywhere. No, why would
I lie? It was a rubbish tip! Eduardo had to clean everything to be able to sow coffee.'

Alongside the families which were either occupying the ICRC premises or
were invited additionally to participate in the land programme, there are also
those who reached the village through kinship ties. Among them were Linda and
Carlos who left Tolima due to high presence of the guerrillas. Carlos explains that
he served in the military, and after he returned to Tolima 'people didn't like it that
I didn't support the guerrillas. One day I was drinking beer and a commander
approached me and asked me why I wasn't supporting them. I said I wasn't with or
against anyone.' Since he did not go to fiestas that the guerrilla organised, he was
accused of being a spy, Linda says.

> They told him to leave or give them four heads of cattle. He was planning to pay
> but I said we should leave. How much longer? We had small children, we had to
> do something. I was afraid they would take them away. Carlos left first and I left
> eight days later. I said I was going to town to cook for my daughter who was at
> school there. I only took clothes not to look suspicious and I asked my brother to
> look after the animals. [...] I would go crazy if we had stayed. One had to think
> about them [the guerrillas] all the time. One needs to think twice to leave the land
> behind, one cries but I'm happy that we left. There are some people who stayed,

who said they would not leave the land, and what happens – they get killed and no one wants to go there, not even their family members, no one.

Carlos took a bus and went straight to Porvenir where his brother secured land as part of the initial fourteen families. He had visited him before so he knew where he was going and what to expect. His brother moved in with his new partner from the neighbouring hamlet and offered Linda and Carlos his *finca*. What they produce, they produce in *compañía* (company), they split it half-half.

Transformations

The point at which people leave varies from being closely related to the death of loved ones, threats, fear for their children's safety, to plain unbearable circumstances and danger in which they live. When I asked him at what point he decided to leave, Fabio corrected me, 'Not that we *decided* to leave, there was no other option left but to leave,' stressing the forced character of their flight. Some escapes are spontaneous, others more planned, yet even the planned escape leaves people with little guarantee. People walk, run, travel by bus, hire a truck or a car, or even fly to places which they hope would be safer. Some travel together, others one by one not to raise suspicion. In some cases families are separated for months, not knowing whether the rest will be able to travel, what the situation is and what the other's faith is. They travel by day, others in the dark of the night, hide, sleep in plastic huts in the open air, on the floor of houses of relatives or acquaintances. The circumstances of violence in the given context, their own personal connections, and means, shape their journeys and routes. The choice of the destination can be random, without a contact that could receive those escaping violence, but people's preferences mostly rest on previous knowledge of a place and/or kinship ties.

My interviewees might have escaped violence, terror or even death, but a number of them nevertheless found little comfort in the journey. The route brought new uncertainties, and in some cases, where there was no food to serve, existential insecurities with little indication of when the potential improvement might come about. The escape, the travel, but most of all the interim stops en route, forever marked the course of life events. Alejandro, whose road to maturity was accelerated, has been working ever since the family left Urabá. He lost some years of schooling, but he then continued his education and has never stopped contributing to the household budget. In similar ways, some of those whose roles of providers were interrupted either because their children or their wives found work more easily, have not managed to recuperate their position in the family completely, which has marked their self-image, esteem and the sense of self. Journeys can speed up the process of growing up through the emergence of new responsibilities, but they can also generate a sense of powerlessness when one's roles and duties are no longer fulfilled.

There are also transformations in leadership. Some, like Don Andrés or Fabio, lose their role with displacement. An official at *Comisión Nacional de la Reparación y Reconciliación* (National Commission for Reparations and Reconciliation,

CNRR)[4] evaluates such a transformation as problematic and deserving more attention.

> There are leaders who come and in some cases reaffirm their leadership, but there
> are many that the city does not accept. For instance, here there are a lot of town
> councillors, who are leaders in their municipalities but here they can't deploy
> that capacity. There also isn't a differential treatment for these leaders and there
> should be. The displacement of leaders who don't have any special treatment is
> great and their skills are lost.

The decline of some means the rise of others. For Juan and Pedro the landfill story and consequent visits to governmental offices meant the initiation of their new function as IDP leaders. They were in their twenties when they left Urabá and were not actively engaged in politics and did not hold any kind of leadership position. Displacement changed this. The old leaders, mostly due to fear of continued persecution stepped to the side, and the two managed to turn the group's struggle into a pillar upon which they have built their political identity, which even almost twenty years after the physical relocation is still one of the most important markers of their self-identification.

Juanita, Don Eduardo's daughter, who also assumed a leadership role, similarly managed to improve her situation and position in the family.

> I feel freer in terms of movement. There [in Tolima] I'd be at home all the time,
> the only person that would leave the house was Patricio [her husband]. He'd leave
> on a Friday to pay the workers and would return on a Monday. He drank a lot
> then. I thought I couldn't leave him, that it was a crime. If one gets married, one
> stays for better or for worse. I once left for four months with my son. I changed
> during that time. I learnt how to do *mercado*. One when one drinks, one forgets
> about *mercado*, it's drinking first. I would leave the house, but I would still have
> to ask for permission. Now, being a leader, I go here and there, if someone calls
> me I go, I don't ask.

For others the struggle for land and persistence gave them personal pride. Cesar for instance describes the occupation of ICRC premises as 'the most important protest in the history of Colombia'. He still keeps a magazine report of the event, proud that he took part in it. Journeys can be highly stressful but for Juanita, Pedro, Juan and Cesar, they brought some positive changes.

Beyond the individual and family levels, group relations have been affected. If the displaced in Porvenir might have never experienced a true unity, the situation was quite different for the displaced in Esperanza. The difficulties that they experienced on their way to the hamlet helped them form a tight-knit community at the time. Fabio reflecting back concludes that 'the community was born out of necessity'. The preference was given to the group and its progress and not to individuals. The support that was generated helped them go through some of the most difficult moments, and it was a driving force that kept them going. Upon arrival to Esperanza, when the displaced were faced with unfavourable reception, drawing on a common story helped group's cohesion and solidarity and has helped them *salir adelante*. At the same time, especially now that the community spirit has been lost, the group myth, which originates from the journey, can be detrimental to relationships. The adoption and perhaps imposition of the single main narrative insinuates prioritisation of certain experiences over others. It is a constant reminder of the sacrifices some of the displaced have made, a call for continuous gratitude, including by the leaders whose leadership legitimacy some of the group began to question.

End of the road? The power to keep in place or remove from place

I walked through Esperanza with Juan. He stopped in the middle of the hill, paused, and pointed his finger to the glimpses of two towns stretching out before us in the valley below. He remembered his initial enthusiasm over the village thinking unbelievably that his potential new home lies not only near the capital but that he can even see two *pueblos* from it. 'We have come far,' he said, speaking of progress rather than only distance. 'We're doing well compared to other displaced, but we still have a long way to go.' Placing his hand in front of him and levelling it with his waist he commented they were only on the first floor. He then moved his hand higher up to show they had been on the fourth or even fifth floor before displacement. 'It is a constant fight,' he concluded. Doña Beatriz, his wife, openly questioned if their journey had come to an end. Speaking about their route to Esperanza and life there she uttered, 'This is the future God gave us but it doesn't mean we have to die here.' When I returned to Esperanza six months later, Doña Beatriz, Juan and their family were not there. Like six households before them, they had left Esperanza. They moved to Bogotá, most likely in search of a staircase which would take them to a higher floor.

After the difficulties experienced throughout the journey to the two villages, many saluted the access to 'tierra firme' (land, solid ground). Alejandra thought that they were in 'paradise', while Martina remembers the displaced saw the land as their 'salvation'. Despite high hopes, people's journeys have not ended. In similar ways in which the migration of the mind may have started before people physically moved, it may continue after resettlement. The following chapters will highlight such cognitive migration to past and new places. But alongside the migration of the mind, actual physical movement has taken place.

A number of the displaced who were primary beneficiaries of the land had already left the plots and both Esperanza and Porvenir have seen a great degree of demographic upheaval. In Porvenir, fourteen displaced households had been allocated land eleven years before fieldwork took place, and yet at the time of research only four of the originally designated beneficiaries remained there, and another came only occasionally to check on how his *finca* was being administered. In Esperanza, twelve displaced households had been allocated land ten years before the study was conducted. Seven of these remained during the first part of the fieldwork and six during the second part, with one household having returned and two others leaving. Some of the displaced households that are still in the two hamlets similarly expressed their wish and/or intention to leave. Yet, in the search of better living conditions and opportunities, people are not free from constraints. Their movements, presence and absence are regulated and controlled through legal means.

The land the displaced managed to secure has come with certain demands and limits which are shaping their journeys. The 'beneficiaries' of the programme are required to cultivate the plot. They cannot lease it, sell it, transfer it, and the land should be used for cultivation of licit produce. There are also certain restrictions related to time. If they wish to have full rights to the land, people need to stay on the property for a period of twelve years. If they leave or sell the land, the officials at Incoder,[5] Bogotá office explain, they lose it as well as the right to participate in any further programmes linked to agricultural development. Certain requirements are necessary and have backing from some of the displaced. Adrián, one of Don Andrés' sons believes, 'There are many people who would exploit the scheme and sell the land were there no time period.' Martina on the other hand is not that supportive. 'I don't agree [with the policy]. If one sees one can't progress, one leaves. I'm certain that my brother [one of the original beneficiaries of land in Esperanza] who worked every day as a rule and was hard-working wouldn't be able to *salir adelante* had he stayed. But he managed to do so when he moved away.'

Incoder officials admit that the Institute has not performed its tasks the way it should have. In an interview with three of its officials, one of the leading figures of Bogotá office assesses:

> Well, I'll be sincere and honest since it can't be hidden, right? From my point of view the Institute when it handed over the land in the last ten years, gave people a handshake saying, 'Good luck, I hope it all goes well.' There is still no sufficiently strong process of monitoring that I could say we have monitoring in place. Only last year we got some funds to start monitoring what happened with the lands in the past ten years at the territorial level. These funds hadn't existed before … With properties which were handed over as a result of direct purchase of the land [the case of the two villages in question], the whole subsidy went to the purchase of the land, not in productive project. Which means that people got there and … [he pauses, claps his hands once] and looked how they are going to care for themselves. In this moment, this is double work for us because we realised there is a world of problems in a number of properties.

Another official whom I interviewed separately, who worked for Incora before and was the president of its labour union for six years supported such observations: 'Bit by bit we are learning. There have been improvements but it is a slow process. The problem of the state is that it doesn't think in the long term; frequently not even in the medium term.'

Despite the 'world of problems', the restrictions of movement remain in place. It often feels as if the twelve-year period needs to be followed at any cost. The context, that these twelve years are accompanied by ongoing conflict and violence, is not considered. Personal dislike of the place expressed through 'excuses' such as 'the wife didn't like it or didn't settle in' are not valid, one of the officers commented. Valid reasons are health and security issues even though the three officials could not agree on the latter. 'The question of security is not clear,' said the head of the unit, 'because people need to provide evidence that a threat really exists. It has to be strongly checked. Who is going to buy the plot if it is insecure?' Unanswered requests for permission to leave the plot on security grounds that Martina and Don Eduardo sent to Incoder, hint that such requests tend to fall on deaf ears.

'In 2009/2010, when I was already a town councillor, I started receiving threats from *autodefensas los Rastrojos* (drug trafficking paramilitary organisation). I left the *finca*. I asked Incoder for relocation but I never received their reply,' explains Don Eduardo. Martina, on the other hand, did not receive direct threats. She felt her life was in danger when she realised that her moves were being followed. In 2007 she travelled to the department of Nariño with the plan to join the guerrillas. She was disappointed with the lack of political consciousness of the contemporary guerrillas. 'I asked the *guerrilleros* why were they there. They said it was for the money and to provide for the family. Then I asked them about the ideology they taught them and they answered that was their ideology.' Martina left the guerrillas and returned to Esperanza two months later. Even though she had not told anyone where she had gone the word came out and she no longer felt safe in the village. Like Don Eduardo, she never heard back from Incoder and like Don Eduardo, she too had to find her own ways of survival – Don Eduardo resorted to short-term physical relocations to Bogotá, and Martina left Colombia. In both cases, their respective families were divided. In order not to lose their farms they have both returned to their hamlets despite the persistent unease. Don Eduardo has launched a *tutela*, suing the government for failing to consider his application. Martina on the other hand feels trapped, and continues to harbour the negative sentiments she cultivates around her life in Esperanza.

The security situation in many parts of Colombia remains unstable and can change. Juanita passed me rules about *orden público*, law and order, allegedly signed by the FARC, Frente 51, concerning department of Cundinamarca, including the two municipalities where Porvenir and Esperanza are situated. Even though no one else made reference to the document, she said it was distributed in Porvenir on Independence Day, on 20 July 2011, but dated March 2011. The guerrillas' presence is not noticeable in day-to-day life and the rules set out in the *orden público* are not being followed to the letter or at all. Nevertheless, the village and its surroundings had a stronger military presence in 2012 as compared to 2011 (see Figure 5). The military was even camping on Don Eduardo's farm for a few days in 2012. According to the commander, this formed part of their usual practice; nevertheless the greater presence might have also pointed to the change in the security situation.

In Porvenir the alteration was noticeable in the increasing number of extortions. Simón, a man in his fifties who lives alone in Porvenir, received threats from people introducing themselves as the guerrillas. He did not believe it was the guerrillas since 'they do things in a different way'.[6] 'They want a part of my earnings

Figure 5 The presence of the military in a municipality neighbouring that of Porvenir before a cultural event.

otherwise they say they will hurt my family. They are hurting the well-being of my family if I give them money!' Simón turned to the police for protection but was disappointed with their reaction. 'They told me not to worry. They are there in their office and I live alone up here. I have no one to protect me.' Simón decided to leave the village for a couple of days to do some rounds to try to find out the origin of the threats. Besides him, his neighbours Don Ignacio and Doña Flor, and Tania and Álvaro, have also fallen victim to extortion. In six months, three people were killed in the surrounding hamlets and a nearby town, two allegedly because they did not meet the extortionists' demands. All this has led to greater cautiousness. Carlos for instance tries to sell his produce less visibly. The extortionists, he believes, keep record of everyone's harvest. 'They count the number of sacks of coffee one sells.' Carlos even holds that due to threat of extortion people do not work as much as they could. 'Forty per cent of people don't work. If one goes to town, one sees people on the street at any time of the day. You go on a different day and you see the same people or perhaps different ones. People don't work. As soon as one has something, they come and take it away.'

Those who wish to continue their journey but cannot due to legal restraints are not the only ones who face the rigidity of policies and who are subdued to the unequal power relations in the process of place negotiation. On the other side of the spectrum are those who were not the original beneficiaries of the land but who bought land from the displaced who had left the respective hamlets. They are free to leave since they are not bound by any contract; yet, none of them wishes or plans to do so. In contrast, they would like to stay. Linda and Carlos are among those 'secondary occupants' of plots who demonstrate their appreciation of the place through emotional and material investment in their *fincas*. Simón,

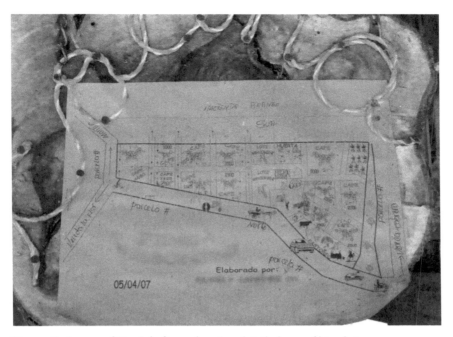

Figure 6 A map of Simón's *finca*, showing detailed use of his plot.

Don Ignacio and Doña Flor keep a map of their plots, where they have carefully outlined what each metre of the land is used for (see Figure 6). They use notices such as 'do not litter', or 'hunting prohibited' and display them on their properties. They have also made changes to their houses; Don Ignacio and Doña Flor have extended the house; they built a bigger living room and a kitchen, which was previously kept outside. Linda and Carlos too have renovated their kitchen. Through their investments the four exhibit a sense of ownership, 'a sense of control over the living area' (Lewicka 2011: 225), as well as their intention to stay.

Yet, their place-making and future life in the place might come to an abrupt end. While the above-mentioned are registered as *desplazados* and in need to find a new place, they were not the originally designated proprietors of the plots they currently inhabit. Their future is therefore uncertain. Colombia has a history of informality and many people do not have papers to prove land ownership. Some displaced hope this informality will work in their favour. Doña Flor believes that by showing the officials they are hard-working, they will be allowed to stay; a sentiment which the bureaucrats do not share. The officials at Incoder territorial unit of Cundinamarca expressed views which point to the opposite:

> They were ripped off. Ripped off. They have no right to this land. They bought a right that never existed … I imagine they signed a buying and selling contract. They are victims of fraud. To us they are invaders from a judicial point of

view. They don't have and won't have any right to the piece of land. None … This land should be returned to Incoder and then Incoder has it at its disposal. … It doesn't matter if the people who bought the land were IDPs, at least initially. There is a way to normalise the matter but it is very difficult … They can be subjects of agrarian reform. I'm not saying they are not. But it's almost as if they started the process anew to get land. It can be this one [the plot in question] or a different one. The problem is, this will sound very sad, but if we allow this to happen [for people to sell and buy properties before the period of twelve years has been accomplished], we are almost inviting land invasions. It would become an absolutely unmanageable problem.

For Incoder 'success is if people stay on the land'. But these need to be individuals who were the original beneficiaries, who need to face any difficulties they may be experiencing on the land, including security issues, practically on their own. The government policy exercises monopoly over people, their movement and territory, their journeys and consequently their place-making project. While the latter is inherently subjective, there are forces 'in place' which go beyond one's ability and wishes that are decisive in the outcome of the process – whether the feeling-at-home continues or not. In the same way that the legislation has the power to keep people in place, it also has the power to compel them out of their place. The fragmentation of the journey, insecurities and the control over people's movement – confining them or compelling them to leave – blur the distinction between the temporary and long-term, potentially permanent, settlement places. Due to this blurred distinction coupled with persistent instability and uncertainty, journeys are embedded in displacement process and not separate from it.

Notes

1 Medellín is the capital of the department of Antioquia; the department within which Urabá lies.
2 The Network's programmes originally addressed poverty issues, but it was eventually also given the responsibility for assisting IDPs.
3 *Acción de tutela* is a mechanism for the protection of fundamental rights of those who live in Colombia. Individuals, without a need for a lawyer, can present them to the court. It became a common mechanism of exercise of one's rights.
4 CNRR was created as a result of 2005 Justice and Peace Law; among others the Commission was overlooking the demobilisation process of the paramilitaries, was in charge of verification of reintegration projects and work of local authorities, was responsible to ensure victims' participation in the process of judicial investigation and realisation of their rights, and to advance reconciliation on the national level.
5 Incoder replaced Incora in 2003.
6 Some other villagers of Porvenir, displaced and non-displaced alike, similarly hold that often people pass themselves as guerrillas in order to exert control or money.

5

The making of a *desplazado*

Displacement in Colombia has a long history; nevertheless, it was only in the mid-1990s when the *desplazados* were born. *Desplazado*, a word that even at the beginning of the 1990s was hardly ever heard, is now an established and frequently utilised expression. It gained prominence after it had become part of legislation and an official category denoting those who have left their places of residence due to violence, persecution and fear. Since then, the term has become part of the general vocabulary, used not only by the policymakers and practitioners but also by journalists, academia, the general public and ultimately by the displaced themselves. The continuous, everyday use of categories and their standardisation, particularly when used on an international scale, give an impression that the categories are self-evident, natural and objective (Starr 1992: 294).[1] Yet, a number of categories are socially constructed, charged with some kind of political or social connotation. Ian Hacking (1986, 1999) convincingly argues that categories have created new ways for people to be. The 'making up of people' affects how they live, how they are perceived, and also how they act.

While some categories can be valorising, the negative consequences of others are numerous. For instance, the categorised are amalgamated into groups that are thought to possess similar interests and identities due to which the various social roles they possess are often hidden or ignored. Categories can rank people according to priority and status. They create and re-create social boundaries between people, dividing them into 'us' and 'them', they include some and exclude others, and they (re)create social inequalities (van Dijk 1998). In this chapter, I focus on categorisation of people as *desplazdos* undertaken by the Colombian state. A number of actors are involved in the categorisation process but the state's categorisation is the most powerful of all. The state has the necessary means to impose categories, shape them and put them to use. It thus gives them weight, grounding and officially compartmentalises those categorised into a certain slot of society.

My aim is not to question the appropriateness of having an IDP category per se; the category is necessary to acknowledge the political and social wrong in a given country which affects a number of people in particular ways. There is a cognitive value in the category (Jaramillo *et al.* 2004). It provokes thinking about the social order and the disorder in the state of affairs in Colombia. It alludes to the breach of human rights. It thus offers recognition of structural difficulties, and the inability of the state to provide protection to its population. Additionally the category speaks of people's persecution and therefore has a political and symbolic meaning. Rather, I analyse the ways in which the category is produced, reproduced and used, the assumptions that it contains, how it can, aided by the scope of the phenomenon, depersonalise those it is supposed to help, and ultimately how categorisation can impact the meta-narratives about conflict and social reality in Colombia. I first look at the historical development of how the category came into being. I then look at the politicised process of registering the *desplazados*, and then turn to the examination of who is perceived as a deserving victim, how people attempt to comply with such requirements and the consequences this can have on recording of history. I conclude with the discussion about how categories can depersonalise people.

The birth of the category

Law 387 of 1997 was the first major law to address displacement. It came into being not necessarily as a result of the government's concern, but was instead influenced by pressures that national and international NGOs and civil society exerted on the government. The nature of the driving force behind the creation of the law helps explain years of government's lack of engagement with the displaced and displacement. Displacement did not appear on national and public agendas due to sudden aggravation of the problem. Pécaut (2001) notes that the society living in a state of neither peace nor war paid attention only to grave acts of violence but not to slow transformation of the society brought about by violence, like the expansion of the guerrillas, drug cultivation and production of new paramilitary strategies. When the presence of the displaced in cities increased substantially new categories had to be invented and public spokespeople started thinking about violence and related phenomena.

The creation of the category had external influences. It came into being as a consequence of numerous factors taking place at the national, regional and international levels. In April 1980, Amnesty International issued a report on human rights violations in Colombia. This was superseded by reports from other international NGOs such as WOLA (Washington Office on Latin America), Americas Watch, and Pax Christi, as well as discussion in the European Parliament and the US Congress (Angarita 2000). The reports exposed the country's affairs to an international audience.

Colombia was not the only country in the region that was facing displacement crisis. Conflicts in Central American countries and in neighbouring Peru contributed to the recognition of states' responsibilities towards the displaced. An important advancement was the plan of action adopted by the governments of El Salvador, Guatemala, Honduras, Mexico, Costa Rica and Nicaragua, which decided to hold an International Conference on Central American Refugees

(CIREFCA) to bring the issue to international attention. The conference, which took place in Guatemala City in 1989, drew attention to the displaced who, unlike refugees, were not under any formal international mandate. Another step forward was the creation of the Permanent Consultation on Internal Displacement in the Americas (CPDIA) in 1992, which included non-Central American countries, such as Colombia and Peru (Weiss Fagen *et al.* 2003).[2] Such international recognition of the phenomenon of displacement helped mobilise Colombian human rights activists.

The character of displacement in Colombia changed in the 1990s. The displaced were no longer mainly leaders of leftist or popular movements; instead, displacement was increasingly used as a military strategy to exert territorial control over the entire population (Osorio Perez 2009). Edilma Osorio Perez explains that the displacement of numerous families began to attract attention, and pressure was exerted on the local and national government and on national and international NGOs to provide humanitarian assistance. The first major achievement by the NGOs was to raise awareness of the problem and to make the government assume responsibility for assisting the displaced. Regional meetings took place with academics who analysed the role of armed actors. The Church, both Catholic and Evangelic, and the media played an important role. The displaced would usually turn for assistance to the Church first, as they perceived it to be 'neutral'. The Church was additionally able to operate throughout the Colombian territory and acted as a mediator in negotiations with armed groups. The media brought displacement closer to the general public through the publication of personal testimonies of those affected.

The government reserved some funding for the provision of humanitarian assistance for the displaced within the Natural Disaster Fund. It treated the phenomenon apolitically, as an aspect of natural disasters, and expected that people would soon return to their homes. In 1995, the Episcopal Conference of Colombia (Conferencia Episcopal de Colombia 1995) undertook the first national study of displacement. The study concluded that one in sixty Colombians had been forced to migrate in the preceding decade. The results of the research were generally accepted due to the legitimacy of the institution, and the research served as a precedent for subsequent studies that focused on areas such as the psychosocial aspects of displacement, education and health provision (Osorio Perez 2009). Displacement was recognised as the most frequent cause of breach of human rights. CONPES, *Consejo Nacional de Política Económica y Social* (the National Council for Economic and Social Policy) formulated two policies concerning displacement and the government eventually passed Law 387 on internal displacement. The law created the policy and administrative category of '*desplazado*'.

Law 387 has been replaced by *Ley de Víctmas*, the Victims' Law, which came into force in the second half of 2011. The Victims' Law was in part a result of fierce critiques of the Justice and Peace Law of 2005 created for the demobilisation of the paramilitaries, which focused on armed actors and offered the demobilised soldiers amnesty. At the same time, the law paid little attention to the victims of paramilitary activity. Hence there were calls for some corrective action. The victims' bill had already been discussed in 2009 during Álvaro Uribe's second administration. However, the Executive Government refused to support it because the bill also recognised as victims those who were affected by the unlawful actions of the state and the military (Céspedes-Báez 2012). With the change in government, Juan Manuel Santos made the bill one of his priorities and it finally became law in June 2011. The Victims' Law is broader in scope compared to Law 387. It recognises other conflict-affected populations, such as victims of torture, forced disappearances, forced recruitment, victims of sexual assault and those affected by land mines.

In relation to displacement, the Victims' Law envisions land restitution and thus represents a step forward from Law 387 in that it assumes a more political response to displacement. A CNRR official also welcomes it due to its recognition of people's rights.

> Colombia has advanced enormously. First, in recognising the quantity of victims that exist in the country and their particularities. But the materialisation [of the law] is complex. On the one hand, we have a country with this many victims, where it hasn't been possible to declare with clarity how many victims there are. And on the other, the levels of inequality. This is something very strange. Something has to lead to a scenario where these differences are negotiated or new conflicts will emerge. So, the Victims' Law, the recognition and the focus on rights, I think its greatest contribution has been the possibility to think at the level of the state that people are subjects of rights.

Nevertheless, the government's efforts are beset with difficulties because the conflict as well as crime persist. The new legislation resulted in numerous deaths of displaced leaders who were campaigning for land restitution, and almost 700 were threatened within a year of the process starting (Semana 2013b). Fabio, who lost land and is eligible to take part in the land restitution, has second thoughts about the process.

> For me it's a good thing but at the same time it isn't recommendable. No one guarantees life to anybody. The president was in Necoclí in Urabá six month ago, giving some things for land restitution and the leader there got killed. So, tell me what is the guarantee? Who guarantees … the state doesn't guarantee life of a person who returns to their land. So I say, what I prefer is, what was lost was lost. Because no one is going to guarantee me life. That's why it isn't easy. It's not an easy topic for the displaced in Colombia. In one way or another these pieces of land that one left, which are now in the hands of irregular armed groups, who are now the owners, who gave them to a *servil* (bootlicker) to have them, but this *servil* who is there is there because he was sent by the group who put him there. And when the time comes when I claim my rights, this group immediately notices me and they can assassinate me.

Additionally, the director of the Land Restitution Unit admitted in an interview for the weekly magazine *Semana* that up to 70 per cent of the land designated for restitution could contain land mines (Semana 2013a). Consequently, even if efforts at an all-encompassing approach which moves beyond the focus on humanitarian assistance are being made, the continuing conflict and crime have severely challenged the process.

Law 387 and the new Victims' Law provide the same legal definition of a displaced person. The difference between the two is that Law 387 refers to a *desplazado*, whereas the Victims' Law speaks of '*víctimas de desplazamiento forzado*' (victims of forced displacement). Both define the subjects of policy as people who were forced to migrate within the national territory, abandoning their location of residence. At the time of the research, the new law and terminology had not yet replaced the term '*desplazado*'. For this reason, but also because I speak of general consequences of categorisation, I make reference to the category *desplazado* rather than to victims of displacement. Whatever the expression is – displaced, victim or something else, the term might lose its explicative meaning in policymaking resulting in homogenisation of varied experiences, reducing people to something measurable and quantifiable (Osorio Perez 2009: 169). As Pedro, an IDP leader in Esperanza, complained, 'If there was a mess before [when the displaced were treated separately], how there won't be one now when they put everyone in the same basket?'

The (non)recognition of status

The category *desplazado* is not a neutral category; from the state's perspective its importance is manifested especially in two ways. First, a greater number of IDPs speaks of continuous political crisis in the country and gives an unfavourable external image of Colombia. This is particularly the case since some of the displaced are the product of state's own breach of human rights. Second, higher number of internally displaced mean more people have, at least in theory, access to limited state resources. Recognition of displacement or victim status is therefore not a straightforward endeavour since the high numbers of the displaced bear consequences.

The rejection rate is not negligible as approximately 25 per cent of applications are declined (CODHES 2011). With the recent peace accord achieved, but very likely continuous cases of displacement, the percentage of rejections in the time of 'peace' might even be on the rise. The government does not keep record of the cases that were rejected or reasons why they were rejected (Brookings Institution-University of Bern 2009). On the one hand the officials are vigilant to trace cases of 'bogus' *desplazados*. An official at the new *Unidad para Atención a Víctimas* (Victim Care Unit), which has under the new Victims' Law replaced *Acción Social* as the main institution responsible for IDPs, with disbelief recounted that during a job interview a former employee of *Acción Social* considered the identification of false declarations his greatest work achievement. False declarations undoubtedly exist. Precarious living conditions and lack of alternatives push people to apply for a status which in theory brings them some relief and assistance. However, the stress on 'achievement' suggests that those declaring displacement are treated as potential liars and that some of the attention is averted to the search for holes in the story. On the other hand, the motif behind rejections is political. Displacement is less likely to be recognised when it is generated by coca fumigation, military or paramilitary activity, opposition to government's policies, and when the declaration concerns intra-urban and intra-shire displacement. In a number of these reasons, the state is partly responsible for displacement, if not directly then through its proxy – the paramilitaries. Therefore, it is clear that the inclusion in the register of the displaced is highly politicised

Some of those, like Fabio, whose status was rejected are strongly convinced this was due to the testimony they gave. 'In my declaration I testified against some people in the military and the local government. Everyone asked me whether I was crazy to do that. But I say the truth has to be told and if they kill me for the truth, so be it.' His declaration of displacement was not accepted. He believes that testifying against the representatives of the government was the reason for his rejection. 'Why else!' he unbelievingly cried out. After Fabio's unsuccessful attempt, his wife decided to declare displacement. In the declaration she omitted the information about the involvement of state actors. Her declaration went through, and their household is now registered as a female-headed household with her featuring as the head of the family and Fabio as one of its members. While he is registered as a *desplazado*, the cause of displacement that was put on record does not reflect the real one.

The rejection of people's applications is made simpler through the structure of the administrative system. It allows for the creation of emotional, social and physical distance between the so-called *declarantes* declaring displacement and those who decide on their faith. The outcome of declarations is not determined by those who collect the statements; from local and regional offices the declaration forms are sent to Bogotá. The officials deciding on people's status never or rarely come into contact with the people they are supposedly helping. Neither do they necessarily understand or know the circumstances and reality of those coming from parts of the country which the clerks very likely do not know.

Amanda, a displaced woman in her forties, mother of seven children who fled Tumaco, Nariño, whom I met in Bogotá and was one of those who fell through the net, shared her view of the government's decision.

> There I was covered by a quilt of violence and it was something *tenaz, tenaz, tenaz* (difficult, difficult, difficult). I first lost my brother and my brother-in-law. Then a persecution most *tenaz* began, until they killed my other brother almost a year later. It was … [she pauses] terrible. He was tortured, massacred, they took him out of our arms. The following day we found him tortured in such a manner … But *Acción Social* says that he wasn't massacred by the paramilitaries but by delinquency. It is very sad that the government plays with the feelings and lives of people. It is very sad to know that the government is perhaps protecting more the causers of violence that those who are affected by violence. While a lot of us, who have lived in our own flesh what violence is, who have experienced persecution, and who know what it is to see a massacre of a family member … there are people who have no idea what it means to live the nightmare, thinking that at night they

are going to massacre me too. And these people are protected by the government, they receive reparations. I have just received a reply from an office in *Acción Social* that I can't receive reparations because the legislative framework doesn't cover me; that it wasn't the paramilitaries who massacred my family members but that it was delinquency. I lived in the *pueblo* for five years. Delinquency, the only type of arms it uses are hunting shotguns, a machete and a basket with which they always walk in the *monte*. Delinquency never massacres. Delinquency doesn't use a high-performance motorcycles, it doesn't take your brother out of your hands and massacres him there in front of your eyes. Delinquency doesn't torture, it doesn't tie you up and drags you with a car, and then hangs you until your neck breaks. Is this delinquency? Delinquency doesn't persecute you and your entire family and gives you a couple of hours to leave the *pueblo*. And if you don't leave, delinquency doesn't start finishing your family members one by one. Never. Delinquency kills who it plans to kill and that's it. Simple and not in the form in which the paramilitaries kill.

The physical distance between the officials and the IDPs who live in different parts of Bogotá, and especially between officials and the displaced in/from other parts of the country, where the reality is very different and often unimaginable to many who have possibly never travelled to any of the conflict regions, does not contribute to either a more humane approach or a better understanding of the phenomenon. Hence some decisions are made without understanding the extent of violence and the impact it can have on people. Categorisation and bureaucratic machinery enable the officials to establish emotional and social distance with the displaced, which ultimately makes the rejection of their status easier.

Performing a deserving *desplazado/a*

Official categorisation of people is a political choice through which states demonstrate their power. The state decides which categories it will use or will allow to be used, what name, priority and status it will give them (Starr 1992: 265). It can equally decide to discontinue the use of certain categories. The state holds monopoly over the norm for membership in the category. It creates a list of criteria and characteristics on the basis of which it categorises people. These are often blanket characteristics with little manoeuvring space, where the rules are clearly defined.

The rigidness of rules, expectations and norms is clearer in cases when categorisation is linked to humanitarian action and state assistance. *Desplazado* is such a category. It denotes a victim which inadvertently brings to mind, and requires, a certain kind of a person. The expectations of exemplary victims can refer to people's clothing and conduct, but victims should also demonstrate economic hardships, humbleness and passiveness. Preferably, they should exhibit purity and innocence. Such prototypes legitimise state's help since it is unlikely that anyone would question why the aid has been given. Nevertheless these anticipations of innocence and purity insufficiently consider and negate the political and social realities in which the *desplazados* are born. Neither do they allow the displaced to be people, who can err, without compromising their *desplazado* status.

Karen, a former employee of *Acción Social* in the department of Arauca, asserts that unlike her colleagues, she took time for people's narratives. 'The declaration process can take up to three hours. It requires patience, which not everyone has.' Karen is among those officials who shows great empathy towards the displaced and their situation. She attempted to increase people's possibilities of having their status recognised. In good faith to help people get a *desplazado* status, she occasionally offered advice about what information declarants can include in their applications. She told me of a man who in his testimony said he worked as a *raspachín*, a person who harvests coca leaves. Karen smiled at the thought of the man's honesty. 'You obviously can't say that in the declaration,' she explained. In the form she changed the man's occupation from a *raspachín* to a *campesino*. *Raspachín* did not fit with who a *desplazado* is, can or should be. Karen was probably right in her expectations that the man's displacement status would not have been confirmed had his application featured his true occupation. Marcela, from Cauca Antioqueño, who is staying in Esperanza, explained that her son's Cristian's application was rejected because he said he was a *raspachín* and an additional reason stated for rejection was that he speaks too fast and illegibly hence the officials were unable to understand him.

Work in coca cultivation might not be seen as compatible with the status of a victim, who is assisted, yet it is part of a number of people's reality. Marcela asserts that 'everyone there [in Cauca Antioqueño] works in coca. The land doesn't serve for anything else. Those who say they didn't work in coca, are lying'. Patricia, Doña Flor and Don Ignacio, and Linda and Carlos admitted to having been involved in coca cultivation. The reasons for involvement in this illicit activity vary, and often point to broader political and structural problems. Some people worked in coca cultivation for the economic benefits it can bring. Doña Flor says it was being 'ambitious to make money through coca' that drove them from Tolima to Cauca, where they spent seven years before they finally left the region. 'All of our neighbours were engaged in coca cultivation and they were relatively well off.' Don Ignacio, her husband, explains: 'It was the only *cultivo* that would grow there. The soil is too acid for anything else. There is also no infrastructure. Those who worked in coca cultivation had money. Those who didn't, didn't.' The couple processed coca leaves into paste. Their buyers were the guerrillas, paramilitaries and also individuals. 'Even if people want to discontinue working in coca, the guerrillas, the paramilitaries, or drug traffickers would not allow them to,' Doña Flor explains. The armed groups partly finance their activities through the drug revenues, therefore they do not wish the coca cultivation to end. These accounts show that the decision to get involved and stay involved in illicit activities is far from simple and most of all, it cannot be isolated from the broader socio-economic context. Despite the importance that work in coca production had in their lives, even if it was the main source of income, as was the case with Doña Flor and Don Ignacio, they did not mention this in their declaration.

The mention of such information, or of any kind of support given to armed actors, voluntary or forced, could have negative repercussions on the outcome of people's declaration of displacement. If categories are the basis for obtainment of benefits, it is not uncommon that individuals adapt their behaviour and self-reference to make them more aligned with official definitions and expectations. Some individuals create a different kind of a reality which they make their own (Hacking 1986, 1999: 168), or in other words they perform their identity (Butler 1999). They 'do' the victim through the adaptation of their behaviour and stories to create an identity they are purported to have and to be. They omit or modify parts of their stories.

Others, play the card of the feminisation of victims. It is arguably more likely that women's status as *desplazadas* is recognised than that of men's. The proportion of households registered as displaced female-headed households is relatively high. In 2008, it was estimated at 43 per cent, with sixty-eight in every one hundred of these being women on their own (UNHCR 2009). Even though in both Porvenir and Esperanza the households consist of men and women, who both contribute to the household income, four out of nine interviewed displaced households in Porvenir are registered as female-headed and four out of seven in Esperanza. The reasons behind this vary. Roberto, for example, left his ID at home, hence Angelica, his wife, declared displacement. Linda and Carlos decided that it would be better if Linda declared since they anticipated that the registration and consequent meetings arising from it would take time. They realised Carlos' day of work can contribute more to the income of the household; hence the cost-benefit analysis they made brought them to the decision that Linda should feature as the head of household. Juanita and Doña Olivia knew their way around the city better than their husbands, and it was easier for them to find the corresponding offices. Fabio's declaration, as mentioned above, was not recognised, consequently Fernanda, his wife, declared displacement. But ultimately a woman's declaration is more likely to be confirmed, or at least that is what the displaced believe. Don Eduardo asked one of the villagers who was aspiring for land whether he trusted his wife. If he did, Don Eduardo's suggestion was that the wife applied, because it is 'easier'. Don Eduardo, among others, based his opinion on the recent experience when he managed to secure food packages for women-headed households – displaced and non-displaced. In Esperanza, an IDP leader, Pedro, similarly holds that it is easier to secure assistance entering through Auto (Order) 092, concerned with the rights of women, victims of displacement. After all, women, not men, are recognised as a group requiring special protection.

Those aspiring to be recognised as IDPs are drawn into the system where there is not much room for explanation or analysis. They have to tell a 'convincing story' (Gatrell 2013: 294). In such cases, performativity of victimhood becomes the best option. This performativity to secure one's status turns into a vicious cycle in which the stereotypes of pure victims are strengthened. The silences and adaptation of stories due to the fear of being excluded from the register reinforce the attributes of an exemplary victim, add to the feminisation of displacement and contribute in part to the decontextualisation of conflict and displacement. The past that the bureaucracy records is a modified past, which is directed by the interests of those with greater power (de Certeau 1988). The category and its assumed attributes help amend the past so that it better fits in with the governmental discourse and with the government's role as a legitimate provider of humanitarian aid. Alongside with the modification of the official past, categories also erase individuals' past and strip them of their biographies. This is what I turn to in the continuation.

The depersonalised *desplazado*

Categories have a functional role; namely, they contribute to bureaucratic efficiency, since they simplify decision making. Simplified procedures are especially welcome in countries such as Colombia, where the numbers of those affected run in millions. Nevertheless, something is lost in the process. Decisions are made keeping in mind an artificially created prototype of a categorised person. They are based on some general assumptions of what it means to be displaced not just anywhere in Colombia but also anywhere in the world. Yet, particularities of circumstances that have led to displacement differ from context to context, as do the circumstances of the environments in which people lived. Through categorisation the displaced are no longer individuals but become universal. The array of IDPs' assumed needs fails to recognise differences among people, such as those generated by age, gender, ethnicity, culture, the different circumstances the displaced find themselves in and their personal histories.

While there are governmental workers who are genuinely concerned with the well-being of the displaced, like the above-mentioned Karen or an employee at one of the municipalities in Cundinamarca who approaches the displaced with an almost mother-like care, there are also those who may forget they are working with people. These are especially those officials who never come in contact with the displaced. The length of conflict in Colombia and the growing numbers of those displaced by it have contributed to thinking of the displaced in terms of statistics rather than individuals: the number of people displaced, categorised by sex, place of origin, place of arrival and the actor responsible for their displacement. Aided with the effects of the category, the displaced have, in short, been depersonalised and their narratives and biographies have been lost. From being individuals with profession, traits and personal family roles, they have turned into mere numbers, or into *desplazados*.

The head of the displacement unit at the former *Acción Social* office recognised such depersonalisation as a problem which he attempted to address while in office and which he believes persists.

> I tell them [the employees] 'we here use numbers, statistics, but you don't work with statistics, you work with human beings'. I send them to the field. Few people have the custom to do so. Let them be there at least one workday. Why? So that when they take the Excel chart and say: 'thirty-two … ah, let's delete this, *no pasa nada* (no harm done)', they know that it is thirty-two lives they are managing. So that they understand that every single thing, every call, every email is important, because there is a human being behind it. They become more aware. This is what I'd like to change because for some [employees] it is a process, for others it is a number and yet for others simply a burden. Nothing else.

It is difficult to escape the grip of bureaucratic machinery, especially when following the rules and laws is the norm of what constitutes a good clerk. The preoccupation with conformity to the rules emerges as 'red tape' (Merton 1940), sometimes unnecessarily lengthening the waiting period to access services. Under Law 387 the average length of time between the initial declaration of displacement and receipt of aid amounted to 109 days (Ibáñez and Velásquez 2009: 442). Some of my interviewees remember having to endure hunger while they were persistently visiting governmental offices waiting to be attended to. Linda even remembers an elderly man who fainted while he was queuing to be seen. 'One could notice he was an honest man, a hard-working *campesino*,' Linda recounts, 'but also that he was hungry and tired.' Pedro, who as an IDP leader frequently comes across people who find themselves struggling to get by while waiting for assistance, demonstrates the situation with the following story:

> One of these days I had to make a *tutela* for a displaced woman. She has leukaemia, terminal cancer, she has a seven-year old daughter, another child, and she is the head of household. She has nothing to be able to do the dialysis, she doesn't have anything. Where she lives she needs to pay rent. We made use of the right of petition, because she hadn't received humanitarian aid for more than two years. They sent her a reply saying that she is programmed to receive help, a reply they send to everyone. They sent her a number 226,213 denoting her turn to receive aid. The same letter said they were at the time at number 1,622. So, when *carajo* (the hell) will she get aid? I called. I said I was calling on behalf of my mother to know when her turn was. This was in June and they said 'look, in about a year she'll get it [the help]' [Pedro laughs]. And this is how they say they are attending to displaced population … For a displaced person to receive help it sometimes takes a year, when they say that it should be immediate. You come to the municipality, you declare displacement, they take two months to say yes or no, and then you wait for another year to receive assistance [laughs ironically]. It's very difficult, but this is how things are.

Under the new legislation, the dissociated approach has not changed; initial stages of implementation of the Victims' Law have revealed that the red tape continues.

Martina invited me to accompany her to the *personería*, the office of the municipal attorney where declarations are collected. She is not newly displaced but under the new Victims' Law she can ask for compensation for the death of her first husband, who was killed when they lived in Urabá. To do so, she needed to fill out the same declaration form as those declaring displacement. She made two trips to Bogotá to present her declaration, but learnt that she had to go to the *personería* where she lived. Upon our arrival to the local *personería* there were no declaration forms. The secretary complained that the central office sends the necessary documentation in limited quantities. As the forms are equipped with a barcode they cannot be photocopied and the *personería* needs to wait to get a new supply. Martina decided to try her luck in a nearby municipality where she used her friend's address as proof of residence. We were greeted by an empty waiting room and four employees chatting. After inquiring why we were there, Martina was told to come back in five days in order to get an appointment for late September or early October – our visit took place on 27 July. Four different trips during which nothing was achieved – the time and money spent, a lengthy waiting time to get the interview and then an even longer time to get the answer – clearly show that the bureaucratic machine is not prepared to treat people as individuals who find themselves in specific circumstances that might demand immediate attention. The scope and the sheer numbers seem to be too much for the state to handle.

Notes

1 It is worth noting that thinking in and using categories to comprehend the world is a normal social practice. We use categories to arrange our thoughts and to make the complex world we are a part of more manageable (Jenkins 2000). Classification helps us focus on certain features of reality while neglecting or ignoring others (Khalidi 2013). We all fall within different categories and categorise others and ourselves, be it by gender, age, profession, ethnicity or religion. Nevertheless, categories have different values attached to them. When the connotation is negative, categorisation may have mainly negative consequences.
2 CPDIA consisted of the Inter-American Commission on Human Rights, representatives of inter-governmental organisations and NGOs.

6

Desplazado: to be or not to be

Being a *desplazado* is 'a burden, a mark of the beast. It's a sign one has. They [people] look at you as the worst possible [person]', says Juan, as he draws on the biblical reference to explain what it feels like to be categorised. The policy category marked him out as different and he experiences the negative consequences of categorisation predominately in the manner others view him and consequently relate to him. Fabio, unlike Juan who is an IDP leader, uses the category and his IDP identity to a lesser extent, similarly points out the consequences the policy category has had on his social world. 'People say "this is a *desplazado*" as if we weren't humans,' he describes his encounters with the non-displaced neighbours, to which his wife Fernanda adds: 'As if we came from a different planet. That's how they look at us.' Despite the 'mark of the beast', despite sensing they are being looked at as 'aliens' and despite the associations of the displaced with liars, guerrillas or thieves, the majority of the displaced use and identify with the category.[1]

When self-identifying as displaced, the voice does not always convey anger, sadness, hurt, or disappointment. Sometimes I could feel a sense of pride, particularly when despite the odds, despite the adverse events the displaced have managed to secure the land, have progressed, or did not engage in violence. Sixteen years after physical relocation and ten years after being resettled, phrases such as '*Nosotros somos desplazados*' (We're displaced) or '*Soy desplazada/o*' (I'm a displaced) frequently echo in the two villages, particularly in Esperanza.

The state might be the first to impose the system of formal categorisation, but it is not the only entity responsible for its dispersion. While the first instance of categorisation normally happens on the state level, the category moves beyond institutional domains and spaces and enters people's everyday lives. The state, practitioners, the media and the non-displaced are all involved in the process of external categorisation. IDPs too contribute their share to the life of the category through internal categorisation. *Desplazado* has become part of their social identity, and it has moved from being a policy category to being a 'category of practice' (Brubaker and Cooper 2000). Through self-identification as *desplazados*, the displaced are contributing to the category's meaning, circulation and life.

There is something in the manner in which being a displaced is conveyed. Spanish has two verbs which correspond to the English verb 'to be', namely *ser* and *estar*. '*Estar*' refers to temporary character and '*ser*' to a more permanent one. When referring to themselves as *desplazados*, the displaced employ the verb '*ser*'. Language creates realities and the use of the verb '*ser*' may give a connotation that to be displaced is something permanent and fixed (Osorio Perez 2009: 177). In certain cases, listening to people's self-identification, this durability of identity becomes apparent. But what is the incentive behind self-identification? What is the motive that encourages people to refer to themselves as *desplazado/a* despite the negative connotations the category bears? Most importantly, what can self-identification and self-understanding as *desplazado/a* tell us about the manner in which displacement is experienced?

Categorisation homogenises the displaced. Yet, engagement with the category – the meaning given to it, when and how it is used and by whom – alludes to important differences among the displaced. The displaced people's views, interpretation and application of the category reveal how they experience displacement and also provide insights in people's biographies. Similar to some other contexts (Brun 2003; Zetter 1991) in Colombia too the displaced use the category instrumentally. Nevertheless, cases when individuals persist identifying themselves as *desplazados* when they no longer receive assistance and do not strive to do so, demonstrate that self-identification happens for reasons other than those of promise of assistance and can have a deeper symbolic meaning. The chapter explores the instrumental and non-instrumental recourse to the category. It examines self-categorisation and self-understanding as a categorised person to demonstrate the heterogeneity of experiences as well as differences in the understanding of what displacement is.

Programmes of assistance, new political roles and mobilisation

One of the outcomes of being inscribed into state register as a *desplazado* is qualification for programmes of assistance intended to lessen the consequences of loss and help people in their search for stability. Among others, the displaced in Colombia receive state support in areas of education, housing, health and productive projects. The assistance is not automatic but rather requires a great amount of persistence and knowledge of the system. It is often during the attempts to acquire access to state funds that the displaced self-reference themselves as *desplazados* even if they otherwise do not actively engage with the category. Angelica and Roberto are such an example. They live on the last *finca* in Porvenir, with only mountains and forests stretching out further up the hill behind their house. Theirs is a big family with seven children. Roberto works as a *jornalero* on neighbouring farms, and Angelica stays at home, running errands. Rarely would they self-identify as *desplazados* in our conversations. It is obvious that having had to leave their village in Tolima has affected them, but at the same time they appreciate their new *finca* and Porvenir's better location. Even if sense of displacement is not as prevalent in their case as compared to some other IDPs, the couple and their family uses the category if they need help. Angelica and Roberto's sixteen-year old daughter gave birth and was to marry a seventeen-year old youth, who is also registered as a displaced. Angelica explained they were planning to build an extension to their house for which they were going to apply for state subsidy available for the displaced. They use the category for the purposes of positive discrimination, even if they otherwise do not identify with the category to a great extent. They are therefore not likely to identify themselves as IDPs in any given situation; they rather choose the appropriate setting.

Alongside these occasional instrumental applications of the category, there are some who self-identify with the category because self-identification is essential for their acquired formal identity. Displacement has finished some local political positions and careers, but it has also opened ways for new political engagements, such as being an IDP leader. To be able to advocate for IDPs' rights, to apply for state support, and to simply give legitimacy to their role, displaced leaders stress their belonging to the category and use it to reach their aims. These are the displaced whose work revolves around the study of legislation, identification of loopholes and application for assistance. Occasionally being an IDP leader turns into people's main activity. Through their agency, inventiveness and resourcefulness the displaced challenge the rigid and impersonal structure. Allen and Turton (1996: 10) interpret such people's ingenuity as a defence against dependency and an expression of degree of control over their lives. Their agency goes against the 'popular image of the welfare recipient … [who is] passive, lethargic and indolent' hence such behaviour is denoted as inappropriate or undesirable.

The four leaders, Pedro and Juan in Esperanza, and Don Eduardo and Juanita in Porvenir, regularly self-identify themselves with the category and to greater or lesser extent do so for instrumental purposes – they use it to mark their status within and outside displaced communities, to give greater legitimacy to their opinions, concerns and lobbying, and as the basis from which they apply for assistance programmes. They also use the category to mobilise people in order to achieve their aims. Don Eduardo, who was attempting to be re-elected as town councillor in the 2011 local elections used the category *desplazado* in his electoral motto. Being based in a region where coffee is one of the main produce and a coffee grower himself, while at the same time trying to secure support from others, his motto read 'working for the interests of coffee growers and the displaced'. Don Eduardo who has a history of promoting people's rights which reach back to Tolima, his place of origin, is genuinely concerned with the IDPs' situation. His effort for greater equality is in line with his political convictions. Nevertheless, his reference to *desplazados* during the election can also be interpreted in instrumental terms. Leaders of supposed collectivity call on people to identify with one another cognitively and also emotionally (Brubaker and Cooper 2000; Melucci 1995). They play the collectivity card when they organise protests, apply for assistance or when they are trying to pursue political career.

Despite numerous examples of instrumental use, a number of displaced in Esperanza and Porvenir no longer receive assistance and indeed no longer wish to apply for it. Applying for help requires time, effort and knowledge of available programmes that not everyone has. Some no longer ask for assistance simply because they do not wish to depend on aid. Nevertheless, their self-identification as *desplazados* is recurrent. The heterogeneity of applications and interpretations of the category, which I discuss below, speaks of diversity of experiences and understanding of displacement.

Beyond instrumental use – *desplazado* as self-understanding

Some uses of the category defy policy purposes. Yet, they contribute to the dispersion of the category and tell us much more than any legislation about how displacement is experienced or what it means to people. The displaced do not self-identify as such only with the objective to fall within policy programmes and initiatives, to demonstrate belonging to a particular group of people, or indeed to aim to look for similarities with others. The displaced rather engage with personalised non-instrumental uses of the category which are not policy or time bound. While those who use the category instrumentally may stop identifying themselves as *desplazados* once they for any reason stop qualifying for governmental or non-governmental assistance, those who employ the category to express deeper emotional state or belief, are likely to continue to do so years or decades after physical relocation. Ironically it is the exact word which is used in policy that people use for expressing the untellable, unexplainable or the non-understandable experiences, emotions and interpretations.

Self-reference as a *desplazdo/a* often reflects affective identification; in such cases the use of the category speaks of people's self-understanding, of their sense of self and of their social location. It is at once both the cognitive and emotional sense that individuals have of themselves and their social environment (Brubaker and Cooper 2000: 17). Self-reference is also directly related to people's interpretation of what displacement is and what it has meant for them. It is another confirmation that displacement is not about physical relocation but a process of loss, instability and adaptation. The term is sufficiently vague in its meaning that it offers itself to various interpretations and applications. The expression at the same time has sufficiently strong emotional connotation to convey part of feelings and emotions, which are otherwise difficult to capture in words.

For many displacement is beyond description. Doña Flor tells me that it is difficult to understand it if you have not lived through it. 'How should I put it? It's like when a family member dies and you say how sorry you are but only when it happens to you, you really know what it's like,' explains Doña Flor looking at a photo of her son placed on the cupboard. The choice of comparison was not accidental and there were parallels between how the two events were experienced. She lost her son in a car accident two years earlier but unlike before the accident, she only now understands what it means to lose a son. Like displacement, the loss has left her with a vacuum, confusion and initial numbness. She never mentioned her son during my first extended visit in the village but upon making the comparison, she explained she was slowly getting to terms with his death.

Unsurprisingly, other people's attempts at describing displacement similarly echoed its negative weight and the long-term if not lasting consequences. For Doña Beatriz who lost four family members, 'displacement is one's worst enemy. One needs to leave from one day to another and doesn't know where to or what will one do. One never recovers.' Fabio, who lost his active political participation fighting for the rights of workers and for greater equality and who lost any faith in the state describes displacement as 'ugly. It stays with one like a psychosis. I'm not the person I was before. I feel I'm not. I was … a free person. I still suffer from trauma even though they helped us. I haven't been able to overcome it.' His wife Fernanda, Doña Beatriz' sister, who also lost her sister, mother and father says 'displacement is a challenge. One needs to go from one's place and never go back. Even if one goes back it's never the same. Your family is no longer there. They might have been killed.' For Alejandra, whose mother disappeared, to be displaced is 'to be here, struggling. It is when they kill your parents, take your land and make you leave the place where you were. Displacement can never be overcome. Here, in my mind, it's going on. I say that all the suffering I've been through is because of displacement.' Camilo, Alejandra's adopted brother, who left Urabá when he was thirteen and who unlike Alejandra did not lose any family members, has nevertheless been permanently affected.

> Displacement is a wound that never heals. One needs to be really strong to get through it. The elderly lost their roots, I lost my culture. I feel I have a hybrid identity, not really belonging anywhere. I don't feel with this here [with the *finca* in Esperanza]. Displacement is a very individual experience. It affects everyone differently. I felt impotent. Impotent seeing my parents struggle and impotent seeing my sisters having to walk to school such a long way and I couldn't do anything. This, what you call best friend, I don't have [due to migration from one place to another].

His uncle, Alejandro, who was two years older than Camilo when he left the region, was similarly affected by his parents' struggle. He decided to help contribute to family income, but as a result he was bereft of his childhood. He is a very good-humoured man who tends to give a funny twist to his stories, or at least accompanies them with a deal of laughter. But despite the seeming lightheartedness, his narratives capture a pool of sacrifices and hardships.

> When we settled in Irra my father didn't have stable work or income. I felt I had to help. I started working in a mine together with some local children. It was dangerous. I was once almost caught in a landslide [he now laughs at his luck or incredulity of the conditions]. At one time the river current almost swept away a friend of mine … I took up jobs that others didn't want. I worked in a shaft for instance. It was dangerous but also extremely solitary.

His accelerated route to maturity is what has affected him most in the process. The loss of childhood has become the essence of what he associates displacement with. Similarly to some others mentioned above, Alejandro's interpretation of displacement is reflected in his use of the category *desplazado* as a way of self-understanding. Who he is and who he perhaps might have been had it not been for conflict and displacement.

Alejandro's preoccupation for his parents mirrors their preoccupation for him and his siblings. Doña Olivia, his mother, when reflecting on displacement, among other things, laments that her children lost a future which would have been built upon years of struggle, efforts and work.

> Displacement is something terrible I wouldn't wish to anyone. All the work of youth, future for children, for the old age is lost. It's tough. One doesn't leave only material things, one leaves friendships, doesn't know if they are ever going to form relationships with their family again. To be without knowing what one will do is horrific. Displacement is something very … who wasn't displaced was killed. I still feel displaced. I haven't recovered my way of life, my routine. I wouldn't be fighting so much for myself, but for my children. I've lived what I had to live. More than material things I've lost my spirit. Spirit is worth a lot. As much as the government helps, I can never overcome. One never feels as if one has recovered.

Besides the loss of life's work and spirit, Doña Olivia and her husband Don Andrés see in displacement an explanation for their ailments. Don Andrés faults displacement for his two heart attacks, while Doña Olivia blames displacement for her daughter's mental disability. For her and her husband, the starting point of displacement was his imprisonment in 1979, the year when their daughter was born. He was imprisoned for eighteen months during which she visited him regularly and pressed for his release. 'I came home at six, seven in the evening and would leave again in the morning. The girl had let herself go. I don't know, she fell ill because of this,' Doña Olivia explains. Since her daughter's condition is unlikely to improve, Doña Olivia will very probably experience a persistent sense of displacement. The understanding of her own social position is influenced by that of her daughter. Through saying she is *desplazada*, she is also alluding to the permanent consequences she believes displacement has left on her daughter and indirectly on her.

Don Fernando, Doña Olivia's brother, also understands displacement to be the source of afflictions. He uses displacement to explain why his wife no longer loves him. In Urabá he worked on a *bananera* for twenty-five years. He often worked long hours in order to provide for his family. After leaving Urabá, Don Fernando, his wife and children went to Cartagena, a city on the Atlantic coast, one of the largest recipients of the displaced. 'Violence there was poverty,' he says. He was unable to find formal work and he started working as a street vendor, selling eggs and some other groceries in poor barrios.

> I would get up at three in the morning and go to the market to sell. It was hard … Out of one hundred people there are two or three who have money, the rest are poor. Poor. They wouldn't have breakfast till noon. One is in a bad condition but there are others who are worse off. I, displaced. But there are people originally

from Cartagena … no. I would sell them things cheaper so that their children would have something to eat.

To complement the earnings, Don Fernando helped unload rations in a local school. Nevertheless, his work did not cover all the household expenses and his wife, who had not been in paid employment before, looked for and found work.

> My *señora* suffered so much that her love [for me] ended … Old age caught me. They wouldn't give me work. I started selling on the street [working as a street vendor]. My wife got work and she is still working. She got tired of the fact that one doesn't earn enough to complete one's duty. And love faded. Her love. I still love her.

As a man coming towards the end of his middle age period, and culturally the main bread winner, Don Fernando was among those particularly hit. As Margaret Walker (2009: 52) rightly concludes '[s]ome forms of violent harm or loss precipitate further losses that enlarge the impact of, and may in the end be worse or less manageable than, the original violation or loss itself'. Don Fernando's inability to fulfil 'his duty' as a father and husband had negative consequences on his family life, his self-perception and his self-worth. Spending his days alone in Esperanza, working and attempting to send some money to his family in Cartagena, Don Fernando not only says but also feels he is displaced. Rather than only using the category instrumentally – Don Fernando is trying to access some state programmes, including subsidy for housing with Pedro's help – his claim of being *desplazado* involves much more, among others, his tarnished self-image as a man.

Sense of displacement, which ultimately affects the manner in which people understand their social position, can vary or be stable. When it varies it is circumstantial and can reappear with the change of conditions. If displacement is experienced as 'a loss of stability' as Don Eduardo defines it, any subsequent challenge to stability is likely to renew sentiments of displacement and is likely to be assigned to displacement. Juanita, for instance, upon my first visit to Porvenir insisted she felt well in the village and wanted to stay there. Upon my second visit this was no longer the case. It was not only that the security situation got worse, but her fifteen-year old daughter got pregnant, which spoke specifically against Juanita's beliefs and it destabilised her efforts aimed at a better position of women. Juanita no longer felt comfortable in Porvenir or indeed in her household. If before she insisted she wanted to stay in the village and was demonstrating signs of place attachment, she later asserted she felt displaced. She left the village and engaged in a new search for stability in Bogotá, away from her family. While her daughter's pregnancy was not related to displacement, it resurfaced as the sense of displacement, destabilising Juanita's place-making process. People's self-understanding and self-identification as *desplazado/a* can vary through space and time.

Alongside these ailments, the diseases, tainted self-worth and loss of crucial periods of one's life, the understanding of oneself as a *desplazado* and consequent authoritative claim to the category also has a different spin. Being displaced is not considered neutral even in the eyes of the displaced themselves. Some displaced link the self-understanding of their position and situation to their religious and political beliefs and convictions. A number of the displaced turn to them to search for the meaning to displacement. When convictions are sufficiently strong, inter-pretation of one's position is understood as a kind of confirmation of one's dedica-tion to political and religious principles respectively. Being displaced thus takes a symbolic and status role.

Religion is an important referent in the lives of the majority of Esperanza and Porvenir's inhabitants. Religious convictions are seen through biblical references people make as well as the weight given to 'God's will' in the course of the everyday. 'It has all been written,' commented Doña María when we were watching the news one morning. Two news stories reported one after the other covered two sep-arate cases of murder where men killed their respective wives and children, one committing suicide in the end and the other attempting to do so. Doña María who was standing at the open door, the only source of light in the room, was affected by the report but did not look surprised. She uttered: 'The Bible says that men will fight their children, children will go against their fathers, nation against nation,' referring to Luke 12:53 and Matthew 24:7. Others too interpreted a number of other incidents as God's act or divine justice. Doña Beatriz who was maltreated by one of her employers in one of the jobs she took on during her journey to Esperanza, believes God punished her employer by burning down her employer's business two weeks after the woman refused to help Doña Beatriz. Fabio is thankful to God for the land that he has: 'not Incoder, not the government, it was *mi diosito* who gave me this land,' he asserts. Ultimately, God permitted displace-ment to take place.

Despite such a prominent role of religion in the majority of people's lives, it was the *cristianos* who made a stronger link between displacement and religion. *Cristianos* are members of the Evangelical Church, which has in recent years seen a growth in the number of its followers. They refer to themselves as *cristianos* in order to differentiate themselves from Catholics. The connection some make between displacement and faith does not refer to the role of religion in conflict, but rather to the writings of the Bible and to sufficiently powerful faith. Like Doña María, Doña Isabel and her husband strongly believe that, 'Everything has been written in the Bible: the war, the earthquakes, the floods, and displacement.' Quoting Daniel 12:4, 'many shall run to and fro', Doña Isabel explains, 'We came here and people from Bogotá go to Urabá.' All these events are the sign of 'Jesus' coming'.

Daniel, a *cristiano* missionary, appreciates the experience of displacement. 'It is necessary to feel the pain to know one is alive,' he comments. 'I have learnt a lot from the process including that life needs to be valued. God sent us displace-ment with a reason. I also teach my children to accept it like that.' Rafael, another missionary, likewise believes that events like displacement happen for people to learn from them:

> No death or suffering is without reason. One learns more from experience than theory. Massacres happen in order to prevent greater massacres. Look at the Titanic. It sank so that more deaths were prevented. God sometimes takes innocent people in order to punish bad ones. Children, for example, who are innocent, who haven't done anything bad, die. This occurs so that parents reflect on themselves. How many times does one hear them saying, 'If only God had taken me'? All this is done to punish the parents.

He believes that God purposefully allows innocent people to lose their lives or to be displaced in order to change the relationship people have with the armed actors. 'People realise that in reality these armed groups cannot protect them, so they withdraw their support.'

Besides the inevitability of displacement, as specified in the Bible, displacement is understood as a proof of one's faith. There are only two options: 'one can either believe in God or follow Satan,' Doña Isabel explains. The Bible says that those who believe in the former will be persecuted. Hence, their displacement, Doña Isabel and her husband Don Jorge interpret, is a sign of their true faith. Their self-understanding as *desplazados* has been highly influenced by their religious beliefs. At the same time, displacement has contributed to their self-understanding as religious followers. Even though they are true believers, God, while also protecting them, allowed displacement to afflict them due to the sin of mankind, concludes Doña Isabel.

As seen from the above examples some understand displacement as being completely apolitical, however, others interpret it as inherently political. They too use their displacement as a confirmation of their beliefs – political rather than religious. Politics and religion are not mutually exclusive: those with political affiliations might also believe in God. Martina affirms that only 'a communist communist [referring to staunch communists] doesn't believe in God'. She herself, who is just 'a communist', believes there is a higher force. Nevertheless, for her and some other IDPs, political convictions are stronger than religious ones and she has no doubts about her displacement being political. Political interpretation of displacement has particularly been seen with those interviewees who arrived from Urabá, where the specific socio-economic and political background of the conflict greatly affected people's biographies. Participation in major political and social movements, such as membership in the *Unión Patriótica*, or labour union activism, has left an impact on people's sense of being displaced.

Fabio maintains he was politically persecuted, that he was displaced because he is a communist. 'The traditional political parties [the Conservative and the Liberal] were for upper and middle classes, but the UP wanted a political party composed of the poor.' However, he argues, 'in Colombia, anyone who is leaning towards the left is said to be a terrorist.' Fabio not only ascribes his displacement to his political engagement but in his mind his displacement also shows his faithfulness to politics. He asserts he is not like those who have 'poor political consciousness and change sides. People who are firm in their political beliefs, who have [genuine] political consciousness were either killed or displaced'. Hence, as he sees it, those who stayed behind and survived either gave in or never really understood what the struggle was about. Displacement or death, in contrast, shows faithfulness to political ideology. The term *desplazado* therefore has a very specific meaning for those who used to be politically engaged like Fabio, Martina and also Don Andrés. They embraced it and are not likely to discontinue its use; not only because being a *desplazado* confirms their political convictions, but because they believe the struggle for greater equality in the country must continue.

The identification with the category *desplazado* in such circumstances gains importance for two reasons. First, people express the feeling of being displaced because their political activity has been curtailed and they are not able to participate in the struggle. This is due to the fear that they might be displaced again, and also to the new context they have found themselves in. The political environment in Cundinamarca, the region of resettlement, does not reflect the one in Urabá. Its inhabitants are not of the same or similar political stance, hence political participation or even political discussions are difficult. Don Andrés feels that his political views, if he voiced them, would not be accepted in the village. Second, by stressing that they are displaced, people draw attention to the government's past and present wrong-doings. If they did not stress their displaced identity, which they understand to be a political status, this might present a form of betrayal. It would take away the severity of the past and current socio-political affairs and it might give an impression that the situation in the country has improved. It is therefore desirable to stress one's *desplazado* status notwithstanding the negative connotation that the category has.

All these different interpretations of displacement – be it as referring to people's condition, situation, affliction or even symbolic status, make a complex but also strong basis for people's self-understanding. The *desplazado* identity becomes vital for people's sense of selfhood. There is then something permanent in the process of self-identification. On the one hand, people are trying to make sense of why they were compelled to leave their homes, they are trying to find explanations and reasons for their current situation; and on the other, they are trying to sustain identity that some might find essential for their sense of self.

Overall, the word *desplazado/a* does not always convey the same meaning. The circumstances, the experiences and even people's biographies determine the emotional value and meaning given to self-identification. Self-understanding rests upon memories of violence and suffering; it is a combination of protagonists who fought for a cause and defied violence, of believers who will be awarded for their faith, and of victims whose rights have been breached and whose lives have been modified beyond imagination. Besides the personal memories, accounts and senses, these identities are influenced by macro-influences such as past and recent debates on the category, breach of rights, and the right to protection and restitution. These influence the different shades of the protagonist/victim identity and their expression.

Reference to oneself as a displaced has direct consequence on place-making. The use of the category as an expression of self-understanding is almost never understood, if at all. Owing to programmes of assistance available for the displaced, the government and the non-displaced associate the displaced's persistent use of the category with instrumental purposes for personal gain without considering any other applications of the category. As a result, the often unfavourable relationships between the displaced and non-displaced can deteriorate even further, undermining relational belonging. The different applications behind the category also allude to something else. They bring to light the heterogeneity of people crammed under the same category. When these are put to live together, as the next chapter shows, the negotiation of social landscapes turns into a challenge.

Note

1 Some refrain from self-identification as displaced. Carlos for instance believes it is 'dangerous' to say you have been displaced; people think you are a guerrilla member. Even though he is registered as a *desplazado*, he prefers not to identify himself with the category. On the one hand, this is due to safety and on the other, he says, it is because the category does not allow for any differentiation among those categorised. It groups him together with some people that he does not get on with and would prefer not to be associated with in any way.

7

Displacement hierarchies: IDP community under question

After the first run of vote counting, Don Eduardo did not get a place in the local council. Before the election a number of candidates invited their relatives to register their *cédulas* (identification documents) in the municipality where they did not normally live to be able to cast a vote for their family member. Some political parties allegedly organised transportation for people to come from elsewhere and vote for their representative or they paid for people's expenses. Even though some of Don Eduardo's family members came from Bogotá to vote for him, the result was not what he had expected. With fifty-four votes he was told he was three votes short. The bitterness was substantive. Don Eduardo was going for re-election and his wife Doña María and daughter Juanita complained of the ungratefulness of the community. They claimed 'no one from the community' voted for him. In the days before the election, when he was running numerous errands, Doña María reproached Don Eduardo saying that he had forgotten about the family and had only thought about the community. In the light of the result, the house went quieter earlier that night than on previous evenings. The following day Don Eduardo learnt that he got into the council after all. Although she was happy for him, his daughter's first comment was that he should now be working for himself and not for the community as he did until then. But why then the members of the 'community' did not support Don Eduardo if he assists them? Who and what is 'the community'? Could his family be mistaken and that there is no real community in Porvenir?

The word '*la comunidad*' (community) is frequently used by governmental and non-governmental representatives. Sonia, the NGO worker who runs gender workshops in both hamlets, often speaks of what *la comunidad* does, thinks or has. She is referring to the displaced, not to the old residents of the villages, or to both the displaced and non-displaced. Community in her perception is based on the common identity of being *desplazados*, possibly also on their shared location. She is not alone in such thinking; governmental officials often make reference to displaced community. Those displaced from their homes create narratives of shared history, which feed into and pronounce the image of unified communities. Nevertheless, such narratives have become so common that they need to be probed (Colson 2003; Loizos 1999). On the outside, a founding myth might create a perception of a community, however, the examination of decision-making about which aspects get included or excluded from the accounts of supposed shared history shows that it is often specific individuals, rather than everyone, who dictate the content.

Communities of course do not preclude disagreements. Communities are not stable, idealistic groups, where life always exists in harmony. They can be 'fragile, changing, and partial' (Amit 2002: 18). But there is something inherently positive in the concept itself which is what makes it so attractive (Creed 2006; Williams 1976). The idea of community brings together the notion of solidarity, empathy and assistance. It encompasses the ideas of mutual understanding, collaboration and support. 'Sense of community is a feeling that members have of belonging, a feeling that members matter to one another and to the group, and a shared faith that members' needs will be met through their commitment to be together' (McMillan and Chavis 1986: 9). Therefore, rather than thinking about communities in terms of fixed identities, they might be better thought of as characterised by caring relationships (Antonsich 2010a; Carrillo Rowe 2005; hooks 2009).

Instead of assuming that a community, a group or a oneness of those categorised and resettled together exists, we need to examine the 'multiple forms and degrees of commonality and connectedness' among them (Brubaker and Cooper 2000: 21). After all, not all members of the collectivity share common interests or let alone common identity (May 2013; Young 1995). The failure to question the simplistic notion of community and groupness of the displaced ignores people's agencies, their subjectivities, thinking and actions. It discounts the possibility that the displaced have differences which may influence their place-making. It also neglects the hierarchies of power and oppression that can exist, and often go unnoticed and unexamined within the so-called displaced communities.

This chapter explores the too often ignored differences among the displaced. I first look at how the homogenisation of the displaced does not consider disparities among them, which in Porvenir resulted in casualties. I then move on to explore the distinctions that the displaced themselves make to show that while they are all grouped under the same category, they are different one from another. They have created displacement hierarchies, based on criteria of suffering and moral behaviour. The distinction that they are making, especially when it comes to moral hierarchies, demonstrates that they do not share the same ideals and that empathy, while not completely absent, is present only to certain limits. In the last section I look at a loss of a community; at how different world views and hierarchies of power have brought a sense of community, in which everyone used to be as 'one person', to an end.

A community thrown together

Categories homogenise people into 'undifferentiated masses' (Harrell-Bond 1999: 141), within which displaced individuals are simply seen as *desplazados*. Such homogenisation does not allow the groups to be perceived and considered 'as variably solidary, salient, and stable' (Calhoun 2003: 562). It critically fails to recognise that in an artificial grouping – such as *desplazados*, with such a strong political connotation and people's distinct histories – solidarity can occasionally be entirely absent. A shared history is the basis for shared emotional connection, a component element of the sense of community (McMillan and Chavis 1986). It is not necessary that people participated in the history, but they need to identify with it. In Colombia, the various reasons behind people's displacement and the distinct actors responsible for it have inhibited such identification. Those directly affected by displacement are so diverse that they have little in common apart from being victims and categorised as *desplazados*. The lack of shared history and associated differences are big enough to characterise the group by unpredictability and uncertainty rather than stability.

The twelve households that were originally given the basis to start a new home in Esperanza are members of three families. They had known each other from before physical relocation and the core households, which were actively involved in securing the land, invited some others to join them either from Urabá or from a place they had fled to. Initially the displaced did not come across major disagreements but rather functioned as a community in the positive sense of the word. In Porvenir, by contrast, the selection of the fourteen households that were eventually resettled there was not based on pre-selection criteria that considered people's displacement histories. Some were occupying the ICRC premises and others joined after hearing about the opportunity through local government representatives, friends or family members. The mix of people who ended up living together was great. Both culturally, since it comprised of people from regions as varied as La Guajira in the north of the country to Huila in the South, but crucially also politically speaking.

In the few first months after the displaced had settled in Porvenir, a Catholic priest organised *olla comunitaria*, or community pot, for the displaced which few remember with positive memories. The priest's aim, did not work, explains Angelica.

> The intention was to bring us together but it doesn't work like that. We came from different parts of Colombia and on top of it some were *costeños* (inhabitants of the coast). We would cook in a different house every day. Problems soon emerged so they first divided us to two locations – those *de abajo* (from below) and those *de arriba* (from the top). When even such a division did not work the priest left after six months and never returned to the village

The *fincas* are spread on a slope and the geographical feature of the terrain was used to divide people on those from below and those from further up the slope. Perhaps not coincidentally this division also largely reflects political disparities in the hamlet.

The tensions and problems emerging among the displaced were not linked only to different cultural practices, but mainly to their contrasting history of displacement. Those that were settled together were displaced by different actors – by both the guerrillas and the paramilitaries, which made the everyday coexistence soon after physical relocation particularly complex. Conflict was still largely ongoing, the armed actors active, feelings of resentment present and displacement could not be considered a matter of the past.

Incoder's policy is not to mix *campesinos* and *desplazados* on one plot. Those who apply for a certain property have to be either one or the other. 'Nevertheless', Incoder official explains, 'previously there was a mix of everything. There were even cases when victims and victimisers were put to live together, in other words the displaced and the demobilised.' Another official participating in the interview stepped in and commented: 'But this is part of the bet to reconstruct social fabric.' Upon which the first official elaborated:

> Yes, also, but the problem is that they were sent like this, without anything [he laughs]. In Valle there is a very particular case. They sent people from the same region to one *finca* and when they saw each other and recognised each other … There were some *muerticos por ahí* (dead persons in diminutive form). In the process of re-socialisation there shouldn't be examples of this type. But it's not that easy.

Some officials can see the danger or the challenge of putting different groups of people together, but they do not recognise differences within these groups. For instance, the displaced are perceived as 'one group' despite different histories behind their displacement. A third official present in the interview knew the case of Porvenir since she worked with resettled households in the first years of their resettlement, when these varied histories became apparent. She admitted there was 'profound enmity' present among the displaced in the hamlet from the very start and that it was sensible that some resettled IDPs left Porvenir in spite of the legal requirements prohibiting them from doing so.

> Initially, we believed in what we were doing there, in constructing a new society, a group of people who we believed got on well. But as things were coming, institutionally speaking, profound enmities were augmenting until the point there were casualties. This was taken to the *fiscalía* (Public Prosecutor's Office), they detained people from the same community, and on the basis of pressures, people started to sell their plots; plots that shouldn't have been sold. They were making fun of the good faith of the institutions because they made documents, which weren't legal, in front of the notary, but they made documents. As one of them said, they had signatures of people that if something weren't complied with, they had ways to make them comply. It turned into an incontrollable situation. I even found it reasonable that people left because they had children who had come there when they were five or six years old, and they were already ten or eleven and they could suddenly become objects of violence.

Sharing of space and regular interaction do not in themselves erase differences among people, particularly not in politically sensitive environments. These circumstances, perhaps more than any other, require institutional support to bring individuals closer together socially speaking. The potential existing tensions can amount to a continuation of conflict, even if armed actors are not necessarily present.

Nevertheless, the need for land and a place to stay rarely permit much man-oeuvring space in terms of choosing who one lives with. When the opportunity of a plot appears, those entitled to it might have some initial doubts and reservations about it, but in the majority of cases, the offer is gladly accepted. Having been in such a situation, Don Eduardo gives advice to people who are aspiring to receive land. A landless *campesino* whom Don Eduardo was assisting with his applica-tion for the Incoder land programme visited him in his house. When they were talking, Don Eduardo expressed one of his concerns. 'We asked for land for forty-five families. The problem is, these are big *fincas*. Imagine you are thrown together with thieves, *marihuaneros* (marijuana users) and the like. There should be a small number of families and selection should be made,' he concluded. In the same way as he was 'thrown together' with thirteen other households who have in different ways influenced his place-making, he was warning the man of the problems of coexistence that the successful application could bring.

A decade after resettlement, emotions have calmed down, but tensions and disagreements still persist. When I asked Patricia about the relationship with other displaced, she replied: 'Oh Matejita, the whole night wouldn't be enough [to dis-cuss them].' She is convinced her neighbour killed her dog, swears he spits when-ever he passes her house, and claims he even called the police when her chicken crossed to his property. She also raised her concern over the machetes that are faithfully strapped around men's waists. They appear to be an accessory that gives the men a sense of fullness, completeness, and have become a part of their per-sonas. People use them to cut through vegetation, collect yucca; but they can also be used as a weapon.

> All these man walking around with machetes. It's just a question of time who uses it first … It will be a problem here. The *dueños* (the owners, the original bene-ficiaries of the land) want to come back. The land is theirs on paper, but those staying here won't admit it. It will get complicated and now that one pays 20,000 pesos [approximately £5.50] to have one killed … [does not finish her sentence].

Disparities were especially pronounced during the pre-election period. The divide persists between some of those from *arriba*, who were mainly displaced by the guer-rilla activity and those from *abajo*, who were displaced due to the paramilitaries. Doña María said she would not visit those who live *arriba* because they supported a different political party. After the elections took place, she was convinced those from *arriba* were not satisfied with the final outcome. Still discussing the disap-pointment over the lack of community's support, she asserted: 'Those from *arriba* wanted you [Don Eduardo] to *quemarse* (get burnt; an expression used in the con-text of elections, meaning to lose the elections).' In contrast, Patricia, who lives *arriba*, claims that 'the leftists, communists, are all *guerrilleros*, violent, and they want to fight.'

The disparities are visible also when it comes to assistance. Those from *arriba*, Patricia and Ramiro, and Linda and Carlos complain they do not get a share of what is secured. 'They say we are a community, but for every meeting there is, or event, they would always invite the same people and exclude others. And they say community?' Patricia complains. There might be some personal preferences involved when distributing the assistance but beyond that, IDP leaders in both hamlets represent and lobby also for the displaced outside the two villagers. Some of the relief they manage to secure is oriented towards them. Furthermore, they often look towards those who are most in need. Nevertheless, the concept community raises 'obligations and expectations one has to people one lives closest to' and is therefore morally charged (Revill 1993: 128). When these expectations are continuously not met and yet the reference to community is still being made, the sole resentment makes the formation of a sense of community highly unlikely. The persistent internal boundaries between people which affect the ways in which they relate, speak more about the community's absence than its presence.

Hierarchies within displaced communities

Physical and verbal confrontations which have marked the relationships in Porvenir, are not the only features that undermine the sense of groupness of the displaced. While they might not do so explicitly, a number of the displaced have in their minds created boundaries between themselves and other displaced. They are comparing their own displacement to that of others and are at the same time creating an image of what they believe an 'ideal' or a 'proper' *desplazado* is like. Considering the theme of hardships, including the life before and after forced migration and the circumstances that led to displacement, they have created a hierarchy of displacement that reflects some kind of 'degrees' of displacement. Alongside suffering, there is also a hierarchy entailing moral values; it exposes the desirable characteristics *desplazados* should have. In some of these constructions the ideal IDP echoes and reinforces certain traits encompassed in governments' cognition of prototypical *desplazado*. In others these constructions are a response to negative connotations related to the category, yet again in others, they are under the influence of IDPs' self-identification and self-understanding. What they have in common is that they challenge any kind of assumed oneness of the displaced.

Material loss is generally speaking perceived as an essential element of displacement. The government in its legislation addresses the question of restitution, the receiving populations tend to be more understanding if assistance is given to IDPs who demonstrate signs of pressing poverty and, lastly, the displaced themselves to a certain extent measure the severity of their displacement according to material loss. When comparing her own displacement with that of some others, Doña Olivia, who otherwise describes displacement as 'a loss of spirit', concludes that 'some people have gained. There are people, also here, within this community, people who didn't have anything but now they have [she is referring to plots of land]. They've gained by displacement. Us, for example, we've lost.' Although other displaced may have also lost their spirit through displacement, be them rich or poor, Doña Olivia believes her family suffered greater material misfortune on top of that. Greater economic suffering and persistent socio-economic difficulties mark higher levels of suffering. Patricio, Juanita's husband, complains that upon arrival in Porvenir, there was *monte* in his *finca* and he and his family had to 'put everything together' themselves. He said this was not the case with some other IDPs, who 'came with money … They have nice *fincas* with coffee. They have workers. Some came with money, but we, we didn't.' The effort Patricio has put in taming the land has been great. Due to differences in economic abilities and in quality of land that the displaced obtained, Patricio's experience was not difficult just upon arrival but ever since, which he believes has not been the case with some of his neighbours.

When reflecting upon their displacement, the displaced occasionally acknowledge the loss that goes beyond assets and economic position and include loss of family members within and outside their families. In such cases, those who have not suffered loss of loved ones, manage to place others, not themselves or their families, at the top of displacement hierarchies. Even though he and his wife both underwent difficulties throughout their journey to Esperanza, Felipe feels he is not *as* displaced as his wife, who lost her father, mother and sister. He himself has not lost any family members and he thus holds that his displacement is incomparable to that of his wife. Marcela who is one of the recent arrivals to Esperanza concurs with Felipe's statement. While her experience has been 'appalling' there are people who have gone 'through worse things. They've lost family members, which is more traumatising,' she concludes. The near equation of displacement with humanitarian aid has led to great emphasis on material loss. However, when thinking outside the context of assistance, the displaced recognise that more severe types of loss exist which are linked to greater suffering.

Harshness of experience is also based on the 'novelty' of IDP status at the time of their physical relocation. The IDPs from Urabá who now live in Esperanza were among the first ones to be recognised as *desplazados*. Accessing assistance had therefore entailed hard work. If for nothing else, they were many times compelled to explain the term displacement and *desplazado* given that the two terms were still not engrained in the policy, or indeed everyday vocabulary. Since then the number of organisations working with the displaced and policies related to displacement have increased substantially. On account of this Lorena, Felipe's wife, concludes that the newly displaced do not struggle as much as they have. A sentiment shared by Roberto in Porvenir. 'The process is different from when we declared. We had to wait for two months, now it's easier. The government recognises everyone as displaced.' On top of it, Lorena asserts, all recent IDPs get psychological help. It is fair to say that assistance to the displaced has overall improved, nevertheless the rate of rejected IDP applications is high and the proportion of the population that actually receives assistance is relatively small. Even though they are mistaken in their perception, Lorena and Roberto contrast the supposed easiness with which newly displaced receive assistance to their situation to that of their fellow IDPs who had to find their own ways of coping. They therefore suffered more and cannot be compared to current IDPs who, they think, get all the help they need.

Finally, the severity of displacement is assessed against real or perceived threats to people. It is closely related to the causes of displacement, as well as people's self-understanding. An indicator of a real threat to life is the (in)ability to travel back to the place of origin. Martina has developed her own typology of displacement, consisting of three types. The first is 'displaced displaced', an individual, 'a member of our family', who she believes can never return to Urabá. The second kind is the displaced who can travel back even if only for short visits. And the third type is people who remain in the same municipality. She understands her displacement as 'displacement displacement', that of the severest type. She explains:

> I still don't understand how some people were displaced from one part of the country and can go back to that same part. When my mum went to Urabá she had to flee. I can't say I can go to Urabá and that I'll have the same opportunities as others [other IDPs]. I went once. They didn't do what they did to my mum. I didn't go to my town. I went to look for help for my children to study. I visited my uncle, we went to Apartadó for two hours. I didn't leave the car, I was afraid. When my mum went back she went to sell one of the *fincas*. They made her flee … She arrived in Urabá at five in the afternoon. At seven they came to look for her. They came to look for her at the house she was going to stay at, at seven or half past seven [in the evening]. Fortunately she changed her plans and spent the night with the *indios* (the indigenous).[1] The following morning she found out there had been four soldiers waiting to kill her. My mum was never in politics because she's religious. But here, some people go [back] and stay for a week.

Martina's formation of typologies is based on her experience and her self-understanding as a *desplazada* which is linked to her political conviction. While Martina feels her family cannot travel back, some other displaced people in Esperanza can. This, on the one hand, raises suspicions about why the paramilitaries do not threaten them, if they too were displaced by the paramilitaries; and on the other puts the 'degree' or 'severity' of their displacement under question.

Alongside the efforts to seek differentiation on the grounds of suffering, the displaced seek distinction through the establishment of a kind of moral hierarchy. One of the features refers to 'innocence' before and after physical relocation. It reflects the wish not to be included in the group of displaced stereotyped to be guerrillas and thieves. Attempting to show his 'cleanliness' and non-relation to any of the armed groups or any wrong-doing that might have led to his displacement, Simón believes that his displacement was different from that of others.

> I was not threatened or told to leave. I left when things started getting worse and before anything happened. The rest, or at least the majority, left because they had bad habits which they still have. Chicken disappear and this is not a habit people adopted now; they had to have it from before. They like gossiping, they have problems of coexistence. People lack tolerance and are not forgiving. If an animal comes to my *finca* and causes damage I can understand that and I don't make

a fuss out of it. It's a different matter if the owner makes the animal go on the neighbour's land to cause damage but if not, no hard feelings should be allowed to grow. The same happens with dogs. If someone sees a dog on their property, rather than look for the owner and talk to them, they poison the dog.[2] The animal is not guilty of anything. If I go back to Huila, people won't say a bad person has come. They would greet me. I never did any harm to anyone unlike others. If one is a good neighbour the guerrilla doesn't do anything. … In my family everyone is hard-working, clean. There are no thieves, murderers, *guerrilleros* or homosexuals.

Simón shares the general assumption that the displaced are responsible for their own predicament. Since he knows he is also included in the state register and thus also a *desplazado*, he is trying to clear his own name, to show that he does not belong to the same category of the displaced, who unlike him, are not necessarily 'clean'. Even more, he wishes to be taken out of the displacement register. He no longer receives assistance or attempts to do so. He does not wish to appear in statistics that help IDP leaders win assistance projects which, he says, they ultimately do not distribute. Simón, who is very hard-working and who has been very successful in the cultivation of coffee on his plot of land, is building his moral position on the grounds of his innocence as well as his independence.

Dependency on assistance is not something that only Simón critiques. A number of other displaced are making a distinction between themselves and the rest based on the degree of reliance on aid. Not all the displaced still receive assistance, and not all of them want to, but many take pride in not receiving it. Roberto describes those who insist on getting help as *limosneros* (beggars), and Alejandra asserts that unlike some others she 'wasn't made to beg'. Patricia similarly disapproves of persistent use of category to access assistance.

> Twelve years have passed. I have a house and food. But people here still say they are displaced. Why? They are proud of it, as if it were their second name. There are plenty of people who live a lot worse and there are displaced who haven't received any help, but in the hamlet the people won't stop with displacement. I call it laziness. Plenty of the fourteen families that moved here sold their *fincas*, got money and said they were displaced again, just to receive more.

The critique goes not only to *limosneros* but also to people who pass themselves off as displaced in order to receive assistance. 'As if being displaced was something nice', comments Doña Flor, who does not approve of such behaviour. This is not because the displaced believe the non-displaced neighbours do not deserve help. Rather, they are afraid that the category has turned into a commodity which undermines the potency of displacement experiences. Furthermore, the displaced know that displacement entails much more than simply provision of humanitarian assistance, which is what a number of the non-displaced perceive it as.

Greater purity and lesser dependence on aid are two features that help determine IDPs' levels of moral conduct. Besides the two, the morality of IDP leaders is also frequently put to a test. This is especially the case in Esperanza where the displaced feel that IDP leaders have placed their interests before those of the rest, which has slowly led to the disintegration of the once community.

Community lost

Those who resettled in Esperanza came from Urabá. Because of their political convictions and experiences of standing up for workers' rights, their ideals of community, community power and community values are high. They have a history of achievements which they gained through working together. These are, for instance, the improvement of work conditions in *bananeras*, or the establishment of a local school. The displaced largely maintained such supportive spirit after physical relocation. Initially, there were even brought closer together. As Miranda Joseph (2002: vii) writes, communities are 'frequently said to emerge in times of crisis or tragedy, when people imagine themselves bound together by a common grief or joined through some extraordinary effort'. This was undoubtedly the case with the displaced who are now in Esperanza.

During their time living in the landfill Alejandra remembers they were 'united in misery. No one had anything but we worked as a community', supporting each other. They were trying to find ways of bettering their situation through common work and efforts. The community was what mattered. Fabio remembers the sacrifices he made for the rest during the time when they 'lived as one. I'd only have three thousand pesos [less than a pound] and couldn't buy *panela* for my children. I'd use them to go to Bogotá [to visit corresponding governmental offices in relation to land acquisition] and my children drank water [rather than *aguapanela*, water with *panela*, which is commonly drunk],' he recounts. In their efforts to attain land, they were an 'exemplary community,' Martina assesses. 'We even gathered 3.5 million pesos [approximately £900] to pay off the electricity debt that had been there from before our arrival.' As Juan rightly confessed, they could not have attained the plots in Esperanza individually; they needed everyone's support, assistance and involvement.

When they finally received land, it was divided into thirteen plots even though there were only twelve households. They decided to keep one plot as a communal plot where they would organise social events and meetings. When a housing project to provide the displaced with houses was finally passed only ten and not twelve houses were promised. Since the land had contained two houses and an outbuilding, they decided that Don Andrés and Doña Olivia being the eldest would move into one, and Juan and Doña Beatriz would move on the communal plot which had '*la casa grande*', a big house, and an outbuilding, in order to look after the communal plot. The latter couple also got their own plot. In the communal spirit of fairness, a draw established who gets which plot. People first drew numbers to decide the order in which they later drew plastic water caps marked with plot numbers. Collaboration continued. Miguel helped his fellow IDPs financially. He had work so he took out a ten million loan to help the rest pay off the 30 per cent they needed to pay for the land. Some never paid him back what they owe him, he now reflects with disappointment.

The founding myth based on the struggle for land for most of the displaced presents a piece of shared history they can draw on. For those who were involved in communal action in Urabá, the organised struggle presented continued realisation of their convictions and efforts of working for common good. However, falling back on the past is insufficient to maintain a sense of community. Rather than being only a community of memory, community also needs to be one of hope, oriented towards the future (Royce 1968 quoted in; Bastian 2014). Its members need to support each other, nurture its existence and the relationships. This is not the case in Esperanza. After the initial unity the community in Esperanza got displaced by individual interests, which buried any prospects of common future endeavours.

Through the years a divide has formed within the community. It is roughly speaking a division between those who cherish and defend old values of solidarity, greater equality and working for common good and those who have pushed such values aside, or who, while they still help others, do so with a personal interest. It is a split between those who were political leaders in the place of origin and the new IDP leaders and their respective supporters.

The threat of potential renewed persecution put some of the 'old' leaders off visible political engagement, therefore they preferred helping the 'new' leaders develop. Fabio assesses that 'pobre muchachos [poor boys, the two current leaders] didn't even know how to speak.' Despite the initial backing the two leaders lost considerable part of the support they had previously enjoyed. The old leaders do not agree with much of their activities. Even though one of his sons is an IDP leader in Esperanza, Don Andrés is critical of his 'narrow' outlook. He himself is concerned with the broader scope of problems in Colombia. These problems concern inequality and the disadvantageous position of the poor which has ultimately contributed to their displacement. The two IDP leaders, however, focus on IDPs' rights and do not relate their discourse to broader social and political context of the country. Fabio also feels that 'it is fine to work as a leader for the displaced, but this should not be done for personal benefits and this is what they are doing. It has become a business. It is not acceptable to say you will help people if they pay you. There are many people like this. It has become a vice.'

The divide got even deeper and any hopes of future community were lost when Pedro, after Juan decided to move to Bogotá, tried to appropriate himself of the communal plot. He claimed his land is on average smaller than that of the rest. His plot measures around 2.6 hectares, whereas that of his neighbour for instance measures 3.7 hectares. While some of the displaced supported him with the promise that Juan and Pedro will continue assisting them, there were a few who opposed them. Juan and Pedro called for a meeting with Incoder saying they had everyone's signatures that everyone who was included in the land programme agreed that they could sell the communal plot. In the meeting Martina stood up saying that if her signature was there, it was forged.

The disagreement over the plot of land destroyed any dreams of a community and it also allowed some other grudges to surface. Those who believed in community most are those who are also most affected. As Gerald Creed (2006: 13) in his reconsideration of community states, '[t]he fascination with, and desire for, community may be inadvertently generating disappointment, alienation, fragmentation, and segregation.' Fabio therefore finds the whole situation disheartening.

> I am demanding Pedro and Juan for the piece of land they have appropriated. They don't even allow anyone to cross through there! There were different projects when money was won and it disappeared. I never said anything but I won't keep quiet. It is demoralising to see how we went from being like one person to having to confront my own *compañeros*.

Miguel, who previously left Esperanza and moved to Venezuela in part due to poor community relationships, says he is 'disillusioned with *la gente misma* [the people themselves, referring to other IDPs in Esperanza]'. Alejandra complains:

> In misery we were more united. Now everyone does their own thing. There are people who have changed a lot. Now, if someone is suffering from hunger, 'well ok' ... Before they'd give you rice. We don't have reunions. We used to get together every month, now we don't. I was in hospital once for twenty days and no one called me or visited me.

Martina who asserts she was the one who believed most in community projects, lost her faith.

> I don't believe in community projects anymore. I was the one who believed the most that the project would work out. We got projects – ninety-seven, thirty-two and seven million pesos [approximately £24,860, £8,200 and £1,795 respectively]. It didn't work out. Some worked, others didn't, again others wanted to abuse the assistance. Nothing worked and people started losing confidence in each other. Now I believe it would be better to give money to one person and help one person *salir adelante* than like this when no one is in a better position.

With pain in her voice Martina concludes that she has 'lost confidence in people'.

The personal investment that people put into the establishment of a community, has not paid off. The disappointment, discouragement and the sense of betrayal contribute to the continuous sense of displacement. The loss of social landscapes which marked the loss of place in Urabá is once again re-lived. Communal relations, which seemed to be the only firm and stable base to re-create the sense of place and belonging at a different location, have been lost. Those, who place their faith in community action, for whom it represents strength and underlines their world views, have been especially affected. The loss of community presents not only loss of social relationships but it also undermines what they have struggled for, their beliefs and ideals.

The displaced in the two villages challenge any assumptions of unity formed among those who suffered similar violation of their rights. They might share the same category and thus one of their identities. They may also meet the criteria of a shared locality, since they resettled in the same villages. However, neither the *desplazado/a* identity, nor the common locality were something they have chosen. It often feels that more than being a recourse to search for commonalities, the category has opened itself up to scrutiny of finding differences among the categorised. These differences can present a challenge in the process of forming new, constructive relationships.

What is under question, however, is not only the interactions among the displaced but also between the displaced and the non-displaced – the topic of the following chapter. The often unfavourable social interactions with the non-displaced can arguably leave even greater impact on the displaced's social landscapes and the locale.

Notes

1 The indigenous were neighbouring one of her father's *fincas*. Martina describes them as *bravos* (fierce) to the extent that not even the guerrillas would 'mess' with them. The *indios* had a good relationship with her family, hence her mum decided to spend the night there.
2 Doña Flor said about seven dogs had been poisoned in the village, including her dog.

8

Desplazados and their 'hosts': the quest for relational belonging

When I first arrived in Esperanza I was accompanying Sonia to a 'gender work-shop' for displaced and non-displaced 'vulnerable' women. At the time neither I nor the people knew I would return to the village in four months and spend sub-stantial time there. We all thought that mine was a one-off visit. During the work-shop, in the presence of Sonia and the rest of the women, Marta, a non-displaced woman, assured me that the displaced are the locals' friends; they are no longer displaced, she said, but rather have become 'one of us'. Yet, the dynamics of the group did not quite confirm this. The displaced women sat on one side of the room and the non-displaced on the other. *Urabeñas* moreover did not fail to stress that they were not long-term residents of Esperanza; they kept referring to themselves and other *urabeños* as '*nosotros, los desplazados*' (we, the displaced). Women did not mingle or talk either before, during or after the workshop.

Numerous conversations which I later had with women and their families in the privacy of their homes confirmed what the group dynamics hinted at. It became clear that the displaced had become anything but 'one of us', nor was it necessarily something that they were striving for. Considering that it is also the people who make a place what it is and the importance social relations have for place attachment and belonging (Antonsich 2010c; Carrillo Rowe 2005; Lewicka 2010; Massey 2005; May 2013), this chapter continues the focus on relationship building; this time between the displaced and their non-displaced hosts.

Place-making is closely connected with the people residing in, moving in and through space. Landscapes we inhabit are 'social landscapes' and are closely influenced by the relationships we have, or do not have, in a particular setting. They are products of our relationships. Family, neighbours, acquaintances and friends to different degrees shape how we feel in a place, whether we feel wel-come or rejected, with consequences on our sense of belonging. The importance of social landscapes is such that the 'social relations that place signifies may be equally or more important to the attachment process than the place qua place' (Low and Altman 1992: 17). That is to say, people we share places with determine whether we feel welcome, supported and, ultimately, safe.

Not all relations matter in the same way. Yet in small settings, such as rural hamlets, where the number of inhabitants is low and where everyone knows each other, even the weaker social ties bear greater value due to the intimacy of the setting. How those already settled in a place receive the displaced greatly affects the displaced's sense of belonging to the place. At the same time, the arrival of the displaced influences the locals' sense of place. The two villages existed prior to the arrival of the displaced. They are places in history, influenced by different sets of relations and interactions. The displaced brought another layer of complexity to the established relations.

This chapter focuses on social landscapes. It examines how social boundaries between the displaced and non-displaced have been created and maintained, standing in the way of greater social bonding, and consequently better appreciation of the villages of resettlement.[1] I first give a short background to the time when the displaced reached to the two hamlets, which came as a surprise for the locals. I look at how cultural differences and the changing power relations shaped their (non)acceptance. Drawing on theories of categorisation and Goffman's concept of stigma, and influenced by lack of awareness of regional specificities of conflict, I discuss how the displaced have become to be identified with guerrillas, thieves and liars and what implications such stigmatisation has on place-making. I then turn to the policy environment, to show how policies created for IDPs keep the displaced and non-displaced socially distant. The chapter demonstrates that construction of relationships and relational belonging is not based merely on personal liking but draws on a much broader set of political influences, where social and political landscapes intersect.

Unwelcome strangers

When people move from one place to another they need to establish new relationships with those who were there before them; the newcomers need to negotiate their access to the conventional ways of life of the 'established', that is of the old residents (Elias and Scotson 1994: 157). They are not negotiating just physical entry but also interpersonal relationships. The same amount of space becomes shared by more people who might have different cultural habits and practices, and who do not yet have any memories with the place on which they could build a shared place identity. Reflecting upon access, Joan Scott (1988: 178) asks:

> How are those who cross the thresholds received? If they belong to a group different from one already 'inside', what are the terms of their incorporation? How do the new arrivals understand their relationship to the place they have entered? What are the terms of identity they establish?

There are other essential questions to ask – after all, the displaced did not move to an empty space, but one which had been already inhabited. Have the locals' perceptions of the place changed since the arrival of displaced people? How does the change inform behaviours towards newcomers and how does it influence the sense of belonging of everyone involved? How do the particularities of arrival establish the terms along which the relationships are going to be built?

The inhabitants of Porvenir and Esperanza did not know that their two hamlets would see a substantial increase in population. Upon arrival, IDPs represented between 15–20 per cent of the population in both villages at the time. When strangers arrive in substantial numbers, the locals perceive them as a threat to their position in the social hierarchy and to their identity. They see them as affecting the established class, gender, ethnic or religious dynamics (Bauman 2006: 3–4). The disruption of local dynamics was felt in both villages. In Porvenir this was due to the effect the large number of the displaced had on the established power structures, whereas in Esperanza it was also due to the question of race and different cultural practices.

Colombia is a country of regions with their own particularities. These regions have been determined by a wide range of criteria. First, the country's diverse geography of mountain rangers, rivers, rainforest, *llanos* and oceans has undoubtedly influenced the formation of regional distinctions. In addition, regions are also social spaces that have been created as a result of economic, political and cultural control over territory. Inhabitants of particular spaces possess strong sentiments of belonging to these imaginary regional communities (Zambrano 2001: 52) and cultural practices and daily habits vary sharply between them. Each region has unique features, be it food, dialect or music and they serve to shape and maintain identities that are distinct from others. It is not uncommon for people to identify more closely with their regional identity than with their national one.

The majority of the displaced came to Porvenir from neighbouring regions – predominately from Tolima – and the areas share similarities in terms of food, accent and climate. Consequently criticisms about IDPs' (or indeed the receiving populations') behaviour in terms of their respective cultural habits are hardly ever voiced. One of the disapprovals that the displaced occasionally articulate is that people of Cundinamarca are tight-fisted. They claim that in Tolima visitors would always be offered coffee and something to eat – and even a place for the night – but that in Porvenir this is not the case.

The habits of those displaced who were in Porvenir at the time of the research and the non-displaced are similar and generally speaking do not stand in the way of relationship building. Nevertheless, the circumstances surrounding the displaced's resettlement in Porvenir (see Chapter 4) as well as the disruption of the power arrangements in the hamlet have left their toll. Don Sergio, a local, who was the first to make contact with the displaced, faced a rebuke from the rest of the locals, who were expecting him to stand on their side.

> People [the villagers] did not like me for it. And for the first junta elections! The village parted in two – those from Porvenir and the rest. Don Eduardo and a shop owner were the candidates. A war started – they'd be using *chismes* on both sides, both locals and the displaced. Don Eduardo won but it was *duro*.

The 'war' persisted during the following local junta elections when it was again one of the displaced who was celebrating victory. The insertion of the displaced not only in the physical environment but also in a position of power contributed to the locals' resentment, which some of them still feel today.

In Esperanza, in contrast, complaints about 'culture' and behaviour abound; the displaced from Urabá crossed many regional boundaries and their food, clothing, music and other cultural practices differ substantially from the rest of the village. Luisa, a long-term resident of Esperanza in her twenties, even uses 'culture' as the reason why she dislikes the displaced: 'I don't know any of them. I don't like them. It's the culture, I guess. I don't know.' Various aspects of cultural practices are a point of critique. Both the displaced and the receiving population in Esperanza would sneer at each other's food habits. Fabio who married Fernanda shortly before physical relocation considers himself 'lucky' to have married an *urabeña*. He cannot imagine having to eat the food he would have to eat if he had married a woman from Cundinamarca. *Urabeños* find the food typical of Cundinamarca tasteless, particularly the *changua*, milk soup with egg, stale bread and coriander which is usually consumed in the morning. 'How can anyone eat it?!' wonders Don Jorge. In contrast the breakfast in Urabá is 'dry'. Carolina and some other non-displaced admit that the food that *urabeños* prepare is tastier; nevertheless, Carolina at the same time scorns the newcomers for eating beans and/or rice for breakfast, lunch and dinner. While the *cundinamarqueses* (inhabitants of Cundinamarca) also consume rice and beans they do so in what they consider acceptable levels.

There are instances where different dimensions of the same thing are seen as (in)appropriate, and they extend far beyond traditional dishes. 'Appropriateness' of behaviour is particularly challenged when it comes to clothing. The displaced women, since they come from *tierra caliente*, wear more revealing clothes compared to the locals. Through their clothing, however, the displaced offend the locals' sense of morality. Natalia explains that *las desplazadas* provoke sexual ideas in some of the local men. 'Women wear short shorts and sleeveless t-shirts. Men would offer to have sex with them.' There were even rumours that *las desplazadas* will sell sex for two thousand pesos (less than £1). Natalia, by way of apology or explanation, states that the local women are 'more reserved'. Marta complains about the music the IDPs play and their *fiestero* (party-like) character. Lively music is often heard from the houses inhabited by *urabeños*; they like organising *fiestas* for various occasions, including birthdays, New Year, mother's day and the day of friendship. Marta and her husband label the displaced '*fiesteros*' (fun lovers). 'All this different culture that they bring, from music onwards!' They complain that after fiestas *desplazados* sleep till late and do not work.

The latter complaints greatly reflect the stereotypes that Colombians associate with *costeños*, and Afro-Colombians. In Esperanza some of the newly arrived displaced had a different, darker skin tone.[2] In the region of Cundinamarca, whose population has historically been indigenous and white, such a difference is noticeable and can in itself stand in the way of place-making. Despite Colombia's claim of celebrating multiculturality, the blacks are in many respects seen 'as non-nationals as distant from the core values of being (light-coloured) mestizo and white, urban(e), civilised and educated' (Wade 1997: 85). Even if they tend to be perceived as superior when it comes to music, dancing and love making, they are also seen as primitive, underdeveloped and morally inferior (Viveros 2000). The stereotypes of blacks being naturally disposed towards delinquency, laziness, noise, music, partying and sexual power (Navarro 2008: 238) were of no help to the newly arrived displaced. Even if in greater part their skin tone was only slightly darker than that of the locals, they were *costeños* – and many of the stereotypes about whom are similar; those from the interior of the country tend to see them as backward and vulgar. Be it for their skin tone or the fact that they were displaced, they were not welcome.

Alejandra reflects: 'I remember so much the day when I had to go to the shop, this was so painful. My husband was working and I ran out of rice. I arrived there, to the shop at six in the afternoon. I remember I was coming closer and this *señor* [the owner] was closing doors and windows.' The shop reopened after she had left, and she continues: 'In the municipality people would spit as we passed by.'

Both the displaced and non-displaced describe the time of the arrival of IDPs as '*duro*'. Natalia, one of the long-term residents of Esperanza, explains: 'We didn't know them. We were afraid. It was during the time when they would be talking about displacement in the news. People were asking themselves what it was that they had done to be displaced.' Marta remembers her daughter's reaction. 'I had a daughter at school and one day she came home saying, "*Mami*, there are *desplazados* at school, I'm afraid they'll kill me." Since displacement was due to the guerrillas or I don't know who, and us, what?'

The displaced, on the other hand, were fleeing violence and rather than coming across acceptance, sympathy and peace, they came across a different kind of violence – one expressed through rejection. This rejection fostered the sense of displacement as the displaced realised that negotiating their place would be a laborious task. The doors of *tiendas* (local shop) may no longer shut when IDPs come close, and it is generally known that the IDPs have a legal right to be in the respective villages; nevertheless the tensions and social divisions between the displaced and non-displaced in both villages are still felt.

Fear of the displaced additionally originates from another motif. Strangers are thought to possess no history but are people who in the eyes of the receiving population begin to exist only upon their arrival (Schütz 1944). The displaced defy such notion of strangers. The receiving population makes assumptions about the displaced people's history, which generates fear and suspicion among the villagers. Doña Tamára, who together with her husband voluntarily moved from Bogotá to Porvenir, contemplates that if the villagers looked at the two of them as '*bichos raros*', as if they were weird, bizarre, even though they did not flee conflict, 'you can only imagine how they perceive the displaced'.

Coming from Urabá, one of the most violent regions in Colombia, Fabio complains, bears even greater negative connotations. 'It is a burden', agrees Alejandro with remorse. 'People see us as paramilitaries, guerrillas, almost non-human.' Such views have repercussions, since those who are deemed responsible for their ills and considered dangerous for the community cannot generate pity and empathy (Aradau 2004: 258). Below I examine why such beliefs exist, and how the social boundaries between the displaced and non-displaced have been shaped and maintained.

Desplazados: victims or guerrillas and thieves?

It was a pleasant Sunday morning and together with Sonia and village women we sat down to engage in one of the monthly gender workshops. Only one displaced woman was present – Alejandra. The aim of the meeting was to plan a small chicken farm, *proyecto productivo* (a productive project), which the NGO Sonia works for would help finance (see Figure 7). It was around ten in the morning and the workshop had not started yet. Screams were heard. At first we thought that a cow had escaped and that someone needed help in bringing it back to the shed. However, we soon realised that a physical fight had erupted between Marcela, a displaced woman, and Don Alberto, a long-term resident of Esperanza. Alejandra immediately got up and ran to see what had happened, as did Doña Constanza, Don Alberto's wife. Other non-displaced women, including Don Alberto's two daughters, stayed where they were. When the word came that the person involved was Marcela, one woman commented, 'It's obvious, who else? That woman is crazy.' All the learnings women claimed to have gained through the workshops on the importance to 'value themselves as women', of 'relating to other community members', and on 'their rights as women', seemed to have dwindled in that moment.

Figure 7 Long-term residents of Esperanza are building a chicken shed.

There was no sign on any kind of notion of imagined 'sisterhood'; it rather became a matter or 'us' and 'them', that is, the displaced versus non-displaced.

No one but the two people involved knew what had really happened and the versions of their stories differed. Marcela claimed Don Alberto had hit her and scratched her breasts. She lowered her shirt to show two red diagonal lines on one of her breasts. Don Alberto on the other hand claimed Marcela had attacked him. According to the women the two had a history of conflict. They claimed Marcela had tried to provoke Don Alberto before and that she had tried to destroy some of his crops. On a different occasion, Fabio, told me that Don Alberto had had sexual intents with Marcela before the incident which she had refused, and that was supposedly the source of tensions between the two. While the women were espousing negative remarks about Marcela, Carolina, one of Don Alberto's daughters, preferred not to take sides. She commented that her father could get violent towards her mother when he drank. 'Last night he was drinking in the *tienda*. The alcohol might still be affecting him,' she concluded.[3]

After things had calmed down and we started the workshop, Doña Constanza received a phone call from one of the non-displaced neighbours. They advised her to go to the farm that Don Alberto was renting from one of the displaced, since '*los desplazados* had him there' and 'some had sticks'. When she finished the conversation, Doña Constanza expressed her concern: 'They will kill him.' The rest of the women contributed to her preoccupation, emphasising that the displaced were 'revengeful'. This was only one of a number of occasions where the displaced, as a group, were the subject of negative perceptions. They did not need to be singled out and named. Rather, the notion that the *desplazados* were involved in a certain incident usually sufficed to satisfy the locals' thirst for information.

In Colombia, to be displaced is not the same as being a *desplazado*. A number of people have been displaced throughout Colombian history before the category *desplazado* came into force, especially during *La Violencia*. Even today there are people who for one reason or another – be it fear of retaliation, lack of documentation, or lack of information about available programmes – do not register for assistance. They might live in anonymity, and may or may not refer to themselves or be referred to as *desplazados*. For those who are, such identification adds to the complexity of their situation, contributes to extended sense of displacement and ultimately influences their place-making efforts, even if it also means eligibility for assistance. The official category *desplazado* has moved from the policy field and entered a social stage. It tends to be negatively coloured and has direct implications for relationship building, since it encourages negative ascriptions.

The category *desplazado* has helped maintain the divide between people; nevertheless, the negative connotations associated with it cannot be explained by its mere existence. Categories, while resistant to change (Zetter 1991), have a life of their own and are shaped by external influences. The latter determine the undertones the category takes and govern the social and cognitive distance established between the 'us' and 'them'. Some of the perceptions about new inhabitants are often based on prejudices present in collective imaginaries about IDPs and are not questioned (Jaramillo *et al.* 2004: 184). But at the same time, the context in which people live – that which produced the displaced, and the opportunities the category presents – dictate what symbolic value the category and those categorised take. In other words, these conditions determine whether the category becomes just another source of identification or substantially sculpts people's behaviours towards the categorised. With some exceptions, the locals of Porvenir and Esperanza see the displaced as having collaborated with the guerrillas, as thieves, and they not uncommonly label them as liars, as people who have passed themselves off as displaced. All these references and beliefs have implications for the village life. And all of them have an explanation – they can be explained through the lack of knowledge about conflict and displacement particularities in departments other than Cundinamarca, the air of a particular kind of victimhood related with the category, and the potential access to assistance related to the category.

In both villages a number of locals hold that the displaced are responsible for their own misfortune. The non-displaced assume that IDPs have collaborated with the guerrillas and/or were involved in criminal activities such as petty theft. As Santiago puts it, 'no one gets displaced for being good – 80 per cent of the displaced have done something to have caused their own displacement.' His opinion closely resembles that of Leonardo, who is likewise highly critical of IDPs. While he recognises that there are some displaced 'who have nothing to do with it [conflict and violence]', there are also 'many who had links with the guerrillas or *paras* (paramilitaries)'. Santiago even claims that he can identify the '*culpables*', namely those guilty of collaborating with the guerrillas. The *culpables* are the displaced who mobilise, whereas the '*buenos* (the good ones) are left with nothing'. Those who organise and demand their rights, he suspects, do so due to their previous experiences of organisation possibly under the auspices of the guerrillas. In his mind, agency and victimhood do not go hand in hand.

When making claims about the displaced, the receiving populations take themselves and their non-displacement as the point of reference. Conflict and displacement have affected all Colombian departments but to a different extent and in different forms. Colombian regions are as archipelagos (Pécaut 2001), where particularities of conflict in one region do not necessarily transfer into the neighbouring region. What might be a reality for some Colombians is simply unimaginable for others. Lack of (balanced) media coverage does not help with the issue. Armed actors had their presence in Esperanza and Porvenir at different times – the military, the guerrillas and the paramilitaries – but the conflict remained largely latent for these two hamlets. Laura, a non-displaced woman from a hamlet neighbouring Esperanza has nice memories of the guerrilla. Even though they were present in the area of Sumapaz she only remembers seeing two *muchachos guerrilleros* in the hamlet.

> The guerrilla doesn't kill for nothing unlike the paramilitaries. When they came, they'd always explain what their objective was and what they were doing. They'd only meddle with people who caused problems. If people got drunk at local parties and started a fight, the guerrilla would tie them against a tree and leave

them there till the following day. They displaced or killed cattle thieves. They would always warn people and give them a chance to improve.

Despite the latent nature of conflict, both places witnessed cases of displacement. The locals remember episodes of selective displacement, when their neighbours were displaced in the spirit of *limpieza social*. Allegedly, these were cattle thieves, prostitutes or guerrilla supporters, and were removed from the respective hamlets. 'They came to do *limpieza*,' Marta from Esperanza explains. 'In those times one couldn't leave even a needle. They would steal horses, cows, sheep, hens ... everything. That's why they came to do *limpieza*.'

Hugo, a long-term resident of Porvenir, indicates that 'one would meet a guerrilla on the road but one would stay out of their business'. Despite the guerrillas' presence, Hugo was not compelled to leave because he did not 'interfere' with them. Those who experienced displacement were 'people who had some sort of bad history, those who were guilty of something. We would never get ourselves involved in anything and nothing happened', affirms Julia, a local from Esperanza. Since the locals had lived through episodes of selective displacement and were not displaced themselves, and since they do not know the conflict dynamics and the local realities in other parts of the country, they assume that their displaced neighbours were 'thrown out' from their villages of origin for a reason. Believing the displaced were involved in the insurgents' armed struggle, Santiago sees some IDPs' displacement as a natural consequence: 'If one [a person who is now *desplazado*] orders people to be killed, of course the *pueblo* protects itself and gets the person out.'

The perceptions of self-inflicted displacement have consequences for village dynamics and everyday life, both for the displaced as well as for the non-displaced. If something goes missing in the hamlet, the displaced are often accused of being responsible. Petty thefts are not infrequent. During my stay in Esperanza 300,000 pesos (approximately £84), some high-value boots, and a TV set disappeared from three different houses in about a month. The fear of theft is so high that Anita, a non-displaced resident, is uncomfortable with the plans to improve the road passing her house. The current dirt road is almost unpassable, with traffic limited to motorbikes and the truck that comes to collect people's harvest. Better infrastructure might bring some improvement to people's lives but Anita worries that it may also bring more thieves. Natalia and Santiago, long-term residents of Esperanza, confess that before the displaced arrived, 'things would also disappear'. Nevertheless, the displaced are now usually held responsible for any instances of theft in the village. The accusations are so widely spread that Anita suspects some thieves might be taking an advantage of the situation knowing that the displaced will be the first ones to be held suspects.

Alejandra remembers allegations from the very start.

Imagine, until today and knowing that it had been the same before we arrived, that there were thefts, and after we had arrived, they continued stealing and they said it was the displaced. If a chicken disappeared, it was *los desplazados* who took it to eat it. A plantain ... *los desplazados*. The displaced were hungry [they would say] … They came to the house, we thought they came to visit us, two women, one man, and a child, to see if we were making a hen *sancocho* (a type of a stew).[4] And we, I'm not lying, I'm not ashamed, we now live in glory because you know what we were buying when we didn't have money? Bones, porous bones that are no longer useful, that don't have meat, this is what we'd buy. And everyone knew us in the municipality, at the butcher's, 'ah, they're coming for the bone', they already knew us. And that day they came to see if we had a hen, making hen *sancocho*, with a hen that we had supposedly stolen. And when they saw that we were serving soup cooked with a bone they saw we hadn't stolen the hen.

Don Andrés is similarly aware or their 'reputation'. If something goes missing in town [the municipality] they'd say, 'Go to Esperanza, that's where the *desplazados* are.' In Porvenir, the situation is not much different. Simón explains he got engaged in a conversation with a man while they were waiting for a *buseta*. When the man asked Simón where he was going, upon Simón's reply he said, 'ah, you're one of those bandits who attacks cars.' Knowing that the area Simón mentioned was where the displaced resettled, the man associated him with bandits who were attacking cars and buses and some of whom were allegedly displaced. Simón does not deny that displaced individuals can be involved in thefts. He gives an example of a pig that went missing. 'A pig was stolen and the people said it was the displaced who took it. The police came and reviewed every house. Only months after the pig had disappeared, it became known that a *desplazado* was involved. But it was one, not all [the displaced]!'

In Esperanza some IDPs similarly admit that among them there are a few who 'have caught bad habits', as Don Fernando describes it. 'But as I've told you there are more good people than bad. The displaced adults are good people.' The 'bad habits', however, are projected on the displaced as a group. As Don Andrés complains, the accusers don't name people. They say '*los desplazados*'. Both the accusers and the accused suffer consequences. Suspicion with which the locals treat the displaced affects the latter's self-worth and the manner in which they relate to the locals. The non-displaced, in contrast, fear that the displaced will bring conflict in the village and undermine village security either due to their alleged links with the guerrillas or because of thefts. Due to the negative suppositions about the displaced Paula, a long-term resident of Esperanza, concludes that another act of 'social cleansing' might take place and that the displaced will be forced to migrate once again. The suppositions of the displaced people's links to the guerrillas and their involvement in stealing are not the only ones interfering with people's relationship building. The non-displaced receiving population also believes that the displaced are liars; that they have not really been displaced but are passing themselves off as *desplazados* in order to receive assistance.

Desplazados: victims or liars?

Similarly to the governmental image of an 'ideal' *desplazado* (see Chapter 5), the receiving community has also established their own perceptions of what a genuine IDP is like. The perception relates to their appearance, socio-economic state they find themselves in, as well as their code of conduct. Destitution and suffering enshrined in the humanitarian character of the category are among the required criteria. The displaced in Esperanza and Porvenir often fail to meet these constructed expectations, which bears consequences for a more positive relationship building. As Erving Goffman (1990: 12) demonstrated, the discrepancy between a 'virtual social identity' which is linked to a certain category, and people's 'actual social identity' – who they really are – can lead to stigma, which reduces people from being a whole person into a discounted one. The displaced's actual social identity is often not concurrent with their virtual social identity. The difference between the two has placed the authenticity of their displacement into question.

Authentic *desplazados* should be poor and have had to flee at gun point, leaving all their possessions behind. If the displaced do not demonstrate relative economic hardship upon their arrival, the receiving population may perceive them as 'bogus' *desplazados* since they do not meet the hosts' expectations. 'Out of all the displaced families in Porvenir there is only one that has really been displaced,' asserts Hugo. I visited him and his wife in their small house which is located at the edge of Patricio and Juanita's *finca* in the middle of the forest. They do not pay rent but occasionally help Juanita and Patricio with work. The couple had their own *finca*, but they sold it because their neighbours were 'jealous' and they 'couldn't take it anymore,' explains Amanda, Hugo's wife. They used the money to buy a house in Bogotá and they live off the rent they get for the house. Having two school-going children they lead a modest life, and are considering renting a *finca* and work in order to increase their income. Hugo, even though he is staying on a *finca* that was given to the displaced, or perhaps just because of it, expresses his doubts over the displaced: 'If one goes to their houses, they have a television, radio and [they are] displaced? If one needs to leave, one doesn't have time to take one's bed, right?' he asked me without really waiting for my response.

Hugo, like a number of other Colombians, understands displacement as quite literally a 'life or land' (Jaramillo *et al.* 2004: 153) matter, whereas people's departures from the area of origin are more complex than that. Reasons for and dynamics of displacement are multifaceted and vary greatly over time and space. The complexity of staying or leaving reflects the complexity of conflict. In some cases individuals are able to plan their escapes or they may leave their homes before fully fledged violence breaks out. Even if people leave in a hurry, displacement in Colombia is mainly parcelled out in small batches; it is often not the case that entire villages move at once, but rather individuals or families trickle out over time. Family members may stay behind and neighbours too, therefore there is always an option of sending some belongings on. Nevertheless, due to the common perception of an instant flight, some non-displaced find it incomprehensible that IDPs may arrive with more than just a bag of belongings. After all, the displaced and those advocating for the rights often say that the displaced 'have lost everything', reinforcing such images of virtual social identity. But what happens if the material loss is not complete?

The government's response to internal displacement has been largely humanitarian, rather than political. The Victims' Law with its focus on land restitution has been corrective, however, due to bureaucratic obstacles and slow processing of cases, the emphasis for many of the displaced has remained based on humanitarian grounds. Those who are advocating for the displaced people's rights, human rights and humanitarian discourses tend to build their arguments on people's destitution, their needs, and their vulnerabilities. If the displaced fit such criteria, the non-displaced from Esperanza and Porvenir tend not to doubt their plight or hold grudges regarding the assistance the displaced receive. Even more, they might actively engage in assisting the displaced. Such was an example of Marta who in one of the gender workshops introduced her initiative called 'basket of love' for the displaced that were in Soacha, south of Bogotá. A priest showed her a video demonstrating the poor living conditions that the displaced were living in and Marta invited women to contribute towards food and clothing for the displaced. Visible suffering prompted her good will (Fassin 2012).

Unlike the displaced families whose material possessions challenge their genuine displacement status, Don Eduardo' family is, in Hugo's opinion, the only one that has really been displaced. While they have both a television and bed, these are old and, crucially, Hugo assessed Don Eduardo as being poor from his first day in Porvenir. 'He didn't even have *panela* to make *tinto* (coffee)', Hugo explains. 'To sweeten his coffee, he would crush sugarcane.' Don Eduardo stands in stark contrast to Simón, Don Ignacio and Doña Flor, who came to Porvenir with savings, which they used to furnish their houses and inverted into cultivation of land which has now brought returns. 'We only took clothes and photos. We had money in our bank account in Florencia, so we were able to buy things,' explains Doña Flor. Nevertheless, for many non-displaced, poverty presents a constituent element of displacement and its absence delegitimises their *desplazado* status. In their view, relative economic stability and displacement are not compatible.

What could be termed 'insufficient loss' to qualify for a displacement status also has another take on it. In some cases the loss may not have been complete, but in others there might have not been any or only few material assets to lose in the first place. Land is one such example. Displacement is so closely associated with the loss of land that many people see it as its necessary constituent element. Paula speaking about her former neighbour who left Esperanza concludes the following: '*La señora* (the woman) who lived here wasn't really displaced. We talked a lot. She told me she didn't have land in Urabá. She came here because others invited her to come.' Even though Urabá was highly affected by conflict, Paula considers that moving away from violence is insufficient to claim displacement. The perception of land dispossession is so pervasive that Magdalena, who arrived to Esperanza some years later than the rest, initially did not attempt to register as a *desplazada* because she had never owned land. It was only after other displaced from the hamlet explained that she qualified for assistance that she registered, albeit to no avail.

Failure to meet these specific criteria of 'real' displaced, engenders strong beliefs that the displaced are liars. While Patricia, an IDP from Porvenir, argues that 'a *desplazado* is not the same as *maluco* (a mean person, a bandit)', the non-displaced remain unconvinced. The negative categorisation – in addition to the actual and the assumed experiences of displacement – affects the behaviours of the displaced and the non-displaced alike.

In reply to negative perceptions the displaced complain about 'narrow-mindedness' of the non-displaced. Juanita laments that in the meetings she attends as an IDP leader, people question her status. 'If I say I'm *desplazada*, people say we have land and a house, that we are no longer displaced. They think that if one is displaced, one needs to be poor to the point of not having anywhere to live.' Gloria, whom I met in Chocó, also gets affected by comments related to her clothing and jewellery. Before physical relocation she would dress up if she went to Quibdó, the departmental capital. She kept her nice clothes and still cares about the way she looks, however, she heard comments that she cannot really be displaced if she dresses nicely. '*Chocoanos* (inhabitants of Chocó) prefer living comfortably, with a furnished living room even if this means no food. The appearance is important, we are proud,' she asserts, explaining her behaviour.

It is such assumptions and their related comments that have facilitated the emergence of resentment towards the non-displaced. IDPs feel that their hosts do not want them to progress or have a better quality of life than themselves. At the same time, the 'stigmatisers' – the non-displaced – are more likely to keep their distance and maintain the sharp social boundaries between themselves and the displaced. Stories of how displacement came about are not shared, partly as a result of lack of contact, of interest and also lack of trust between the locals and their new neighbours. Not knowing their trajectories, the non-displaced make assumptions about their displaced neighbours' alleged dark history. Consequently, the displaced are perceived as a threat, as a risk to security and the established way of life and people that cannot be trusted.

But even more than the lack of knowledge and understanding of particularities of conflict and people's displacement, what has particularly shaped and maintained the divide between the displaced and the non-displaced is the policy of assistance to IDPs, which is in place. It is in part due to this policy that the non-displaced continue labelling the displaced as the guerrillas, thieves and liars. Tania bitterly remarks that 'one needs to rob or kill to get displaced to get things. My upbringing doesn't allow me to do that.' Through continuous reference to assumed negative histories of the displaced, their hosts attempt to morally challenge the assistance the displaced receive, which they themselves also often need.

'*Vulnerables*' and '*desplazados*': leveraging suffering

In the weeks leading up to the local elections in 2011, political candidates organised a number of meetings presenting their programme. In one such meeting we gathered in a local's house to listen to the candidate for *Partido Conservador Colombiano* (the Colombian Conservative Party). The meeting started with a prayer, which was followed by the candidate's presentation, after which he asked attendees for their comments, questions or concerns. The first one to raise his hand was an elderly man who took the microphone and his words echoed in the small room, too small for such technical assistance. The words did not echo only due to the loudspeakers, but also because of their content, and they particularly affected the displaced who were in the room.

> *Doctor*, the only thing I'd ask you is to think of us [long-term residents with disadvantaged socio-economic backgrounds] if you're elected. At the moment all the help is for the displaced. We've been here all our lives, we've worked here and we're going to die here and we have never received anything. Any help that comes is for the displaced.

He explained his statement and spoke of lack of assistance for the elderly, lack of pension and his inability to work much due to old age. Don Eduardo, Patricio and Juanita, displaced residents of Porvenir, who attended the meeting, remained quiet. Sitting next to them I could feel they were startled. They felt personally attacked, even more so because they knew the man. We started our half hour walk back to Don Eduardo's house in silence. Patricio finally broke the quiet. He usually does not voice his opinion as much as his wife Juanita, and it was clear he was upset. 'What Ricardo [the man] said isn't fair. We haven't received anything. If one doesn't work here, one dies,' Juanita replied, '*Mercados* come but they stay at the mayor's office and they sell them for votes.' She backed part of the old man's words acknowledging that some help does arrive but not necessarily to the right address and not to everyone.

The displaced commonly resettle among the so-called historic poor of Colombia whose socio-economic position may be similar to that of the displaced or worse. Spending a couple of days with Silvia and her three children on her *ranchito* – a house made of wood planks, unsuitable building material for the *tierra fría*, with earthen floor, two rooms and a simple kitchen, with no bathroom or running water, and no land attached to it – it was easy to see why some of the non-displaced were complaining (see Figure 8). Silvia, perhaps surprisingly, was not among them. In Esperanza and Porvenir IDPs' 'hosts' are families that lack socio-economic stability. They often do not have land of their own; sometimes they do not even have a house. To make a living, they administer other people's farms or work as *jornaleros*. The uncertainty of their situation is such that Doña Pilar compares her position with displacement. Together with her husband they administer a plot of land and she additionally works *jornal* two to three days a week, leaving the house at 6.30 a.m. and returning home at 4.30 or 5.00 p.m. She and her husband are paying back a loan they took out and invested in land cultivation, but their crops failed.

> I'm not saying that there aren't *desplazados* who need help. I'm saying it's unfair that the government doesn't consider everyone's situation. We're also displaced in a way. Few of us have land. We can be sent away any day [from the *finca* they are administrating]. But the debt [in their case the bank loan] stays with us. My only comment is that it is unjust. They don't think about us, vulnerable families. That's how we're called, right?

Figure 8 Silvia's *ranchito*. The house has no running water and there is no land attached to it.

Her previous landlord asked her family to leave the *finca* where they had been staying because he decided to sell his farm. The family had to move and find another way to make a living. Doña Pilar, who is in her fifties, finds it increasingly difficult to find a *jornal*, because employers prefer younger people. For now, she still manages to get work pruning blackberry bushes, a task for which *patrones* (bosses, owners) prefer people with experience. However, she is developing arthritis and suffers from pain in her hands, making such work increasingly difficult. Doña Pilar thus knows she could do with some extra help.

Not being used to (academic) attention and interest, the non-displaced were quick to tell me about their hardships. Those who possess land would emphasise the difficulties they went through to get it and how draught and excessive *invierno* (periods of heavy rain) can ruin the crops. Octavio explains he started working as a bus driver's assistant when he was seven and has not stopped working since. He arrived in Esperanza in his teens, when everything was *monte* and he had to clear the land of trees and other vegetation. In the absence of machinery, changing *monte* into arable land was highly laborious. 'I have faced many challenges in my life, including hunger.' When I asked his wife not to serve me too much food for lunch, he interfered, reflected on his own experience and said: 'Food should never be turned down because you never know when you may be deprived of it.' His wife Edilma complained: 'All the government sees is that we have land. But no one thinks what happens when the harvest is bad, about the expense [that maintaining land entails] and the little money we get for the crops.' She also remembers years when life was even more difficult, when she was with her first husband who drank all the money and she had two jobs to help her children *salir adelante*.

A number of other women likewise emphasise past or current problems within their families, both with their parents, partners but occasionally also with their children. In some instances, as was the case with Adriana, who is originally from Sincelejo, Sucre, a city on the Atlantic coast, and who now lives in Porvenir, the difficulties were such that women were forced to leave.

> I'm finishing my *bachillerato* (highers), because my father would not allow me to study more than five grades. He was drinking and he would hit my mum. When I was sixteen, I got tired of it and I left for Bogotá. I worked in *casa de familia* and in restaurants. I liked working in a restaurant. I left because the owner's sister was jealous or something and it became unbearable to work there. I couldn't find work and my mother would get angry because I couldn't send her money. I met my husband when I didn't have a job. He's more than twenty years older than me. He invited me to a baptism and I accepted. I came to Porvenir for a couple of days and he said he could see I was suffering without a job. I had two children and he offered me to move in with him. I was in a horrible situation, without a job, my mother was angry ... so I said yes but now I regret it. I don't like living in the countryside. I'm afraid of animals, I didn't know anything about land cultivation and the *finca* is very remote [from the main road one needs to take a steep, in rain very slippery, path to her house which takes about twenty minutes downhill and thirty minutes uphill]. I think twice if I need to go anywhere. Even more so in the afternoon, since it gets dark after 6.00 p.m. [...] My husband drinks and I am desperate. I want to leave. Sometimes with him, but more often alone with my four children. But I have nowhere to go.

These stories are just a small sample of a much broader repertoire of narratives about domestic violence, migration in search of employment, working as domestic servants, the state of landlessness, and living in deprivation in general. The non-displaced recount these adversities with a purpose: they wish to highlight their situation and vulnerability in relation to that of the displaced. They wish to make a case for why they find the government's policies unjust, for why their plight should be considered and why the government and NGOs should pay them more attention.

Particularly in urban contexts, the non-displaced complain about the worsening of their living conditions after the arrival of the displaced. These acute tensions arise due to the significantly restricted physical space available in slum areas, to the limited access to public utilities and jobs, and to the insufficient number of spaces for children in local schools. In Porvenir, and even more so in Esperanza, the trend is more nuanced than this. Rather than emphasising a decrease in the quality of life since the arrival of the displaced, non-displaced communities in these villages instead stress their persistent and life-long vulnerability to assert their need and right to receive assistance.

In making their case, the non-displaced refer to themselves as '*vulnerables*' (the vulnerable). Paula describes the latter as 'people from the hamlet [excluding the IDPs] who have nothing', while Marta uses it to refer to 'us women, who were born here'. The NGO's usage of the term in the gender workshops has consolidated it. It is predominately women participating at the workshops and IDP leaders who use the word to distinguish themselves from the displaced and non-displaced respectively. The non-displaced find its particular value in that it stresses their persistent vulnerability.

Policies of assistance are commonly designed thinking of the displaced in a vacuum, separating the displaced from other influences such as the social environment in which they find themselves in. With the aim to control resources, the government directs humanitarian assistance to groups that fit certain predefined criteria; in so doing, however, the system fails to see beyond their 'beneficiaries' (Bakewell 2000: 104), that is, beyond those that the government identified and categorised as victims or in this case *desplazados*. As Oliver Bakewell rightly points out, there is a disconnect between policymaking, assumptions and looking for solutions to forced migration at the national or international levels and the events taking place at the micro-level, in the village life itself. What might work in the policy world, does not necessarily translate into an effective approach on the ground. Esperanza and Porvenir are two examples of such a disconnect. They have become a podium for victimisation, a stage for assumptions, where the aid system is in the eyes of the non-displaced perceived as more effective than it actually is, and a platform where further resentment between the categorised and non-categorised is nurtured with lasting impact on the place-making endeavours.

The displaced are prioritised in policymaking; programmes of assistance that are available to the non-displaced of disadvantaged backgrounds are usually also available to the displaced, while those available to the displaced are not necessarily available to the non-displaced.[5] The assistance for the poor non-displaced works through a system 'Sisben', *Sistema de Selección de Beneficiarios de Programas Sociales* (System for Selecting Beneficiaries of Social Programmes), which identifies, classifies and selects potential beneficiaries. Based on a number of criteria related to housing conditions, available services, school attendance, demographic characteristics, and affiliation to the social security system and durable goods, people receive points which puts them into six different levels. Those who find themselves in Sisben 1 and 2 are subject to most national and local programmes. Low points help you get involved in the programme but are often not sufficient for their continuation. Natalia and Clara both complain that if they wish to receive assistance from *Familias en Acción* (a government welfare programme concerning health, education and nutrition) they need to attend workshops and courses. While Natalia asserts she values the training they receive, it comes with a price.

> I know education and training are good but I lose time out of work if I go. For now it still pays because I get subsidies for three children [aged between eight and eighteen], but when it goes down to one, I'll no longer go. They taught us to make cheese and yogurt but who will I sell them to? They teach us things but we

don't have material, nor the market. The same with the chicken project. The NGO and the Lutherans both gave us money for chickens. We're thirty women with one hundred chicken each. Who's going to buy 3,000 chicken? ... Some people know how to get governmental programmes but you need time for that. If I miss a day of work, this might mean we won't have enough food for next week.

People are fearful of progressing to a higher level of Sisben, which would result in lesser access to assistance. The fear is such that Edilma is hiding the washing machine her son gave her. Edilma, who doubts she could have afforded a washing machine, keeps it outside the house under a sheet of plastic. Together with coloured TV sets, refrigerators and ovens, washing machines fall among durable goods and can influence Sisben points. 'Sisben doesn't permit people to have decent lives,' Carlos rightly criticises the scheme.

> They come and check the floor, roof. One needs to live in miserable conditions and it's difficult to change people's thinking. I am in a process of renovating my house and because of it people say I have too much money. Due to the politics of the state, people prefer drinking what they earn rather than investing the money. They will drop out of Sisben if their house is decent.

In contrast to having to hide assets 'los desplazados have a motorbike' as Marta likes to stress, and they do not attend all the meetings, which Clara asserts are a pre-condition for the continuity of help, and they still receive assistance.[6]

Various issues are at stake that contribute to the locals' bad humour regarding IDPs' access to aid. One of the main ones is the mistaken belief regarding the extent of help. Despite the policy of assistance many displaced in Colombia receive little or nothing because of a lack of information on available aid or a lack of persistence. Estimates about the actual access to assistance are as low as one third of those eligible (Elhawary 2007: 7). A study (Mendoza Piñeros 2012) showed that the displaced included in the state register in 2007 enjoyed only 57.2 per cent of their rights and those who were not included in the register, 49.2 per cent. The indices that the author of the study considered were education, health, diet, housing, income generation, humanitarian assistance provision and identification. Despite lack of access to relief, some displaced in Porvenir and Esperanza still receive some sort of support. The distribution of aid can be sporadic and is often related to specific projects, but it does not reflect what the non-displaced believe IDPs get.

Local perceptions are exaggerated. Fabian and Paula, two of the non-displaced, quote a sum of 800,000 Colombian pesos (approximately £205) as being transferred monthly to the accounts of two IDPs they know, both of whom they additionally believe to be 'bogus' desplazados.[7] 'One of them has been buying branded goods ever since he started receiving assistance,' claims Fabian. Fabio, an IDP, quotes the same sum of money as the amount he gets annually. For Linda and Carlos the amount is one million pesos a year (approximately £260), which they will receive throughout a seven-year period. Fabio also explains he does not receive the money automatically but needs to apply for it on a regular basis and the assistance is subject to governmental approval. The locals do not know this. They rather mistakenly believe that the displaced receive assistance in a fairly straightforward manner, as something automatic for simply being registered as displaced. As the long-winded trajectories to Esperanza and Porvenir (Chapter 4) testify this is far from the truth. Securing aid requires persistence, time, knowledge of legislation and available programmes. As Juan confirms, 'if we kept quiet, we wouldn't receive anything.'

The perceptions of ease of access to assistance are fuelled by some of the experiences the non-displaced have when they attempt to find help for themselves. Reflecting on her visit to *Desarrollo Social*, governmental social development office, Doña Pilar complains that even the governmental organisations that are there to help low-income families have sent her away:

> It's the first thing they ask you. I went to *Desarrollo Social* the other day with the documentation. Upon getting there they asked 'Are you a *desplazada*?' I said I wasn't. I was told to wait and when the official returned he said, 'We only have programmes for the displaced at the moment.' The same thing happened to my daughter-in-law. I sent her to *Familias en Acción* to apply for help because her baby son's weight is low. They asked her whether she was displaced and told her they only helped the displaced.

Pedro, an IDP leader ascribes such behaviour to planned and thought-through local government tactics.

> We've had problems with the community and the municipality because the municipality were saying they couldn't give anything to the vulnerable population, to poor *campesinos*, and mothers heading households, because they give help to the displaced. But they also weren't giving any assistance to us. It was to enter into a clash with the poor of the municipality and the displaced.

Doña Pilar's husband attributes such comments to corrupt officials who siphon off the funds for their own gains instead of distributing them among the poor. Local government officials' corrupt practices are not unusual so his comment bears some weight. Not everyone, however, doubts officials' words. The clerks' statements generate suppositions about what the scenario would be like if there were no displaced people in the country. The comments suggest that were there no displaced, more assistance would be earmarked for the non-displaced. This is also the belief Natalia has. 'If more *desplazados* come, they [the government] will forget about us [the non-displaced] completely,' she asserts. The historical lack of attention paid to the poor, however, undermines the rationality of such assumptions.

The imagined mode, delivery and amount of assistance, coupled with restricted opportunities push some to try and pass themselves off as being displaced. Paula and Carolina both claim someone suggested they did it, but Carolina refused saying, 'it would be making fun of misfortune of other people.' Others were thinking of doing so. Natalia and her husband Santiago, landless famers who do not have their own house, but have five children and whose sixteen-year old daughter gave birth at her mother's great distress, wanted to register as *desplazados*. During the days I spent with them, meat was never present on the table, the main source of protein was an egg. She served us *guatila* (chayote), 'it is *papa de pobre* (poor people's potatoes),' explained Natalia apologetically. It saves her some pesos she would otherwise spend on potatoes. Natalia admits she approached IDP leaders asking them to help her acquire the status of a displaced person. 'There was time when I didn't even have rice to give to my children. I went to one of the IDP leaders and asked him to help me get the letter. He advised me not to do it. He said that if the government made an investigation in a few years, I'd go to jail.' The leader instead offered to help her with some food. The displaced leader still gives her a bag or rice or a bottle of oil every now and then, but the leaders received 'trucks of help' complains Natalia, drawing attention to the small share that she gets. She directs her disappointment towards the displaced and not the government or NGOs who are the ones who administer the programmes in the first place.

In their complaints about *desplazados*, the long-term residents once again take grudges against the displaced as a group. This is despite the fact that only a small number of IDPs are in a position of sufficient power through which they can implement clientelistic practices, and despite the fact that not all of them still receive assistance. Even if some displaced 'work hard' to show they are 'good people', as Don Andrés puts it, these individual attributes and performances remain ignored or side-lined since people judge individuals by their group membership (Tilly 1998: 7). As a result of persistent tensions, the displaced also adopt words of 'lower human value' (Elias and Scotson 1994: xxi) to describe the villagers. They do not single out individuals but describe them collectively as 'jealous', 'envious', 'cold' and 'ungrateful'. Through these words, the displaced express bitterness and disappointment with how they have been received by the villagers. Many of the displaced therefore still feel unwelcome, which contributes to their feeling out of place.

The categorisation and the architecture of the aid system generally perpetuate the boundaries that exist between those categorised and non-categorised. The locals see the displaced as people who, apart from physical relocation (as contrasted to displacement), have not suffered as much as they themselves have, and yet they are the focus of governmental attention and NGO concern, at least in theory. They project the resentment they hold onto the displaced and not on the government, its poorly designed policies, neglect and its failure to tackle poverty. Unlike the government, the *desplazados* are near (physically, as well as in relation to their economic status) and constitute an easy target. The policy of assistance to IDPs has further perpetuated negative sentiments and continues shaping villagers' social landscapes and the manner in which they relate to one another even after more than a decade.

If more displaced came to the village, Clara, a long-term resident of Esperanza, says she would feel displaced. She deems the displaced would be taking away her space. Clara is not necessarily referring to physical place; her statement rather reflects her cognitive and emotional state. Upon entering a new location, IDPs need to negotiate their social belonging. Acts such as sharing with others, engagement in conversations, impression of support networks and empathy, help generate the sense of being welcome in a certain place and help generate a sense of affinity. When these are absent, prospects of relational belonging are dim. At the same time, place-belonging of those who were there prior to IDPs' arrival has been challenged; not only in the respective villages but ultimately in the Colombian society, since the poor non-displaced feel their long-life adversities are not of sufficient governmental interest. In their attempts to secure their own position and right to be at a certain place, the displaced and non-displaced stress respective groups' virtues and undermine the other group's merits, which makes the sharing of the same space an unattractive option.

Notes

1 Even though the chapters in this book refer to relationship building and tensions that exist between the displaced and non-displaced on the one hand and among the displaced on the other, it is fair to say that tensions exist also among some of the non-displaced. In Esperanza for instance Paula and Marta have, according to the villagers, been in conflict since secondary school and their conflict has now been passed on to their children. While the tension between the two affects their sense of place, these tensions run along personal lines and are not structural in nature such as tensions between the displaced and non-displaced.

2 The great majority of the displaced from Urabá who arrived to Esperanza are not direct Afro-Colombian descendants but are of mixed race. Race mixture in Latin America is complex and does not produce only mulato (combination of black and white), zambo (combination of black and indian) and mestizo (combination of indian and white). Nevertheless, *negro*, *indio* and *blanco* are the three powerful sources of identity (Wade 1995: 22).

3 *Tiendas* are small shops selling mainly foodstuffs during the day which convert in a local bar in the evening, particularly on Saturdays. They are places where predominately men socialise. On one of the nights when Alejandra agreed to take me to a *tienda*, I was one of only four women there. The displaced in Esperanza largely avoid night visits to *tiendas*. Fabio is the only one who would occasionally go. Alejandra avoids the shop even during the day, and prefers sending one of her sons to do the shopping. She says she prefers to avoid the villagers.

4 *Sancocho* is a typical Colombian stew made of fish, chicken or beef. It also contains plantain, potatoes and yucca.

5 National and international organisms, including the Colombian Constitutional Court have recognised the need to prioritise the displaced. The Constitutional Court in its sentence T602/03 argues for the prioritisation on the basis of IDPs' uprootedness, destruction of material base which supported their life project, and effect displacement had on their social fabric. Other groups such as the historically poor, the elderly, children, the ill or people who are deprived of liberty should benefit from permanent state programmes (Jaramillo *et al.*, 2004).

6 The motorbike Marta is referring to is Doña Beatriz'. She bought it with the money she received for the death of her husband.

7 As a point of comparison, the minimum salary for 2017 was set to 737,717 Colombian pesos, or approximately £190.

9

Taming the land

Day after day a number of peasants in both hamlets, displaced and non-displaced, engage in physically exhausting activities which bring little or no returns. Their days start before the dawn and *campesinos* often continue working tirelessly until it gets dark. They pick the thorny blackberry bushes twice a week, rain or shine. The heavy boxes of tree tomatoes test their endurance and strength. Their feet may get trapped in the rocks on the steep rocky terrain while they stretch high to bring the few Arabica coffee plants that have not been destroyed by diseases closer to pick its red fruits. Lack of machinery contributes to hardships since everything is done by hand. Diseases, such as rust attacking coffee plants, climate instability with uninterrupted *invierno* or droughts at the other extreme, and the market structure, where the intermediaries are better off than those cultivating the land, create insecurities. The returns are so low that at times *campesinos* prefer to leave the tomato to rot on the vine, blackberries to overripen and fall to the ground, and to give the zucchini to cattle rather than sell it. In such circumstances forming attachment to land can be a challenging task.

In this Chapter I examine the role that location as one of the aspects of place (Agnew 1987) plays in place-making. I examine the physical environment, where people's farms and their natural features are located. I do not conceive of landscapes as merely a 'visual idea' where the viewer is outside the landscape (Cresswell 2004: 10). Visual sights can indeed speak a thousand words about the meaning given to the natural environment. Plots that are attended to – where tree tomatoes have had their leaves taken off, and blackberries have been pruned to control their growth – are contrasted to plots that are mostly grown over. Such displays reflect the relationship people have with their land.

Beyond the visual, physical landscapes are incorporated in people's everyday activities; they therefore crucially influence people's belonging. For peasants, who have strong ties to the land, physical environment is of particular significance. The environment provides not only shelter but also economic subsistence and the basis for their *campesino* identity. Rather than on visual sights, the focus of this chapter is thus on how landscapes are called into meaning through projects (Schein 2009), how they influence the locale, the setting for everyday interaction (Agnew 1987), through how people 'interpret, use, practice and reference the landscape' (Rose 2002: 456) – on how they make landscapes matter, or indeed, how they fail to do so.

The displaced managed to obtain land where they resettled, nevertheless, this has not necessarily translated into land attachment. Land ownership might be the most powerful example of economic attachment to place (Low 1992: 170), yet the land does not always meet people's needs and answer their aspirations. There is a difference between belonging *to* and belonging *with* a place (Schein 2009) – the former refers to ownership and the latter reaches further – it expresses membership. At the same time, landless peasants might not have the legal papers to demonstrate their belonging to a place, but they might belong with it.

Just as for places in general, physical landscapes hold multiple meanings for different groups of individuals. They can relate to land through a number of dimensions: physically through work and food, materially through the provision of subsistence and land ownership, socially through family members, family and cultural practices, cognitively through construction of identity, through emotional investment and future plans with and for the place. Physical landscapes and investing them with meaning therefore cannot be considered in isolation since they intersect, overlap and are influenced by social, political as well as psychological factors. As Rose argues, 'landscape is not just related to, but is *reliant on*, other social processes' (Rose 2002: 465, emphasis in the original). Land attachment therefore brings together location, locale and sense of place (Agnew 1987).

Before I look at the difficulties that some displaced are facing in their attempts to form attachment to the land, it is fair to say that the non-displaced share many of the challenges the physical environment poses. Yet there are some distinct differences between the displaced and non-displaced and the way they interpret the land. The non-displaced who have been born and raised on the land, have been facing the same or similar challenges throughout their lives. The cycles of rain, drought, good and bad harvest, the physical exhaustion, poor returns, atrocious intermediaries' rates have been a continuous companion of their place-making process. The peasants complain over the harshness of life but have at the same time mostly reconciled with what it has given them. For most the great majority it is the only life they have known. While they complain over the state of affairs, they at the same time understand and accept them as a 'normal' part of their place-making. The displaced on the other hand, have a point of comparison with the place left behind. This comparison can result in resistance to form greater attachment or encourage further search for a more suitable environment. Additionally, if part of the non-displaced's attachment comes from family history and knowledge of the land passed down as heritage, this is not the case with the displaced, at least not with the first generation. The displaced's reading of the landscapes therefore differs from that of the long-term residents in some crucial ways.

Generally speaking, the displaced in Porvenir have in their majority managed to generate a deeper degree and higher level of affective relation to land in comparison to those resettled to Esperanza. Below I consider how the sense of continuation with the life people used to know, the quality of land, exchange system, people's family role and their attainment of the role in relation to land have conditioned the meaning they have given to the physical landscapes.

No shelter but central geographical location

The farms to which the displaced have been resettled were two big estates partitioned to fourteen farms in Porvenir and thirteen farms in Esperanza in order to accommodate the displaced families. The size of the *fincas* ranges between just under three hectares and slightly over four hectares per farm. If the land is of lower quality, the farm is usually somewhat bigger compared to *fincas* of higher quality. When the displaced arrived in the respective villages, the landscape that awaited them was one of mostly uncultivated land without many, if any, installations. 'When we arrived, there was nothing, it was *monte*. We had to buy plantain. It was so difficult to buy it while I knew that on our *finca* in Tolima it was dumped,' reflects Linda on the situation in Porvenir. Doña María remembers that they first lived in a house made of cardboard cartons, with plantain leaves and plastic used for the roof. Doña Flor and Don Ignacio who are secondary occupants, moved to Porvenir once the houses had already been set up. They had a roof over their heads, but 'the house was so neglected that there was grass growing inside it,' remembers Doña Flor.

In Esperanza, apart from the two houses that had already been there, the majority of the displaced had to do with the open skies. Fabio remembers the day of the arrival with bitterness. It was raining and he made a make-shift hut out of plantain leaves for his family. 'That night we went to sleep wet and with our clothes on,' he remembers, 'Like dogs. We went to bed like dogs.' After some persistence, the displaced managed to secure small huts, made of plastic sheets, without insulation and without windows (see Figure 9). They stayed there for about two years until they acquired their current houses through the international community's assistance. The plastic huts, reminders of cold nights, are still present on most of people's lands. They use them for storage, or they form part of outdoor kitchens, or have been turned into animal stalls. It took a couple of years before small houses dotted the hilly terrain and a couple more for electricity instalments. The latter is in most cases not officially provided. People rather informally 'hang' themselves on the system. Martina, who asked for electricity to be legally provided but was turned down, unbelievably remarked 'We are in twenty-first century and I live without *luz* (light, but people use the expression to refer to electricity)!'

The great majority of the displaced in both hamlets came from remote parts of the country. Even though some miss rivers and mountains that stretched through their areas of origin, the vicinity of their new residence to the capital is generally interpreted as an improvement to their location. They see Esperanza and Porvenir as being closer to progress, and development and as having a larger presence of the state. 'If there was no electricity in our village [of origin] when there were six hundred people living in the area,' said Carlos, 'with three hundred having left, the prospects of bringing electricity to the zone, are close to none.'

Figure 9 The first 'housing' given to the displaced soon after their arrival.

The displaced are certain, probably rightly so, that more assistance comes to Cundinamarca than to other parts of the country. Don Fernando came to Esperanza because in Cartagena, where he settled after he had left Urabá, there was no prospect of relief. Linda registered her displacement in Bogotá. She is convinced that acquiring assistance is easier in Bogotá and that help is more reliable. 'Not all of the assistance that arrives to Porvenir reaches the people,' she explained, 'due to corruption in the local government.' Generally speaking, the displaced have welcomed the central location of the two villages of resettlement. They have found utility in the better access to assistance, greater presence of Cundinamarca on the country's development map and closeness to governmental offices. They therefore appreciate the location not just because of its situatedeness on the physical map but because of the socio-political system within which it operates. The central location, however, for some IDPs also coincided with a climate belt and soil properties different from those at the place of origin. This distinction has had a greater effect on their day-to-day lives than the proximity of the capital. The implications of these differences have in some cases been inherently negative.

Disruption and continuity

Continuous iterative farming practices result in an embodied knowledge which ties peasants to particular places (Cheshire *et al.* 2013: 64). Rural farms often see land and knowledge being passed down to subsequent generations. Looking at landscapes from a 'dwelling perspective' landscapes become a 'testimony' to the lives of those who once lived there and who shaped it (Ingold 1993: 152). They are an intersection of space and time. Farms turn into a treasure trove of memories bringing added value to the economic and utilitarian relationship of land cultivation. With displacement there is a rupture. Land is lost and with it the embodied knowledge, the possibilities to put an imprint on the land to be taken forward by the generations that follow, and memories linked to the landscape are disrupted. The tie to the land in the place of origin was potentially very strong and on a new plot of land, *campesinos* attempt to re-create it, or at least come close to the lost sentiment. Farming is only one of the daily activities peasants engage with at the locale, yet its contribution to a positive sense of place is crucial. Farming can help reconnect the displaced with their culture. It helps people pursue projects relevant to their *campesino* identity. Farming and engagement with the landscape therefore also give people sense of purpose, continuation and progress, all the features necessary for overcoming the sentiment of displacement.

The path to achieving this is not straightforward. Landscapes, soil and terrain differ from location to location. Work and the engagement with the land might be distinct from what people used to know, as can be the conditions of trade, which has repercussions for people's livelihoods. Places that are largely different from the place of origin demand greater adaptation; they challenge beliefs, knowledge, exchange systems and use of natural resources (Nesheim *et al.* 2006: 100). The degree of familiarity and disruption influences the smoothness of adaptation and the way in which places are experienced and appreciated. The greater the change the bigger is the test to the knowledge system. Great disruption can even require one's reinvention as a farmer.

In the two hamlets, the test of one's farming capabilities, beliefs and experiences varies extensively. In Porvenir 'everything is exactly the same as in the part of Tolima where I came from,' asserts Juanita. 'The climate, the food, the crops. Just the people are less sociable.' Daniel, Carlos and Linda found their place of origin warmer but, generally speaking, the change in terms of climate, food and produce was small. While those who were from departments more remote to Cundinamarca had left the hamlet, the displaced who were in Porvenir at the time of the research had some previous knowledge and experience with the cultivation of coffee, the main produce of the area. Some engaged in coffee cultivation in the place of origin, others spent some time working on coffee plantations working as *jornaleros*, or helping out their family members. The familiarity with the crop allowed them to apply their previous knowledge to the production of the land. They have therefore experienced some sense of continuity when it comes to land cultivation. This continuousness has helped reduce what would otherwise feel like a completely alien place.

In contrast, the displaced in Esperanza did not experience any similar 'insideness' (Rowles 1983) with the land. They left *tierra caliente* and resettled in *tierra fría*, which has been a great change in the ecosystem. Arrival to a relatively moderate climate of Cundinamarca from a hot Urabá, presented a shock for many.

The varied and dynamic Colombian landscape and geography mean that people, even though they stay within one country, may have crossed a number of internal borders, where they encounter largely distinct cultures and environment. Pedro is very critical of how little consideration government officials give to the differences between the places of origin and resettlement. He explains:

> How can they throw us in a working environment that we don't know? We are *campesinos*, but there are *campesinos* from Nariño, from *tierra fría*, how are they going to put them to work to Tolima where there is *tierra caliente* for instance? They are *campesinos* but it's not the same. They are *campesinos* of different zones. Unfortunately, or fortunately, Colombia has many different climates, due to which *campesinos* have many customs. Just because we are *campesinos* they can't throw us in the same basket [...] I had an argument with the authority because he said '*desplazados* are lazy'. So I told him, 'Go to Sibaté where they cultivate potatoes and strawberries and replace the *campesino* there for one day.[1] We'll see how long you last and if they don't call you lazy.'

Different climate requires cultivation of distinct crops or even different cultivation practices of the same crop. Even though the displaced had previously worked with maize and cattle, the unsuitability of the cultivation practices to which they were accustomed resulted in a very negative outcome, Pedro continues:

> Don Andrés started to sow, since he saw such beautiful soil. He threw the seeds and the maize was this little [he uses his hands to demonstrate its size]. There [in Urabá] you would sow, and it grows, you don't need to use fertilisers or anything. And Don Andrés said, 'And well, what is this? What happened?' Bad seeds, I don't know what. The neighbours started saying: '*Señor*, did you loosen up the soil, did you fertilise it?' And we, 'No.' 'No, *señor*, don't be wasting your money in this. Here you need to loosen up the soil with a mattock, fertilise it with poultry manure, and add lime.'[2] And we said that the person who told us this was jealous [he laughs]. We had cows, and the ten died. We didn't know why. Did they get ticks, did they have temperature, was it the change in climate? We didn't know this. We had to go to SENA for counselling.[3] How to cultivate the *finca*, how to keep animals. They gave us this training. But it was *duro*, how they dropped us here, how they released animals on the pasture without any kind of assistance ... Here, one had to devote time and learn anew. It's *muy duro*. For instance, my father had two *fincas* there, and having to come here and make all the effort that he had done without any assistance. We had to learn through making.

Pedro's mother, Doña Olivia similarly laments, 'The cows died because we didn't use vaccination. All cattle died and we were left with a debt. We lost a lot. It was a chaos to come from one part to another with no one telling us anything.' This expensive and tragic outcome affected people's impressions of the land from the very start. The failed cultivation attempts live vividly in people's memories – nearly as much as the landfill story. The disruption with past lives for *urabeños* was complete. It was partly this disruption which determined the lack of land attachment to what some still perceive hostile land.

Even a decade after resettlement, the displaced have still not managed to form strong links to the land. Farming practices, the exchange system as well as social contexts in which the landscape is used, differ greatly from what they were accustomed to in Urabá. Cultivation opportunities in Esperanza are limited and the crops cultivated are of low market value. People mostly dedicate themselves to the cultivation of blackberries and tree tomatoes, while some cultivate peas, beans and zucchini (see Figure 10). These crops cannot compare to the agribusiness production of bananas and plantain cultivation in which the displaced were involved in Urabá.

Blackberries, the most widely cultivated crop, fetch a low price. The money that farmers receive for a box of blackberries varies between 5,000 and 25,000 Colombian pesos (approximately between £1.40 and £6.60), depending on the season. High season means lower price and vice versa.[4] In the high season, the owners of plots or administrators of *fincas* need to hire day workers to help them pick the fruit or help with its maintenance. *Jornaleros* typically have no land of their own and receive on average twenty-thousand pesos a day (approximately £5.50) for their work. The amount is not high enough to improve *jornaleros'* socio-economic situation, and is at the same time a relatively high cost for the farmers who hire them, considering the cost of fertilisers, seeds and the payment they receive for the crops.

In any season, be it high or low, the peasants need to pay for the transport of crops to the Bogotá market. Road conditions are poor and people do not have cars

Figure 10 Cultivation of blackberries.

or any other means of transport, hence, they turn to intermediaries. Besides paying a low price for the crop, the intermediaries charge the peasants one thousand pesos (approximately £0.27) for a wooden box in which the blackberries are kept, and an additional thousand per box for the transportation. Despite such poor conditions of exchange, the peasants do not organise in unions, like they did in Urabá. The involvement in blackberry production does not create the conditions for political engagements, like working in *bananeras* did. Beyond the lack of familiarity with cultivation, the meaning and role of the physical landscape in Esperanza has shrunk compared to physical landscapes of Urabá also in this respect.

Farming requires money and peasants in both hamlets express concerns over the costs related to cultivation, from fertilisers to seeds. Juan explains: 'It's expensive to cultivate here. The seeds they sell are all imported and they are only good for one season. The price of produce varies on a daily basis. It's not the *campesino* who sets the price and one gets tired of it. You buy seeds, you buy fertilisers and you get almost nothing.'

The architects of land programme did not consider such expenses and the necessary start-up capital when the displaced were resettled to their perspective plots. Drawing on his own experience with resettlement, Juan further commented on the current land restitution policy, saying:

> The government gives you land and then what … In my opinion, they will give *campesinos* land and nothing else. One needs to get professionals to assess what can be cultivated and present papers, photocopies. All this costs money. When you start off, you need to pay for everything and it doesn't always bring profit or returns on investment. What will happen is, they will give land and *campesinos* will eventually leave.

The altered engagement with physical landscapes has also taken toll on people's practices and habits linked to social and cultural spaces. The latter are essential for identity construction and attachment (Yuval-Davis 2006: 203). The change of location modified people's diet. While the displaced attempt to follow *costeño* cuisine as much as possible – some prepare *arepas* with pure maize, with no salt, butter or cheese, eat eggs with tomato and onions, occasionally have rice and beans for breakfast, and include fish in their meals – they have had to make certain modifications. The fish is not as frequent on the plate and it is usually canned as opposed to the fresh fish they would eat in Urabá. They need to buy plantain if they wish to eat it, and for the same reasons coconut is now only rarely used in cooking. When I was leaving the field, the displaced prepared a fish *sancocho* with coconut rice, which was a treat for both me and them.

Besides its influence on diet, the new location does not permit the same kind of engagement with medicinal plants. Don Andrés grew a variety of them in Urabá and brought two to Esperanza. '*Penicilina*' survived. To a visitor, a green bush growing on the side of the house, appears as any other plant. Yet Don Andrés introduced it to Esperanza. It is used for the healing of small wounds and gastritis. Alejandro, his son, explained Don Andrés would take the plant with him wherever they moved. The climate, however, was not suitable for the other plant he brought, so it died. Don Andrés and others cannot apply the knowledge of alternative medicine they learnt in Urabá in Esperanza since climate and soil in Esperanza gave birth to plants which are not known to them. If they wished to continue practising alternative medicine, they had to acquire the necessary knowledge anew.

Altered use of physical space also affected customs. Fabio with an air of disbelief recounts that in Esperanza it is not permitted to cross a *finca* which is not yours. This was something common in Urabá and inevitable in cases of big properties. Iris, a non-displaced villager, with a similar incredulity to that of Fabio complains that the displaced would cross someone's land without asking for permission first. An act she thinks is unacceptable. The perception of properties as private entities, access to and use of these spaces, which are in Esperanza, often clearly demarcated with a line of wooden sticks connected with a wire, has challenged the old system of norms. As Jean puts it, '[t]he physical landscape may not become legible to new arrivals without the ability to "read" the social landscape' (Jean 2015: 50). Acquisition of land in a new territory requires one to learn how the land and landscapes are used in that particular setting to be able to negotiate one's own engagement with them. Landscapes shape human activity but in turn, human activity too shapes physical landscapes. Where productive use, practices and habits are substantially different, adaptation to the new way of life requires more effort and emotional labour and the establishment of a positive relation to land is more challenging.

Tierra muerta

Sense of attachment is closely linked to quality of life. The latter is conditioned by a variety of factors: livelihood opportunities, prospects for personal development, social support network, existence of spaces for reflection and relaxation and so on. In rural contexts the feature related to physical landscapes that stands out the most is livelihood prospects. In earning their subsistence, peasants more than anyone else depend on the land. The socio-economic situation, the materiality of social life, and sense of economic security influence people-place relationships (Antonsich 2010b; Cross 2015; Lewicka 2011; Low 1992). In other words, the more the physical conditions allow an intended use, the higher is place dependence. The opportunities the place offers in terms of meeting people's sustenance provisions, and the effort required to make a living, condition how they perceive and appreciate the place.

Good quality of life is not something characteristic of Esperanza. Days are long and filled with heavy physical work. Even though farmers engage in cultivation activities, they need to buy most or all of their food. The climate and soil are not suitable for the cultivation of potatoes, rice or plantain. An occasional yucca grows here or there but apart from that whatever is served on the plate is purchased. On one of the cloudy days when I helped Julia fertilise the blackberries she cultivates on a rented plot, she complained over the non-generous nature of the place. She is originally from substantially warmer Llanos and married to Esperanza. 'Life was easier in Llanos. We had potatoes, plantain, yucca and cows. We had everything to eat. And here? What can one eat? Blackberries? Mosquitos?'

'This is *tierra muerta* (dead land),' assertively concludes Doña Isabel. She draws upon biblical reference of Isaiah (51:6) and the land before the end of times. In contrast, 'in Urabá you'd throw a seed and in a couple of weeks, you'd have a plant. Here, no. You need to wait and wait and wait and use fertilisers.' Her reading of non-fertile landscape is not a lonesome case. Martina and her family tried with the cultivation of different crops – granadilla, beans and, most recently, avocado. She describes her past organic granadilla production as the nicest and best kept crop in the village, and yet she says: 'I couldn't get back on my feet.' In 'Urabá it was different', confirms Doña Olivia.

> Cultivating in Urabá was a delight. The land was fertile, there was no need for *químicos* (chemicals), fertilisers. How much have we lost? There's no way … Plants gave one what one needed. We're ruined also because of this. One ate clean there. My husband cleaned the territory, he sowed maize, beans. He didn't fertilise the land. We lost everything.

The use of fertilisers is Esperanza is not meagre. To increase growth and instil life in the 'dead' soil, farmers fumigate blackberries at least every fortnight and fertilise them every two months. The amount of chemicals used in the production is such that people do not eat fruit while they pick it. When I did so, a nine-year old girl reminded me that I needed to wash the berries first since they are unhealthy due to *químicos*. Similar to Doña Olivia's reference to 'clean' food, a displaced woman I met in Quibdó, the capital of Chocó, spoke of how she missed natural, organic food she consumed at home. The meaning given to landscape is thus experienced also through the body. On the one hand through the work invested in the land, and on the other through the consumption, or lack of it, of the land's fruits.

The poor quality of soil and sometimes unpredictable climate, the physically exhausting work which does not yield many returns has generated different reactions among the displaced. Adapting and learning from trial and error requires willingness and persistence not everyone has. Some displaced say they 'got bored' of cultivating land. Doña Isabel and her husband recount that the rain killed the blackberries and maize would not grow so they gave up. For now they manage to get by with the money he makes working as a dentist on call. Pedro and Juan with their families dedicated themselves to lobbying for IDP rights and programmes of assistance. They have put farming on a side track. Their choice, however, has affected social relationships within the hamlet. Juan's farm is located in the centre of the village, and the village road passes right next to it. Their decision to not cultivate land, has contributed to tensions with their non-displaced neighbours.

When I walked with Natalia, a landless peasant, through the village towards the farm she and her husband were administering, she paused at the last curve before two hills embraced the road which started to descend. The central Esperanza was laid out in front of us bathing in the sun. Natalia pointed towards Juan and Doña

Figure 11 The plot described as 'the best' in the hamlet, which is no longer cultivated.

Beatriz' *finca*. There were no crops growing there. Instead, we saw the remains of past cultivation of tomato trees and blackberries. An odd plant was fighting off the weed and wooden support structure was resisting the weather influences (see Figure 11). 'They have the nicest *finca* in the village,' Natalia said, 'and they don't cultivate it'. Rather than anger, her voice conveyed pain and disappointment. Her husband shares her feelings. 'Why do people want land if they don't work on it? ... People who don't plan to work the land shouldn't fight to get it. Look at them – the majority sold, let the land or left.'

The physical environment directly intersects with social landscapes and place-making. The lack of meaning Juan and Doña Beatriz have found in and given to the landscape has affected their relations with the non-displaced, especially the landless peasants who dream of being able to cultivate their own land. The visibility of the uncultivated *finca* has reinforced the stereotypes of IDPs' dependence on assistance and their supposed laziness. When the non-displaced complain about *desplazados* in general, they do not take into the account the efforts of those displaced who, like themselves, are trying to get through the often unfavourable cultivation conditions, but draw their conclusion on few examples.

'Boredom' with the cultivation, as those who do not cultivate the land describe it, is also affected by another emotional process affecting place attachment – resistance. Forced migration can create initial 'frozenness' (Papadopoulos 2002), where the experiences of flight, violence and loss of family members restrict individuals' functioning. The frozenness can be temporary but it can also persist, and it can express itself through different means. One such is resisting to adapt to new cultivating conditions. Resistance is evident in cases where, even after spending all of their adult life outside the region of origin, some still claim the land is unsuitable for their own agricultural practices. Camilo, for instance, left Urabá when he was thirteen years old and was just entering the productive years of his life. Despite having spent half of his life outside Urabá, he maintains, 'This is not our *tierra*. It will never be. We don't know how to cultivate it.' He consciously decided he would not relate to the land and he also moved away. His only connection with Esperanza is through his parents and grandparents who are still there.

Those who came from Urabá remember what they now see as better times. Life in Urabá had not been easy even before violence broke out. Don Fernando remembers he worked long hours. 'I worked till 11:00 p.m. or midnight to sustain my mother, niece with special needs, daughter and my wife.' Nevertheless, the land gave him and others enough to live on. 'On *la tierra mia* (on my land, back in Urabá) I'd do *mercado* every fifteen days when I got a salary. Here, I need to buy it every day. *Mercaditos pequeños* (small grocery shopping). Oil for 500 pesos [approximately thirteen pence].' The displaced now, probably more than before, see the past land as paying back the fruit of their work. A sentiment that that they do not experience in Esperanza.

The green lush of coffee plantations

Soil quality and cultivation conditions are generally speaking better in Porvenir than in Esperanza. This is true in relation to food for consumption, especially yucca, plantain and garden vegetables, as well as for cultivation of crops for sale – coffee. Carlos praises the quality of soil in Porvenir. 'I like the soil in Porvenir because it is rested, new, fertile. In Tolima the soil is tired.' The displaced were resettled on previously uncultivated land, which was 'fresh' on the displaced's arrival. Partly due to that, the generation of place attachment in Porvenir seems to have been more successful. The land is still providing some of the displaced with sufficient means of subsistence and better economic conditions compared to the peasants in Esperanza, which is visible through the diet.

Unlike in Esperanza, where in certain households an egg would often be the daily source of protein, in Porvenir a piece of meat, either red meat or chicken, would normally be found on people's plate every day. Nevertheless the process has not been without its difficulties. The peasants are struggling with the climate, crop diseases, and some of them also with physically difficult terrains to work on. While the returns on coffee are higher than those on blackberries, the climate change influences its production. Patricio recounts he lost four thousand plants due to lack of rain at one point, and Álvaro, a non-displaced villager who bought his *finca* from a displaced woman, with regret remembers a year when he picked only 120 kg of coffee. Despite such difficulties, people nevertheless persist in coffee cultivation; the available assistance to promote coffee growing has been of help.

Coffee is ranked the country's fourth biggest export item and certain incentives are available to coffee growers in the form of government loans and grants. One of the schemes is a blend between credit and a subsidy. The coffee growers, Patricio explains, receive six million Colombian pesos (approximately £1,600) and repay 2.7 million pesos (approximately £720). Credits are not easy to secure because in the past some people spent the money on drinking, he adds. Álvaro agrees. 'Due to alcohol the funders changed their strategy. Under the new scheme one needs to plant the plants first to receive part of the credit. The rest is released in instalments if the work is carried out.' Some of those who previously did not cultivate the land have also taken up the scheme. One such couple are Angelica and Roberto. Roberto said he could not afford to cultivate his *finca* even though he had one. Ever since their resettlement he has made his living as a *jornalero*, working on neighbours' *fincas*. The coffee growing scheme has encouraged him to try. He planted 1,500 coffee plants by himself and was planning to plant 5,000 more.

Despite the availability of the scheme there are stark socio-economic differences among those resettled in Porvenir. Don Eduardo and Doña María's *finca* is full of rocks, very steep and does not bring many returns (see Figure 12). If they have *jornaleros*, they can only afford to hire elderly men, some of whom live in an old people's home nearby. They do not cost as much as younger workers, yet they still present a substantial expense. Juanita and Patricio's *finca*, which is positioned just above Don Eduardo and Doña María's farm, is similar but it is already less rocky. After their *finca* comes to an end, the surface levels out almost entirely, the rocks disappear, and lush patchwork of coffee plantations can be seen on the left and right side of the path. Don Ignacio and Doña Flor, Simón, Ramiro and Patricia and Carlos and Linda who hold land there, have planted their *fincas* to the last available corner (see Figure 13). Simón, comparing his *finca* to that of Don Eduardo assesses: 'I can make 800 holes a day to plant coffee, but Don Eduardo can only make fifty due to bad soil and terrain.' The cultivation success is such that some of enumerated manage to store the coffee they pick and sell it during the low season when the price of coffee is higher; something that the rest of the coffee growers in the hamlet cannot imagine. Don Eduardo and Doña María also cultivate some sugar cane and they produce *panela*. They store less *panela* than they consume and need to buy it once it runs out. When I asked him why they did not store more, Don Eduardo explained: 'We need to sell it so that we can pay for the transport and the workers.' They mostly live from hand to mouth, hence they find it difficult to save for a rainy day.

In contrast, as many as eight *jornaleros* skilfully engage in coffee picking of dense bushes on Don Ignacio's and Ramiro's respective *fincas* in high season. The plants are so compacted together, that it is impossible not to touch the surrounding bushes while finding your way through the plantation maze. Don Ignacio and Simón have between them been able to buy some of the machinery necessary to process coffee, saving themselves much of the physical work. The size of plastic huts where they dry coffee beans in the warmth of the sun is incomparably larger than that of Patricio and Juanita's or Álvaro and Tania's hut for instance.

Figure 12 Coffee plantation planted on a steep terrain full of rocks.

Stable provision of livelihood has undoubtedly influenced their wish to stay in Porvenir, which at the same time confirms that they have established a deeper level of connection to land. Nevertheless, as discussed previously, the place attachment of Don Ignacio and Doña Flor, Simón, Carlos and Linda, but also of Patricio and Juanita, and Álvaro and Tania is in the hands of the state, which sees them as 'invaders'. They are in threat of expulsion from the land even though the first five enumerated have largely been successful in turning their *fincas* in Porvenir into meaningful places.

Relational place-(non)attachment

Doreen Massey convincingly argued that places are 'constructed of particular interaction and mutual articulations of social relations, social processes, experiences and understandings' (Massey 1993: 67). Relationality refers not only to the relations between places linking global to the local, it also concerns the way we experience places through others. We can feel the place and nurture placebelongingness (or not) through people close to us; through how they experience place and the opportunities it offers them. We can only appreciate and understand the value and attention given to physical landscapes if examined in relation to the stage of people's life and their social role (Barrett 2009: 89) – that is their role in relation to others. Displaced are not merely displaced and peasants. They are also

Figure 13 One of the nice *fincas* in Porvenir, where the cultivation of coffee has been successful.

parents, some of them with dependent children. If they fail to see positive results of their work and they are unable to realise their social role, they can experience the inability as a personal defeat. This can affect their sense of displacement as well as generate resentment towards land. In contrast, if land provides sufficient conditions for the fulfilment of parental roles, individuals are likely to imagine the future with the place – not only for themselves but also for the generations to come.

Linda and Carlos miss the vast space they had in Tolima, which gave them plenty of room to keep numerous animals. They say they owned about two hundred hectares of land which allowed them to have cattle and horses. This is not possible in Porvenir where they need to make the most of their four hectares, which they thus use exclusively for cultivation. 'If you have a horse, you can't have a cow. If you have a cow, you can't have a horse. *Cultivos* come right up to the house,' explains Linda. Despite contracted space they would like to stay in Porvenir. They have two grown-up and two school-aged children. The land and the coffee that they grow currently give them enough to provide for the two dependent children and they would like to stay at least until their children finish their schooling. They are partly experiencing their belonging through their children. More exactly through being able to realise their priority – providing children with access to education.

In Esperanza, despite the numerous challenges, some share such sentiments. Fabio, for instance, draws on his identity as a father to keep him going. His and Fernanda's, his wife's, situation is different from the rest. They became a couple just before leaving Urabá. While they had their own individual pasts and place attachment to Urabá, their common path after physical relocation, and birth of their son, in many ways presented a new start. If they lacked technical knowledge of the land, they have managed to develop an emotional link to the place since the *finca* holds memories of prominent positive family events (Riley and Harvey 2007). The pair are engaging their teenage son in cultivation. Like others, Fabio fumigates and fertilises his blackberries in order to encourage growth. But compared to villagers who only rent a plot, he uses substantially less *químicos*. Rather than short-term exploitation of land, he is thinking of its sustainability for the next generation: Fabio wishes to pass the *finca* on to his son.

Others wish to move, or have already moved for exactly the same reason – they do not perceive the land as giving them a sufficient financial base. Alejandra and her husband both found work in different parts of the country. He works in an illegal gold mine in the department of Chocó and she works in Bogotá. At the same time, their two children aged nine and thirteen live in Esperanza. Alejandra pays someone to look after them; however, the childminders change rather frequently. During my fieldwork this was first a twenty-year-old girl, who was then replaced by a two-year older young man who stayed with them only for a few months, and finally the boys' grandmother temporarily moved into the house. Unlike the boys' father, who is largely absent, Alejandra returns to Esperanza every weekend. While Alejandra swears she moved away for the boys' sake, they are largely left to themselves. The separation of families, which might have not taken place as an immediate result of conflict and physical relocation, came about as a result of failure to endow the physical landscape with meaning. Juan and Doña Beatriz cited the search for more favourable conditions to provide their daughter with a better education as the main reason for leaving Esperanza. The lack of future plans with the land is also common among some non-displaced. In Esperanza, almost as a rule, people imagine the future of their children in the urban environment. In part this is because of lack of resources such as land to pass on to them, but partly also due to the difficult work that farming entails.

Don Andrés, who arrived to Esperanza in his early sixties, never managed to tame the land and re-establish the position he had held within the community and the family. The new conditions coupled with his age and health problems, which he ascribes to displacement, have taken their toll. He questions his role as a farmer since he can no longer work, and also reflects on his limited power to protect his children and grandchildren and direct their choices. When the guerrillas were luring one of his sons to join them while they were in Urabá, Don Andrés prevented this through offering his cattle, something he can no longer do. He recounts the story vividly and uses direct quotes as if the situation were unravelling while we spoke.

Ah, and what do you need? Money? What is it that you need? Sell this cow, and get some money. Go and take two of my cows, any you want. Say what it is that you want. But let me be with my son. You need something to offer. If not, the boy is lost. But if I don't have anything to back up my son with ... oh, my son ... he goes [joins the guerrillas]! You see, this is how it happens. This is what really happens here in Colombia.

'Subversion in many parts comes from poverty,' he says. 'If one is poor, one can't stop the risk.' Don Andrés no longer has the same ability to negotiate the future of his children or the same ability to stop his children or grandchildren from taking '*mal camino*' (go astray). He has been unable to give meaning to the landscape which has undermined his protection capacities and maintains him and others in poverty. His situation does not go by unnoticed. Martina for instance laments, 'He had forty to fifty head of cattle in Urabá. He would be taken care of for the old age. It hurts me he has to beg for cigarettes now.' Relational displacement therefore works also in the other direction – from children to parents.

Connection to a physical space through a family member can be influenced also in the absence of dependent children, but it is still influenced by a person's life stage. Doña María's children are all married and have moved away. She wishes to leave Porvenir because she feels that her husband has worked himself too hard on the steep land full of rocks. 'Eduardo is working too much. He has *obreros* (workers) but the work doesn't yield results. Our children also say we should sell. I'd like to go to Líbano, but Eduardo prefers Ibague to open a *negocio* (business, reference here is to a *tienda*, shop) but without alcohol. I don't like *tiendas* where they sell alcohol ... He has worked enough.'

Doña María's work has largely remained the same as in the area of origin – she stays in the house and does household chores. Despite her non-involvement with land cultivation, she has a strong stance towards the plot. She relates to the land through Don Eduardo. He normally gets up just after five in the morning and works till dusk. All of this, she believes, is for nothing. Her own attachment to the place is interlinked with that of her husband. Knowing that he is getting older and that he will not be able to sustain this rhythm for long, and that even at the current level of engagement his work is hardly repaid, she finds it difficult if not impossible to appreciate the place.

Physical landscapes are never just the built environment; they are inseparably interlinked to social and cognitive worlds. It is impossible to understand the depth of an individual's attachment to land if we do not consider the subjective and emotional meaning they give to it. The inability to tame the land has taken its toll on people's *campesino* identities. With little prospects of establishing strong ties to the land, and further tarnished sense of self, the grounds for a persisting sense of displacement are fertile.

Notes

1 Sibaté is a municipality in Cundinamarca, south of Bogotá and Soacha.

2 Lime is added to soil to reduce its acidity, it improves the soil's structure, and increases nutrient availability.
3 SENA, Servicio Nacional de Aprendizaje, or the National Service of Learning, is a public institute which provides vocational training.
4 As a point of reference on the size of the box – it took me eight hours to pick about 4 boxes. Those that are experienced are faster, but the quantity of blackberries ready to be picked is limited, especially in low season.

10

The remains of the place and times left behind

The everyday life in the two villages unfolds in its set ways. In the absence of recurrent incidents it is easy to become oblivious of the broader context and conflict fought in the country's periphery. Any extraordinary occurrence, however, quickly unsettles the supposed tranquillity, invites greater awareness and increases the heartbeat. One evening in Porvenir, in the time approaching local elections, a helicopter was flying low above the hamlet and its sounds could be distinctly heard. I was in the kitchen with Doña María, preparing dinner. The helicopter's even cutting of the air drowned out the sound of burning wood in the open stove, and of the boiling beans and potatoes in the pots. Doña María, who was attending to the food, raised her head and looked at me crying '*¡Dios mio! ¿Qué es eso?*' (My God! What is this?). The uneasiness the sound of the helicopter caused filled the kitchen. Doña María did not try to hide her concern. Don Eduardo was not home yet and perhaps more than being worried for our safety, her thoughts were with him. She wished he were there, knowing he was safe or simply be there if anything happened. Her uneasiness reminded both of us of the continued complex reality of the context we were in, despite the seemingly dormant character of the village life. Besides, Doña María's reaction indicated that her past experiences influenced how she experienced the present uncertainty. Had there been no conflict and had she not been affected by it, her and my reaction would have very likely been that of a simple interest, if at all, and would have not arisen in fear.

Displacement brought with it physical separation with the place of origin; in some cases a physical distance of several hundred kilometres. It brought rupture at various levels: different social landscapes with new neighbours, new customs and new social roles, distinct physical landscapes with new crops, management systems and cultivation specificities, and it also brought changes and challenges to individuals' identities. Nevertheless, despite the distance and the novelties, the place left behind has remained present at the very personal dimension. Years of experiences and life spent, be it in Tolima, Urabá or somewhere else, have not been erased with displacement. They persist through memories. Memories are 'produced out of experience and, in turn, reshape it' (Lambek and Antze 1996: xii); they can give certain experiences greater emphasis and value than they had in real time.

Memories elicit emotions. In the context of displacement, the sentiments arising from memories run largely along two quite different strands. On the one hand the loss, the instability and uncertainty have led to emotional escapes to a familiar, even if prettified past, resulting in nostalgia. On the other, those who hold memories of extended time caught in violence, in the rule of terror, silence and suspicion, exhibit traces of fear embodied through greater cautiousness, alertness, and distrust. Past and experiences of past places influence people's sentiments, guide their decisions, shape their reactions, and ultimately also impact the emotional value they give to new places. After all, memory and the sense of place are interconnected.

Longing for lost time and place

In their narratives most people have constructed two different images of the place left behind. One of displacement, of terror and violence, of curtailed freedom of movement, of limited opportunities to use their own land in the way they wished, of a place where Alejandro found it more unusual not to have to get off his bike to pass a corpse on the way to school than to do so. But alongside these images, they also constructed a fantasy place where time sits still. It is a place of opportunity, better economic conditions, genuine social relations, where life was 'sabroso'. Only a few do not share this fantasy. This might be because their lives have been filled with hardships and they perceive their current situation as an improvement of their past lives. Angelica is one of those whose memories of Tolima are linked to her difficult childhood.

> My mother left my father because he was maltreating her. She got married again and my step-father raped my sister and nearly raped me. I was sent away to town to work in a house of some woman. But she wouldn't take me because I was a minor. I was fourteen or fifteen at the time. I went back home and went to live with my current husband. There was nowhere else to go … We got married when I was fifteen and the same year I gave birth to my first child […] Where we lived there was no electricity, no roads. One wouldn't see a soul for days. It was so isolated that one would get scared of a car or would not know how to get into one!

Angelica has little to be nostalgic about, since neither her childhood nor her adulthood hold a treasury of beautiful memories. This is also probably one of the reasons why she is relatively happy in Porvenir. Any references to a fantasy place of origin were therefore absent from our conversations.

The nostalgic memories were similarly not present when individuals did not have the chance to get to know their place of origin in the absence of violence. That is, when they were born and raised in the context of conflict. Camilo was a child when the paramilitaries entered the region and he spent most of his childhood in paramilitary presence. The memories of violence prevail in his mind. When I asked whether he missed Urabá, he responded with disbelief, 'I don't have memories with Urabá. What should I miss? How I had to run *pa'l monte* when I was five?' He also resents the fact that Martina, his mother, sometimes left him, his sisters and his father alone while she engaged in political activities. For security reasons, she would not tell them where she went or when she would be back. In his opinion Urabá has not given him anything he would long to go back to. Camilo's narrative speaks of generational differences in which memory operates among people. Possibly because of a troubled childhood and his mother's occasional departures, he focuses only on the negative aspects of the place left behind. He did not know the region when it was still 'healthy'.

Others, who might mention the positive aspects of the past but without embracing them strongly, are the highly religious people, like Daniel, Doña Isabel and Don Jorge, who concentrate on their afterlife, their future. For them the 'unsatisfactory present' is seen as merely an 'antechamber to some better state' (Chase and Shaw 1989: 3). 'If there is no justice on land,' asserts Don Jorge, 'there will be justice in heaven'. Both he and his wife have accepted their current situation, and are hoping for a better life which follows. But alongside these individuals, there are the majority who expressed greater belonging in the past (May 2017) than in the present.

Physical relocation has in a number of individuals awoken a kind of retrospective place-belonging. What they might have taken for granted before, has retrospectively received greater appreciation and value after it had been lost. Dissatisfaction with lives in the place of resettlement, be it in relation to livelihood, social relations, or food, has awaken nostalgic memories of the past which is often idealised, and in which there is no presence of memories of violence – violence seems to belong to different times, to a different sphere.

'The most difficult thing for me has been the cold. I would cry. *Me da rabia* (It makes me furious) … And the economic condition,' says Doña Beatriz reflecting on her process of adaptation in Esperanza. Upon saying this she disappeared to her room and came out with two photos of her and her husband from the time when they were in Urabá. In the photos, both are wearing nice clothes, she is wearing make-up and her hair is nicely done. She silently looked at the two photographs for some seconds and said, 'If I didn't like a dress, I'd put it on once and give it away'. She used the photos to stress the downfall in the economic position, which now only lives in her memories. She is not alone in her nostalgic remembering of her past welfare. Don Andrés, who lost two *fincas* where he was cultivating plantain for exportation, with even stronger remorse in his voice said: 'People see me well from the outside but inside I have pain. I never lacked anything where I lived, now I don't even have a peso in my pocket. Only God is with me, no one else'.

Present instabilities are not the only reason why memories escape to the past; so is an insecure and unstable future. Adrián who lost ten hectares of land where he grew plantains did not receive a plot of his own in Esperanza but lives with his parents Don Andrés and Doña Olivia. He would like to stay in the hamlet, because he is, as he says, *amañado* (settled). However the land is not his and his parents would like to sell it. Not knowing where he will go, and lacking any guarantees that he will get land of his own, has evoked strong sentiments of past nostalgia.

Life was peaceful. One had work, there were a lot of sport activities – football ... one's community. One lived well. There were a lot of fish. You could go fishing. There was money to buy meat. There were labour unions so rights of *obreros* were protected. We got salary on time, the working conditions were good. One could leave the door open and nothing happened [no one stole anything]. One for example forgot to lock the door and in the morning everything would still be there. There are *gamonales* (caciques) in any part of the world, in towns, cities. But there weren't many [in Urabá]. They would steal cattle but there weren't many [thieves/incidents]. Public force [represented by the guerrillas or the paramilitaries] itself would put them away.

Adrián feels general insecurity about his future, which is why memories of what he now perceives as a stable past abound. Even though at the time, at the then present, future was unknown, looking back at it, one realises the '*now* known consequences for what was *then* the unknown future' (Lowenthal 1989: 30, emphases in the original), and past becomes a comforting escape.

Relational remembering

The displaced in Esperanza exhibit greater nostalgic stories of the past than those in Porvenir. This is partly due to generally speaking higher levels of satisfaction with their current lives among the displaced in Porvenir. Since not everyone experiences a strong sense of lack, the admiration of the past is not present to the same detriment. There is also something else which contributes to the emphasis on the past which was lost and shapes the memory. The mode through which memories are evoked in Esperanza and Porvenir differ.

Individuals hold their own memories, influenced by their own past experiences, which surface as a response to the given trigger in the environment or an emotional state they find themselves in. But memories are not isolated. They are influenced by relationships and social circumstances in which the remembered event takes place (Misztal 2003). Where there is a high concentration of the displaced, memory plays a different role than in cases where the displaced are dispersed. As Malkki (1995) shows, memory has a distinct effect on historical identity, the imagination of homeland, and the myth of return depending on the place composition. The displaced in the two hamlets live in similar circumstances both in terms of their numbers as well as physical positioning. Since they were resettled on what used to be one big property, they live on a sort of an island, with the difference that the long-term residents live closer to the displaced's houses in Esperanza than in Porvenir. Despite these similarities, relational remembering is far greater in Esperanza.

The displaced in Porvenir do not share much besides the category *desplazado* and familial ties which stretch to two households. In Esperanza in contrast, the displaced's similar background and shared history reaching back to times before physical relocation help maintain memories alive. They do not participate in any kind of formal commemoration practices in which they would remember the past and past events. Nevertheless, the past is remembered through others in ways that go beyond institutions and artefacts. Memories are maintained in less structured, informal ways.

On my last night in Esperanza Martina, Miguel, Fabio and Alejandro gathered in Alejandra's house where I was staying to bid me farewell. We sat in the kitchen and the night gave way to memories of past times. One story led to another, and narratives were accompanied by nods of agreement, complementing sentences, 'do you remember' encouragements to remember specific events, and at times what seemed to be genuine reminders of stories that might have already been dormant, or temporarily dormant in some people's minds. Some stories were recollections of violence but even these were accompanied with laughter denoting the disbelief at one's own luck to be alive to tell the tale and the plain absurdity of the circumstances in which the killings happened. But the majority were anecdotes, longing memories of spending time hunting and fishing, and sharing space with the *indios*. In Esperanza it often feels that the mere presence of people who formed people's social landscapes in the place of origin is enough to keep some memories of the past alive. Their daily chance and arranged meetings are a constant reminder of the encounters in a different time and space.

(Un)productive nostalgia

Nostalgia can help people survive (Boym 2001; Valis 2010). Through retaining the memory of home, there is an illusion that one can and will return home, which keeps people going. But nostalgia can be productive even when no return is envisioned. Even without the expectations of return, the displaced initially had a 'drive', to re-create their past sense of home in the present. Productive nostalgia 'refocuses on the desire for home and its enactment in practice rather than solely in narrative or the imagination' (Blunt 2003: 735). Such desires for home, to re-establish the lost sentiment, undoubtedly helped the numerous displaced who have been successful in their place-making efforts in Porvenir.

Productive nostalgia, however, has in some cases waned with time. Persistent fall backs, disillusionments with the physical, social and also political environment, reduced some of its productivity. For those who hope they will move once they have spent the required twelve years on the land, nostalgia can still be a pushing factor, informing their hopes for the future. It pushes them not to be easily satisfied with what they are given, but rather aim to restore what they now believe was 'some golden age of "homefulness"' (Turner 1987: 151). For others, however, the unlikelihood that the current social, political, economic and personal circumstances change substantially, and the limited and constrained options to employ the productive nostalgia at a different location have reduced the sentiment to one that predominately embodies the sense of loss. The persistent remembering and retelling of what is now interpreted as a comfortable past life, lacking in want, only highlights the current sentiments of physical and financial insecurity, of the absence of plans and immediate change. Nostalgia, therefore, can also impede the place-making process. Rather than being a bitter-sweet memory, where the loss is accepted and no regrets are taken (Dickinson and Erben 2006), nostalgia can leave an unpleasant sentiment.

The constant comparisons between past times in a past place and the place of resettlement highlight the deficiencies that the latter has. Since these are unlikely to change, some displaced continue forming belonging from afar (Fields 2011; May 2017) to the place and time left behind, possibly at the expense of forming belonging to the current one. Nostalgic reminiscence is a constant reminder of what are perceived better times in a different place, which was forcefully taken away and which has provided a better basis for belonging than the one they are currently in. These memories, however, are only a partial representation of past. Among others they do not encompass the terror and violence which actually contributed to the loss of place. These experiences too continue affecting people's place-making.

Violence and fear

Exposure to 'sadistic' violence, witnessing killings, threats to one's life and persistent sense of insecurity have left consequences on people's ways of being. This is especially the case when exposure to such an environment and circumstances was prolonged and when fear had built up over time, as was the case with the displaced who came from Urabá. As Peter Loizos (2002: 45) rightly put it, flight from violence does not traumatise but is an additional experience in people's lives. What has lasting effect is suffering or witnessing violence that might accompany flight. Bearing witness to extended violence and atrocities can have permanent consequences on the sense of displacement and people's aims at restructuring their lives (Riaño-Alcalá 2008). A woman in her early eighties whom I met separately and who was displaced during *La Violencia*, told me that even after all the decades that have passed she still has fear of the countryside and *el monte*. Pretending that individuals may not be affected by violence and the fear they experienced for their lives denies people's humanness, negates the role the past plays in the present, and undermines the influence the past has on people's current struggles, achievements and senses.

Fear, some hold is inherent in human society (Garretón 1992: 13); it is common to fear death, losing a job, or losing a partner. 'We have a right to fear,' asserts Joanna Bourke who adds that 'a world without fear would be a dull world indeed' (Bourke 2005: 390). The fear experienced as a direct threat to one's life, as that caused by living in the context of violence, extrajudicial killings, disappearances and torture, can be paralysing (Salimovich *et al.* 1992). Doña Isabel describes the time when she and her husband Don Jorge were still in Urabá. Don Jorge is a dentist and one day, when he was on their *finca* nearby, and she was in town at home, some men got to the *finca* asking for his services. The men later turned out to be the guerrillas.

> They came to look for him asking if he was a dentist. He said he was. They told
> him he should make a list of things he needed to work and that they would go

and get them off his wife. Off me. He thought it was his end and even his guts froze. He made a list and the two men came to our house to look for me. Imagine, they knew where we lived! I gave them the things. I was so afraid I couldn't walk. I crawled on all four to mount the stairs. I started praying to God and angels to protect him.

The notion of adrenalin, the unknown but anticipated horror weakened Doña Isabel, requiring a good deal of strength to be able to actually move.

Derivative fear

In the absence of sounds of gun shots, house raids, and constant rumours carrying the scent of death in the hamlets of resettlement, people do not experience the same kind of numbness Doña Isabel experienced. Yet, they are still affected. In people's minds, events of violence are not seen as part of an archive but as having the potential of becoming alive again (Das and Kleinman 2000).

Fear is dynamic and comes in many forms. Once it is experienced in a certain situation, it lessens with time. It is most fearsome when it is impossible to identify what the danger is and where it lies. Once the menace has been survived, people gain more confidence. They either learn to repel the menace or learn their limited ability to come out unharmed and learn what pain or loss they need to accept (Bauman 2006: 1). The change in the nature and level of fear is not abrupt but gradual. The resulting 'derivative fear' while lesser in form still affects and guides people's behaviour, even in the absence of direct threat to life and integrity (Bauman 2006: 3). The displaced, from initially having a stronger sensation of fear, have gradually transformed the sentiment into one of cautiousness, lack of tranquillity, vigilance and restraint. They normally respond to and address these sensations through the recycling of survival practices they used in the place of origin.

Soon after physical relocation, the fears were intensified. Some real or perceived threats were new, others were old but were nevertheless experienced in a different, unknown environment when the knowledge of the microgeography of the place was still weak. In certain circumstances individuals fear spontaneously rather than instinctively and it is the education and experience that shape their immediate response (James 1997). At first, any situation that was reminiscent of a threat in the place of origin provoked a strong reaction. Numerous anecdotes refer to the time of arrival in Esperanza, when the displaced sensed fear, and would hide or run. Alejandra reports:

> One day I woke up, happy. I had my hen, throwing them maize, when I saw a group of people approaching in a line. Look, you won't believe me, but I took my children and started running. One [child] was walking and I held the other one. I said, 'They're coming to kill us, they are coming to attack, to throw us out!' Supposedly it was the guerrillas who wanted to know about us, where we came from. It was the only time they came. Never again.

Alejandra similarly started running during Christmas celebrations, when she heard fire crackers. Now, she says, she no longer runs, but goes to the other extreme. She does not leave the house during Christmas since she believes the noise that the firecrackers produce may be used to mask the noise produced by guns. She fears that people are being shot during that time.

She was not the only one affected by familiar clamour. Alejandro similarly recalls how noise generated fear in him. For a long time he and his family would hide if they heard a sound of a motorbike or a car. 'This is the way they [the paramilitaries in Urabá] used to come – by motorbike. We'd all hide and wait for the motorbike to pass.' He remembers how in Esperanza he 'nearly slept by the road' once as a result of this fear.

> I was on my way home from town with my nephews when a car passed us and stopped after a curve. We hid and waited. We were there for almost an hour and the car didn't move. We didn't know what to do. I was the oldest of the group and said we should continue. When we passed the car, we saw it wasn't the paramilitaries. It was a couple making out [he laughs] ... But it stays with one ... the fear.

Alejandro no longer hides at the sound of the motorbike or a car. He might notice them more than other people with a different history, but the nature of his fear has changed.

Those forcibly displaced tend to mistrust more than those who have not lived in violence (Daniel and Knudsen 1995). The displaced have lost their usual way-of-being, are facing new circumstances and consequently see the world differently. Because of the past experiences of violence, erosion of familiarity and flight, Daniel and Knudsen argue, forced migrants develop agitated state of awareness. Rather than exhibiting fear in its purest form, it is partly expressed through greater vigilance.

It is not unusual that in a small village context, any new arrival or a passer-by attracts attention from both the displaced and non-displaced. During our conversation in front of his house in Porvenir one afternoon, Simón suddenly paused to follow the movement of a motorbike which passed us. Simón did not recognise it. 'When a stranger comes, we call each other [the neighbours] to identify who the person is, who they came to see. We'd be doing this until we find out,' he explained. While the non-displaced look at unknown people with suspicion, thinking that they might be thieves, the thoughts of some of the displaced are more severe – they worry that their lives might be in danger.

Two unknown men on motorbikes were seen in Esperanza one afternoon. I was with Martina when Fabio called her saying there might be *sicarios* (hitmen) at her *finca*. At the time, Martina was not living at home but was staying at Alejandra's *finca* looking after her two grandchildren. While no similar concerns were heard from the non-displaced, Fabio and Martina began a discussion about who the two men were possibly after. Upon my question how they knew they were *sicarios*, Martina based her answer on her past experiences of life in Urabá. She said: 'No one [in the village] knows who they are. One knows how this [contract killings] functions and what they [*sicarios*] look like.' The threat might have been only perceived, nevertheless, it disturbed the calm of the day, or even days. It took some of mine but also of Martina's sleep (we were staying in the same room), as we stayed awake listening to the sounds of the night to detect any movement or any unusual noise.

Greater vigilance and cautiousness relates not only to unknown visitors but also to some infrequent residents of Esperanza. The displaced express concerns about two *finca* owners, who do not live in the village permanently. They bought the *fincas* and use them as an occasional retreat from the city. The displaced believe that one of them has links with the paramilitaries, while the other is a retired official of the *Departamento Administrativo de Seguridad*, DAS, the Colombian former Administrative Department of Security. Juan explains:

> It's quieter [in Esperanza compared to Urabá], but not that much. Retired government officials buy *fincas*. One can't talk to them about these things [displacement] like the two of us talk. There are people from DAS. One can't talk to everyone. We talk within our community but not to outsiders. There are many *infiltrados, paras*. They know we were displaced but they don't know how.

Some DAS employees were under investigation for corruption and their collaboration with the paramilitaries and drug traffickers. Since the IDPs in Esperanza left Urabá mainly as a result of the paramilitary activity there, the presence of these two individuals in the village contributes to IDPs' uneasiness. The degree of discomfort is even greater when these two individuals receive visitors, because questions arise regarding what they might be doing. If the two officials in question realise that the IDPs were active members of *Unión Patriótica* or were displaced by the paramilitaries, they fear they might have to move again.

The rule of silence that people practised in the place of origin continues. The conversations remain limited, as do contacts. Lorena says that the receiving population does not know their stories, and even if they asked, the displaced are not likely to share them. The absence of information sharing influences the process of place-making. The receiving community has created their own understanding and explanation of why the displaced left their areas of origin – they believe the displaced are responsible for inflicting displacement upon them. 'Not speaking can entail accepting someone else's story about what happened to you' (Winter 2010: 8). A vicious circle is created where certain stereotypes about the displaced exist, but which are not being challenged in part due to the atmosphere of mistrust or heightened cautiousness which inhibits relationships and impacts people's social landscapes.

Silence is present not only in relation to the receiving populations but continues in relation to the state. Many grow suspicion towards the state and its organs. When I asked Fabio whether he trusted the government, he laughed: 'No, no, no. You can't trust the government. They say nice things but don't carry them out.' Camilo, for his part, openly expressed fear towards the state's armed forces: 'People say that the military protects them. I get frightened when I see the military. In Urabá one knew that if they passed, the paramilitaries would soon follow and kill.' Others, like Don Andrés, on the other hand, remain sceptical when it comes to claiming his rights over the material loss he suffered. A couple of years after his physical relocation a state official working for *Acción Social* advised him not to claim what he had lost if he wanted to live.

> In this country you need to be quiet. If you're not quiet they beat you. The government calculated once 'what was yours, is worth at least 600 million with everything. Well, I'll give you an advice,' she said, 'since they saw you there, [I'd advise you to claim] two or three million and that's it.' She told me I better keep quiet if not they will pay someone a million or two and 'bang bang' they'll shoot me. So I kept quiet. One can't claim one's rights. If one does, he is a *guerrillero* until they kill him. One stays quiet, even now.

Don Andrés decided to remain silent, not to exercise his rights, in order not to put his life in danger.

Besides the law of silence, there are some other survival strategies that individuals still consider when they feel heightened tensions and danger. Memory encrypts and stores experiences 'which can be retrieved, or which re-emerge in subsequent practice' (Jones 2011: 876). The tested survival practices come in handy when fear is revived. The row over a communal plot in Esperanza that has divided the once 'community' increased the fears about the means through which the conflict might be resolved. Martina, Fabio and Don Andrés and their families suspect that some of the displaced might have links with the paramilitaries even though they persistently speak against them. 'There are enemies within the community,' Don Andrés asserts. 'I need to leave as soon as possible. The connection here – Urabá … I don't like that they are informing, informing, informing. My family can't go to Urabá; they can.'

During one of the days when the dispute was most intense, Martina's husband Miguel, who was not in Esperanza at the time, called her and suggested that she spent the night somewhere else, not in the house. He was afraid that the displaced with whom she was in conflict would send someone after her. Similarly to the way in which houses had stopped being experienced as safe in the place of origin and people opted for short-term nightly relocations when in Urabá, the house in Esperanza too was interpreted as threatening, as a possible point of attack.

The impact of violence and fear does not end there. The vigilance, heightened awareness and cautiousness are accompanied by restraint. This is restraint from getting involved in political activity, even if such engagement presented the most important part of people's identities in the past. When the area where people live reflects who they are, they feel greater belonging and connectedness to the place (Savage *et al.* 2005). If such reflection is not present and people feel they cannot exercise their identities, their ability to form connectedness to a place will be small. Don Andrés, who had been an active political leader in Urabá, decided not to continue with his political activities. 'I was a local leader and I'd like to continue in politics, but it's too dangerous to do politics in Colombia,' he concluded. He did not perceive Esperanza as giving him the necessary infrastructure and protection to do so. This influenced his liking of the place. People had been sent from Urabá once before to look for him in the village of resettlement, hence he felt the danger very much present. Don Andrés died nine months after I had left Esperanza. He died of old age and disease. His wife Doña Olivia and Martina in a telephone conversation said, 'at least he died as a person [and not like hounded animal] surrounded by his family.' They were grateful that he had not been persecuted and killed by someone sent from Urabá. Their statement reflects the extent to which they still live the conflict, even though they are geographically speaking remote from it.

Fabio too opted for a low political profile and discontinued his active participation in political life or any kind of a leadership role. He is in his mid-fifties, and while he misses politics and would still discuss it with the very limited number of people he trusts, he prefers not getting involved in it. 'I miss political participation but I'm trying to be neutral. It's obvious that the same thing can happen again,' he concludes. He is purposefully limiting what used to be one of the defining characteristics of his identity. He took a temporal and spatial distance from Urabá. In Fabio's case, the anxiety over what might happen, and the fear of political activity based on what has already happened, inhibits him from living his life fully. This in turn prevents him from establishing a closer link to the new place and stands as an obstacle to rendering the place more meaningful.

Despite heightened awareness, people do not live in constant fear. Such a state would not allow them to function properly. Constant fear 'can kill us before we actually die' (Lechner 1992: 26). The displaced continue living their lives albeit at times in a reduced form. Besides the state of suspicion, the derivative fear works in concert with other senses and triggers from the environment. Any extraordinary event, or anything that can provoke the memories of the place left behind, be it sound, smell or sight, can disrupt people's everyday lives. The memory of violence and the impact it left on people's cognitive landscapes still affect them. While fear is lessening in form it continues shaping people's social relations, conduct, and is accompanied by occasional spikes in dis-ease with one's position, location and one's general state.

In many ways the process of unmaking past places is replicated and it inhibits attempts at making the new location meaningful. The accentuated perceptions of threats and their implications for people's social landscapes add an additional layer to the already complex, demanding and challenging place-making process.

11

Conclusion: end of displacement?

'We are *desplazados* for life,' said Carlita, 11 years old, born and raised in Esperanza.

After four years of peace negotiations between the government led by Juan Manuel Santos and the FARC, the two parties signed a peace accord in November 2016. In February 2017, Santos' administration additionally started official negotiations with ELN. Peace negotiations with the guerrilla groups are long due and are a welcome change to the previous government's announcement of the guerrillas as terrorists and subsequent declaration of end of conflict. The agreement is also welcome since it promises some structural changes. Among others, land reforms, and it thus aims to address the agrarian question which has been at the root of the conflict. Nevertheless, it might be too early to celebrate, to proclaim 'peace', or to think that the demobilisation of the guerrillas will bring an end to violence and displacement. Decades-long conflict, a whole generation of individuals who are more accustomed to living in conflict than in peace, the number of people profiting from conflict or from the system as it currently is, the plethora of actors, and regional particularities mean that the materialisation of the agreement will be highly challenging. Interests are multiple, corruption still present, and criminal groups, drug lords and neo-paramilitaries active. The latter, who might be an attractive option for demobilised guerrillas, continue with their involvement in violence, and continue contributing their share to displacement. In the first half of 2017, IDMC reports fifty-six thousand new displacements. But even if the numbers of the displaced did come to a halt, there are millions of displaced individuals for whom displacement is ongoing.

Displacement in Colombia is not a state of exception. The recurrent and persistent phenomenon has rather become normalised. The presence of the displaced has reached a point at which it is taken for granted. The point at which displacement occurs, not only in one person's life, but also in relation to the country's history of displacement and conflict, helps explain whether it is seen as a topic of urgent engagement or as a normalised state of affairs whereby approaches to displacement have become desensitised. In Colombia, in policy, the approach to displacement has been marked by 'institutional thoughtlessness' (Oslender 2016a).

As Ulrich Oslender notes, new laws and administrative bodies are created to deal with displacement but they do not problematise it; instead, displacement continues to be perceived as part of social fabric. Crucially, little interest has been paid to the actual situation in which the displaced find themselves, how they perceive and experience displacement, and how they cope with it. Those, who are in a need of a 'solution', are not in the centre of consideration. At the same time important opportunities for a more profound understanding of displacement, which would lead to more appropriate methods when addressing the phenomenon, are lost.

In this book I aimed to bring people's struggles, achievements, feelings and relations to attention in order to provide a view into how displacement is experienced. Using Agnew's (1987) conceptualisation of place I showed how conflict and violence affected the locale, location and people's sense of place, leading to a processual loss of place and subsequent place-making in Esperanza and Porvenir. People's stories reveal that individuals follow distinct temporalities of displacement. Some left as a means of precaution, soon after violence broke out; others persisted, believing or hoping violence would soon end or in order to defend their territory. Those who spent years caught in violence saw how their places changed, sometimes beyond recognition. For these individuals the transformation of place triggered the process of displacement before they actually physically relocated.

The exploration of the impact violence has had on people's places shows consequences which 'cannot be explained with recourse to the mere history of war itself' (Jansen and Löfving 2009: 11). The political analysis of the warring parties, or knowing who the actor responsible for displacement is, does not say much about what it is like to witness and experience violence, to live in fear, or about people's resourcefulness that helps them survive. It does not tell much about the impact terror has on people. About the undermined levels of trust, heightened sensual awareness and (dis)ease with being in a particular place, in the proximity of certain people, or voicing an opinion. Close examination of violence on the ground demonstrates that displacement is not merely a by-product of conflict but that it can be systematic and planned. That displacement can be an objective, as was the case in Urabá. It also shows that conflict is not a mere background to displacement, but forms integral element of individuals' loss and making of place – political violence shapes people's places before and after migration. The analysis of violence thus helps understand why, for some individuals, physical distance from the conflict is insufficient for their sense of security. For those exposed to terror and violence for a number of years, it is difficult if not impossible to leave the past behind.

Putting people in focus revealed an array of different experiences. Some roles have shifted and relationships transformed. The experiences have not been shaped only by people's gender, age or ethnicity, but also by their biography. Previous history of migration, circumstances in which they lived in the place of origin, and the (in)ability to engage in similar activities pre- and post-migration have affected the manner in which displacement is lived and in which places are experienced. Discontinuation of undertakings, which moulded and nurtured people's identity such as political participation, has been especially detrimental. The varied experiences have, however, been tucked away and made invisible under the homogenising category *desplazado*. A category that affects people's sense of displacement and place-making through the influence it has on individuals' self-worth, who they are, and more than anything through singling them out as a different class of people, separating them from their non-displaced neighbours.

The label *desplazado*, as an example of a macro-order, has impacted the locale, the setting for social interaction (Agnew 1987). Social landscapes have been largely marked by political environment; on the one hand, the policy category *desplazado* has enabled grouping of people together, to draw generalisations about them and to simplify assistance. At the same time, categorisation implies homogeneity of experience and identity and a set of shared needs. It subsumes differences of age, gender and ethnicity and it effaces people's personal biographies. It has additionally legitimised the unequal use of governmental resources, causing tensions between the displaced and the non-displaced. The great majority of the latter worry that the displaced's presence might push them into complete oblivion. Their unstable and occasionally precarious living conditions do not get as much governmental attention as they should, and they look at the displaced who manage to secure assistance with resentment. On the other hand, the changing political context of conflict and displacement has shaped the category's connotations. The displaced are seen as responsible for their displacement and assumed to be guerrillas, thieves and liars. Fear, stereotypes, sense of injustice experienced by the non-displaced, and resentment, lack of understanding and gratitude felt by the displaced, have helped maintain social boundaries between the categorised and non-categorised. These boundaries have inhibited the search for shared history, which would advance the sense of commonalty and affinity between different groups of people (Kriesberg 2001) and contribute to relational belonging. As a result, in their everyday lives, the displaced and non-displaced point fingers at one another and complain about each other's personal characteristics, while structural elements of inequality go by almost unnoticed. The impact of the categorisation is likely to persist even if peace is reached and even if there are no new cases of displacement. Due to categorisation, the two 'groups' are physically close, but they are, at the same time, socially distant.

Social distance is felt also among some of the displaced. Displacement is highly political, particularly when a plethora of actors is involved. In the absence of careful planning of who is resettled with whom, or in the absence of accompanying programmes helping those affected to (re)establish social fabric, disparities can continue for years, as is the case in Porvenir. Tensions can also exist among those who resettle together by choice. The unequal power relations, disagreements with leadership and deterioration of relationships have led to some individuals having a renewed sense of displacement in Esperanza. They may share the category, and location, but the displaced do not necessarily form a community.

Alongside social landscapes there is another essential feature affecting people's everyday setting with consequences for place-making. That is the physical landscape. Paying attention to people's stories confirms that allocation of land is insufficient to address their displacement. Land and housing are important bases to start from but in themselves do not result in successful place-belongingness. Not 'any place is, ultimately, good if it's one's own' (Jansen and Löfving 2009: 13). Several issues are at stake. The process is affected by the sense of (dis)continuity. If land of resettlement requires similar cultivation practices as the land left behind, individuals' identity as peasants is not as affected. The rupture is not as severe as when people are resettled into an entirely new environment in which they cannot rely on their past knowledge and they need to reinvent themselves as farmers. Quality of soil is another important factor of place attachment. Whether peasants feel their work is repaid or not, and whether the plot of land enables them to fulfil their social roles makes a difference. The focus is often not only on livelihood opportunities in the present, but also on hopes and opportunities in the future.

By not listening to the displaced, the government fails to see that some displaced have found or are attempting to find their own solution to their situation. The technocratic approach actively prevents such undertakings and even threatens to unmake place where it has already been made. The legislation controls people's mobility. It decides how long they must stay at the land dedicated for resettlement, for better or for worse, it threatens to punish those who left the plot to look for alternative strategies, and to expel those who were not the original beneficiaries of resettlement. Doña Flor and Don Ignacio, Linda and Carlos, Simón, Juanita and Patricio and their families are among those in Porvenir who found land through their own means and have mostly – Juanita excluded – been successful in their place-making. A number of others have left Esperanza and set off on secondary migration. Some of them might have also successfully started to build a new home at a different location. Yet, their faith of whether they are allowed to stay where they are or not is at best unknown. At worst they will be 'displaced' again; this time not by armed actors or criminal groups but by rigid legislation.

The sense of place and consequent sense of feeling comfortable in a place is thus affected by social landscapes, physical landscapes, the micro-environment where macro-policies have left their mark, but also by people's past places and experiences; both positive, now embodied in nostalgia, as well as negative, those of violence and terror. The memory of fear surfaces up again and again and manifests itself as heightened levels of suspicion, caution and alertness. Various things become clear. First, that displacement is a process in which the loss of place and the making of place are interrelated and influence one another. Second, in attempts to understand and address displacement a longer time frame needs to be considered – extended to life before physical relocation, and including people's journeys and challenges with settlement. The current academic and policy focus on post-arrival or post-registration is not adequate. Finally, people's opinions, feelings and interpretations matter.

Displacement can affect the most intimate part of people's existence. It shakes their sense of self and often transforms it. The influence can be so powerful for some individuals that it is questionable if they can ever overcome their sense of displacement, if they can ever bring it to an 'end'. Nevertheless, they get on with their lives. They try to endow places with meaning despite the adversaries. They look for ways of improving their situation, to *salir adelante*. Not everyone has experienced the same kind of life in violence and not everyone has been affected to the same extent; the clock with which displacement starts ticks at a different pace for each individual towards its uncertain end. Rather than relying on a set of fixed 'solutions' and piecemeal programmes and policies or timetabled end to displacement, the approach to addressing displacement should include politically risky modes of intervention, which are flexible and experimental and which better consider displaced people's views, their own 'solutions' outside policy domains, and wishes (Zetter 2011: 9). If not, there is a danger that taking the decision on their behalf can impede their place-making efforts and only emphasise their sentiments of displacement rather than help them overcome it. The displaced as well as their non-displaced hosts have a lot to share. They only need the opportunity to be heard.

References

Agier, Michel. (2001). 'La política en tiempos de la guerra sucia. Notas sobre la toma del edificio de la Cruz Roja', *Análisis Político*, 42(Enero-Abril): 95–100.

Agnew, John. (1987). *Place and Politics: The Geographical Mediation of State and Society* (George Allen & Unwin: London).

Ahmed, Sara, Claudia Castañeda, Anne-Marie Fortier and Mimi Sheller. (2003). 'Introduction: uprootings/regroundings: questions of home and migration' in Sara Ahmed, Claudia Castañeda, Anne-Marie Fortier and Mimi Sheller (eds), *Uprootings/ Regroundings: Questions of Home and Migration* (Berg: Oxford).

Allen, Tim and David Turton. (1996). 'Introduction: in search of cool ground.' in Tim Allen (ed.), *In Search of Cool Ground. War, Flight & Homecoming in Northeast Africa* (James Currey: Oxford).

Amit, Vered. (2002). 'Reconceptualizing community' in Vered Amit (ed.), *Realizing Community* (Routledge: New York).

Angarita, Carlos Enrique. (2000). *Estado, poder y derechos humanos en Colombia* (Corporación René García: Bogotá).

Antonsich, Marco. (2010a). 'Book review: bell hooks Belonging: A Culture of Place', *Progress in Human Geography*, 34(5): 693–4.

——. (2010b). 'Meanings of place and aspects of the Self: an interdisciplinary and empirical account', *GeoJournal*, 75(1): 119–32.

——. (2010c). 'Searching for belonging – an analytical framework', *Geography Compass*, 4(6): 644–59.

Aradau, Claudia. (2004). 'The perverse politics of four letter words: risk and pity in the securitization of human trafficking', *Millennium – Journal of International Studies*, 33(2): 251–77.

Bakewell, Oliver. (2000). 'Uncovering local perspectives on humanitarian assistance and its outcomes', *Disasters*, 24(2): 103–16.

——. (2011). 'Conceptualising displacement and migration: processes, conditions, and categories' in Khalid Koser and Susan Martin (eds), *The Migration-Displacement Nexus: Patterns, Processes, and Policies* (Berghahn Books: New York/Oxford).

Ballinger, Pamela. (2012). 'Borders and the rhythms of displacement, emplacement and mobility' in Thomas M. Wilson and Donnan Hastings (eds), *A Companion to Border Studies* (Wiley-Blackwell: Chichester).

Barclay, Craig R. and Peggy A. DeCooke. (1988). 'Ordinary everyday memories: some of the things of which selves are made' in Ulric Neisser and Eugene Winograd (eds),

Remembering Reconsidered: Ecological and Traditional Approaches to the Study of Memory (Cambridge University Press: Cambridge).

Barrett, Michael. (2009). 'The social significance of crossing the state borders: home, mobility and life paths in the Angolan-Zambian borderland' in Stef Jansen and Staffan Löfving (eds), *Struggles for Home: Violence, Hope and the Movement of People* (Berghahn Books: Oxford).

Basso, Keith H. (1996a). *Wisdom Sits in Places: Landscape and Language among the Western Apache* (University of New Mexico Press: Albuquerque).

———. (1996b). 'Wisdom sits in places: note on a Western Apache landscape' in Steven Feld and Keith H. Basso (eds), *Senses of Place* (School of American Research Press: Santa Fe, NM).

Bastian, Michelle. (2014). 'Time and community: a scoping study', *Time & Society*, 23(2): 137–66.

Bauman, Zygmund. (2006). *Liquid Fear* (Polity Press: Cambridge).

Bautista Bautista, Sandra Carolina. (2012). 'Alternativas analíticas en el campo de la movilización social en Colombia: la acción colectiva de alto riesgo. Lecturas a propósito de la protesta campesina en el Tolima', *Revista Estudios Políticos*, 41(3): 57–79.

Bello, Martha. (2001). *Desplazamiento forzado y reconstrucción de identidades* (Unibiblos: Bogotá).

BenEzer, Gadi. (2002). *The Ethiopian Jewish Exodus: Narratives of the Migration Journey to Israel 1977–1985* (Routledge: London).

BenEzer, Gadi and Roger Zetter. (2015). 'Searching for directions. Conceptual and methodological challenges in researching refugee journeys', *Journal of Refugee Studies*, 28(3): 297–318.

Bergquist, Charles, Ricardo Peñaranda and Gonzalo Sánchez (eds). (2001). *Violence in Colombia, 1900–2000: Waging War and Negotiating Peace* (Scholarly Resources: Wilmington).

Blunt, Alison. (2003). 'Collective memory and productive nostalgia: Anglo-Indian home-making at McCluskieganj', *Environment and Planning D: Society And Space*, 21(6): 717–38.

Bosk, Charles. (2004). 'The ethnographer and the IRB: comment on Kevin D. Haggerty, "Ethics creep: governing social science research in the name of ethics"', *Qualitative Sociology*, 27(4): 417–20.

Bourke, Joanna. (2005). *Fear: A Cultural History* (Virago: London).

Boym, Svetlana. (2001). *The Future of Nostalgia* (Basic Books: New York).

Brookings Institution-University of Bern. (2009). *Judicial Protection of Internally Displaced Persons: The Colombian Experience* (Brookings Institution-University of Bern: Washington, DC).

Brubaker, Rogers and Frederick Cooper. (2000). 'Beyond "identity"', *Theory and Society*, 29(1): 1–47.

Brun, Cathrine. (2003). 'Local citizens or internally displaced persons? Dilemmas of long-term displacement in Sri Lanka', *Journal of Refugee Studies*, 16(4): 376–97.

Butler, Judith. (1999). *Gender Trouble: Feminism and the Subversion of Identity* (Routledge: New York; London).

Calhoun, Craig. (2003). 'The variability of belonging: a reply to Rogers Brubaker', *Ethnicities*, 3(4): 558–68.

Carrillo Rowe, Aimee Marie. (2005). 'Be longing: toward a feminist politics of relation', *NWSA Journal*, 17(2): 15–46.

Carroll, Leah Anne. (2011). *Violent Democratization. Social Movements, Elites, and Politics in Colombia's Rural War Zones, 1984-2008* (University of Notre Dame Press: Notre Dame, IN).

Castillejo Cuéllar, Alejandro. (2000). *Poética de lo Otro, para una antropología de la guerra, la soledad y el éxilio interno en Colombia* (ICAN, Universidad Nacional de Colombia: Bogotá).

CCJ. (2010). *Colombia: La metáfora del desmantelamiento de los grupos paramilitares. Segundo informe de balance sobre la aplicación de la ley 975 de 2005* (Comisión Colombiana de Juristas: Bogotá).

Celestina, Mateja. (2016). '"Displacement" before displacement: time, place and the case of rural Urabá', *Journal of Latin American Studies*, 48(2): 367-90.

Cernea, Michael. (1997). 'The risk and reconstruction model for resettling displaced populations', *World Development*, 25(10): 1569-87.

Céspedes-Báez, Lina M. (2012). 'Colombia's Victims Law and the liability of corporations for human rights violations', *Estudios Socio-Jurídicos*, 14(1): 177-213.

Chakravarty, Anuradha. (2012). '"Partially trusting" field relationships opportunities and constraints of fieldwork in Rwanda's postconflict setting', *Field Methods*, 24(3): 251-71.

Chase, Malcolm and Christopher Shaw. (1989). 'The dimensions of nostalgia' in Christopher Shaw and Malcolm Chase (eds), *The Imagined Past: History and Nostalgia* (Manchester University Press: Manchester).

Cheshire, Lynda, Carla Meurk and Michael Woods. (2013). 'Decoupling farm, farming and place: recombinant attachments of globally engaged family farmers', *Journal of Rural Studies*, 30(April): 64-74.

Chomsky, Aviva. (2008). *Linked Labor Histories: New England, Colombia, and the Making of a Global Working Class* (Duke University Press: Durham, NC).

Clifford, James. (1997). *Routes. Travel and Translation in the Late Twentieth Century* (Harvard University Press: Cambridge, MA).

CODHES. (2011). *Boletín de la Consultoría para los derechos humanos y el desplazamiento* (CODHES: Bogotá/Quito).

———. (2013). *Dato: numero de personas desplazadas por municipio y año de llegada* (CODHES: Bogotá).

Cohen, Jeffrey. (2000). 'Problems in the field: participant observation and the assumption of neutrality', *Field Methods*, 12(4): 316-33.

Colson, Elizabeth. (2003). 'Forced migration and the anthropological response', *Journal of Refugee Studies*, 16(1): 1-18.

Conferencia Episcopal de Colombia. (1995). *Desplazados por la violencia en Colombia* (Conferencia Episcopal de Colombia: Santafé de Bogotá).

Creed, Gerald W. (2006). 'Reconsidering community' in Gerald W. Creed (ed.), *The Seductions of Community. Emancipations, Oppressions, Quandaries* (School of American Research Press: Santa Fe).

Cresswell, Tim. (2004). *Place: A Short Introduction* (Blackwell Publishing: Oxford).

Cross, Jennifer Eileen. (2015). 'Process of place attachment: an interactional framework', *Symbolic Interaction*, 38(4): 493-520.

Daniel, E.Valentine and John Chr Knudsen. (1995). 'Introduction' in E.Valentine Daniel and John Chr. Knudsen (eds), *Mistrusting Refugees* (University of California Press: Berkeley, CA/London).

Das, Veena and Arthur Kleinman. (2000). 'Introduction' in Veena Das, Arthur Kleinman, Mamphela Ramphele and Pamela Reynolds (eds), *Violence and Subjectivity* (University of California Press: Berkeley, CA,/London).

de Certeau, Michel. (1988). *The Writing of History* (Columbia University Press: New York).

Dean, John and William Whyte. (1958). 'How do you know if the informant is telling the truth?', *Human Organization*, 17(2): 34–38.

Dickinson, Hilary and Michael Erben. (2006). 'Nostalgia and autobiography: the past in the present', *Auto/Biography*, 14(3): 223–44.

Downs, Roger M. and David Stea. (2011). 'Cognitive maps and spatial behaviour: process and products' in Martin Dodge, Rob Kitchin and Chris Perkins (eds), *The Map Reader: Theories of Mapping Practice and Cartographic Representation* (John Wiley & Sons: Chichester).

El Tiempo. (2000). 'Toma de Cruz Roja afecta liberación de niño', *El Tiempo*, 14 January 2000.

Elhawary, Samir. (2007). *Between War and Peace: Land and Humanitarian Action in Colombia* (ODI: London).

Elias, Norbert and John L. Scotson. (1994). *The Established and the Outsiders* (Sage: London).

Escobar, Arturo. (2008). *Territories of Difference: Place, Movements, Life, Redes* (Duke University Press: Durham, NC).

Fassin, Didier. (2012). *Humanitarian Reason. A Moral History of the Present* (University of California Press: Berkeley CA/London).

Feld, Steven and Keith H. Basso. (1996). 'Introduction.' in Steven Feld and Keith H. Basso (eds), *Senses of Place* (School of American Research Press: Santa Fe, NM).

Feldman, Allen (1991). *Formations of Violence: The Narrative of the Body and Political Terror in Northern Ireland* (University of Chicago Press: Chicago).

Fields, Desiree. (2011). 'Emotional refuge? Dynamics of place and belonging among formerly homeless individuals with mental illness', *Emotion, Space and Society*, 4(4): 258–67.

Fujii, Lee Ann. (2010). 'Shades of truth and lies: interpreting testimonies of war and violence', *Journal of Peace Research*, 27(2): 231–41.

García de la Torre, Clara Inés and Clara Inés Aramburo Siegert. (2011). *Geografías de la guerra, el poder y la resistencia. Oriente y Urabá antioqueños 1990–2008* (Universidad de Antioquia: Medellín).

Garretón, Manuel Antonio (1992). 'Fear in military regimes' in Juan Corradi, Patricia Weiss Fagen and Manuel Antonio Garretón (eds), *Fear at the Edge. State Terror and Resistance in Latin America* (University of California Press: Berkeley, CA/Oxford).

Gatrell, Peter. (2013). *The Making of the Modern Refugee* (Oxford University Press: Oxford).

Geertz, Clifford. (1996). 'Afterword' in Steven Feld and Keith H. Basso (eds), *Senses of Place* (School of American Research Press: Santa Fe, NM).

Giraldo, Carlos Alberto, Jesús Abad Colorado and Pérez G Diego. (1997). *Relatos e imágenes: el desplazamiento en Colombia* (Cinep: Bogotá).

Giraldo, Fernando. (2001). *Democracia y discurso político en la Unión Patriótica* (Centro Editorial Javeriano (CEJA): Bogotá).

Goffman, Erving. (1990). *Stigma. Notes on the Management of Spoiled Identity* (Penguin: London).

Goodhand, Jonathan. (2000). 'Research in conflict zones: ethics and accountability', *Forced Migration Review*, 8: 12–15.

Green, Linda. (2004). 'Living in a state of fear' in Nancy Scheper-Hughes and Philippe Bourgois (eds), *Violence in War and Peace* (Blackwell: Oxford).

Grupo de memoria histórica. (2013). ¡BASTA YA! Colombia: memorias de guerra y dignidad (Centro Nacional de Memoria Histórica: Bogotá).

Hacking, Ian. (1986/1999). 'Making up people' in Mario Biagioli (ed.), *Science Studies Reader* (Routledge: New York).

Hardin, Russell. (1992). 'The street-level epistemology of trust', *Politics & Society*, 21(December): 505–29.

Harrell-Bond, Barbara. (1999). 'The experience of refugees as recipients of aid' in Alastair Ager (ed.), *Refugees: Perspectives on the Experience of Forced Migration* (Pinter: London).

Heidegger, Martin. (1977). 'Building dwelling thinking' in David Krell (ed.), *Martin Heidegger: Basic Writings* (Harper and Row: New York).

hooks, bell. (1991). *Yearning: Race, Gender, and Cultural Politics* (Turnaround: London).

———. (2009). *Belonging: A Culture of Place* (Routledge: New York).

Hylton, Forrest. (2006). *Evil Hour in Colombia* (Verso: London).

Hynes, Tricia. (2003). The issue of 'trust' or 'mistrust' in research with refugees: choices, caveats and considerations for researchers. Working paper (UNHCR: Geneva).

IASC. (2010). *IASC Framework on Durable Solutions for Internally Displaced Persons* (The Brookings Institution Project on Internal Displacement: Washington, DC).

Ibáñez, Ana María and Andrea Velásquez. (2009). 'Identifying victims of civil conflicts: An evaluation of forced displaced households in Colombia', *Journal of Peace Research*, 46(4) 431–51.

ICRC. (unknown). *Desplazamiento – mujeres y niños en el conflicto armado. Protección de la población civil. Complicación de lecturas* (ICRC: Bogotá).

IDMC. (2017). *Global Report on Internal Displacement* (Internal Displacement Monitoring Centre: Geneva).

Ingold, Tim. (1993). 'The temporality of the landscape', *World Archaeology*, 25(2): 152–74.

James, Wendy. (1997). 'The names of fear: memory, history, and the ethnography of feeling among Uduk refugees', *The Journal of the Royal Anthropological Institute*, 3(1): 115–31.

Jansen, Stef. (2009). 'Troubled locations: return, the life course and transformations of home in Bosnia-Herzegovina' in Stef Jansen and Staffan Löfving (eds), *Struggles for Home: Violence, Hope and the Movement of People* (Berghahn: Oxford).

Jansen, Stef and Staffan Löfving. (2009). 'Introduction: towards an anthropology of violence, hope and the movement of people' in Stef Jansen and Staffan Löfving (eds), *Struggles for Home: Violence, Hope and the Movement of People* (Berghahn: Oxford).

Jaramillo, Ana María, Marta Inés Villa and Luz Amparo Sánchez. (2004). Miedo y desplazamiento: experiencias y percepciones (Corporación Región: Medellín).

Jean, Melissa. (2015). 'The role of farming in place-making processes of resettled refugees', *Refugee Survey Quarterly*, 34(3): 46–69.

Jones, Owain. (2011). 'Geography, memory and non-representational geographies', *Geography Compass*, 5(12): 875–85.

Joseph, Miranda. (2002). *Against the Romance of Community* (University of Minnesota Press: Minneapolis).

Kelly, Tobias. (2009). 'Returning to Palestine: confinement and displacement under Israeli Occupation' in Stef Jansen and Staffan Löfving (eds), *Struggles for Home. Violence, Hope and the Movement of People* (Berghahn: Oxford).

Kriesberg, Louis. (2001). 'Changing forms of coexistence' in Mohammed Abu-Nimer (ed.), *Reconciliation, Justice, and Coexistence: Theory and Practice* (Lexington: Oxford).

Lambek, Michael and Paul Antze. (1996). 'Introduction: forecasting memory' in Paul Antze and Michael Lambek (eds), *Tense Past: Cultural Essays in Trauma and Memory* (Routledge: New York).

Lammers, Ellen. (2007). 'Researching refugees: preoccupations with power and questions of giving', *Refugee Survey Quarterly*, 26(3): 72–81.

Lechner, Norbert. (1992). 'Some people die of fear: Fear as a political problem' in Juan Corradi, Patricia Weiss Fagen and Manuel Antonio Garretón (eds), *Fear at the Edge: State*

Terror and Resistance in Latin America (University of California Press: Berkeley, CA/ Oxford).

LeGrand, Catherine. (1988). *Colonización y protesta campesina* (Universidad Nacional de Colombia: Bogotá).

Lewicka, Maria. (2010). 'What makes neighborhood different from home and city? Effects of place scale on place attachment', *Journal of Environmental Psychology*, 30(1): 35–51.

——. (2011). 'Place attachment: how far have we come in the last 40 years?', *Journal of Environmental Psychology*, 31(3): 207–30.

Lewicki, Roy. (2006). 'Trust, trust development, and trust repair' in Morton Deutsch, Peter Coleman and Eric Marcus (eds), *The Handbook of Conflict Resolution. Theory and Practice: Second Edition* (Jossey-Bass: San Francisco).

Lewicki, Roy and Barbara Bunker. (1996). 'Developing and maintaining trust in work relationships' in Roderick M. Kramer and Tom R. Tyler (eds), *Trust in Organizations: Frontiers of Theory and Research* (Sage: London).

Lewicki, Roy, Daniel McAllister and Robert Bies (1998). 'Trust and distrust: new relationships and realities', *Academy of Management Review*, 23(3): 438–58.

Loizos, Peter. (1999). 'Ottoman half-lives: long-term perspectives on particular forced migrations', *Journal of Refugee Studies*, 12(3): 237–63.

——. (2002). 'Misconceiving refugees?' in Renos K. Papadopoulos (ed.), *Therapeutic Care for Refugees: No Place like Home* (Karnac: London).

Low, Setha M. (1992). 'Symbolic ties that bind' in Irwin Altman and Setha M. Low (eds), *Place Attachment* (Plenum: New York).

Low, Setha M. and Irwin Altman. (1992). 'Place attachment: a conceptual inquiry' in Irwin Altman and Setha M. Low (eds), *Place Attachment* (Plenum: New York).

Lowenthal, David. (1989). 'Nostalgia tells it like it wasn't' in Christopher Shaw and Malcom Chase (eds), *The Imagined Past: History and Nostalgia* (Manchester University Press: Manchester).

Lubkemann, Stephen. (2008). *Culture in Chaos. An Anthropology of the Social Condition of War* (The University of Chicago Press: Chicago/London).

Machado, Absalón. (1998). *La cuestión agraria en Colombia a fines de milenio* (El Ancora Editores: Bogotá).

——. (2004). 'Tenencia de la tierra, problema agrario y conflicto' in, *Desplazamiento forzado: dinámicas de guerra, exclusión y desarraigo* (Universidad Nacional: Bogotá).

Madaleno, Isabel Maria. (2010). 'How do southern hemisphere residents perceive the world? Mental maps drawn by East Timorese and Mozambican islanders', *Scottish Geographical Journal*, 126(2): 112–36.

Magolda, Peter M. (2000). 'Accessing, waiting, plunging in, wondering, and writing: retrospective sense-making of fieldwork', *Field Methods*, 12(3): 209–34.

Mainwaring, Ċetta and Noelle Brigden. (2016). 'Beyond the border: clandestine migration journeys', *Geopolitics*, 21(2): 243–62.

Malkki, Liisa (1995). *Purity and Exile: Violence, Memory, and National Cosmology among Hutu Refugees in Tanzania* (University of Chicago Press: Chicago; London).

Massey, Doreen. (1993). 'Power-geometry and a progressive sense of place' in Jon Bird, Barry Curtis, Tim Putnam and Lisa Tickner (eds), *Mapping the Futures: Local Cultures, Global Change* (Routledge: London).

——. (2005). *For Space* (Sage: London).

May, Venessa. (2013). *Connecting Self to Society: Belonging in a Changing World* (Palgrave Macmillan: Basingstoke).

──. (2017). 'Belonging from afar: nostalgia, time and memory', *The Sociological Review*, 65(2): 401–15.

Mayer, Roger, James Davis and David Schoorman. (1995). 'An integrative model of organizational trust', *The Academy of Management Review*, 20(3): 709–34.

Mazurana, Dyan, Lacey Andrews Gale and Karen Jacobsen. (2013). 'A view from below' in Dyan Mazurana, Karen Jacobsen and Lacey Andrews Gale (eds), *Research Methods in Conflict Settings* (Cambridge University Press: New York).

McMillan, David W. and David M. Chavis. (1986). 'Sense of community: a definition and theory', *Journal of Community Psychology*, 14(1): 6–23.

Meertens, Donny. (2010). 'Forced displacement and women's security in Colombia', *Disasters*, 34(2): 147–64.

Melucci, Alberto. (1995). 'The process of collective identity' in Hank Johnston and Bert Klandermans (eds), *Social Movements and Culture* (University of Minnesota Press: Minneapolis).

Mendoza Piñeros, Andrés Mauricio. (2012). 'El desplazamiento forzado en Colombia y la intervención del estado', *Revista de Economía Institucional*, 14(26): 169–202.

Merton, Robert K. (1940). 'Bureaucratic structure and personality', *Social Forces*, 18(4): 560–68.

Miller, Kenneth E. (2004). 'Beyond the frontstage: trust, access, and the relational context in research with refugee communities', *American Journal of Community Psychology*, 33(3/4): 217–27.

Misztal, Barbara. (2003). *Theories of Social Remembering* (Open University Press: Maidenhead).

Montoya Arango, Vladimir, Andrés García Sánchez and César Andrés Ospina Mesa. (2014). 'Andar dibujando y dibujar andando: cartografía social y producción colectiva de conocimientos', *Nómadas*, 40(Abril): 191–205.

Navarro, Marta. (2008). 'Discriminación racial, procesos de exclusión y desigualdad en las mujeres afrocolombianas: reflexiones a partir de un estudio de caso en la ciudad de Buenaventura' in Liliana Suárez, Emma Martín and Rosalba Hernández (eds), *Feminismos en la antropología: nuevas propuestas críticas*. Serie, XI Congreso de Antropología de la FAAEE (Ankulegi antropologia elkartea: San Sebastián).

Nesheim, Ingrid, Shivcharn S. Dhillion and Kristi Anne Stølen. (2006). 'What happens to traditional knowledge and use of natural resources when people migrate?', *Human Ecology*, 34(1): 99–131.

Nordstrom, Carolyn. (1995). 'War on the front lines' in Carolyn Nordstrom and Antonius C.G.M. Robben (eds), *Fieldwork Under Fire. Contemporary Studies of Violence and Survival* (University of California Press: Berkeley, CA).

Ortiz Sarmiento, Carlos Miguel. (2007). *Urabá: pulsiones de vida y desafíos de muerte* (La Carreta Social: Medellín).

Oslender, Ulrich. (2007). 'Violence in development: the logic of forced displacement on Colombia's Pacific coast', *Development in Practice*, 17(6): 752–63.

──. (2008). 'Another history of violence: the production of "geographies of terror" in Colombia's Pacific coast region', *Latin American Perspectives*, 35(5): 77–102.

──. (2016a). 'The banality of displacement: discourse and thoughtlessness in the internal refugee crisis in Colombia', *Political Geography*, 50(A1–A2): 10–19.

──. (2016b). *The Geographies of Social Movements: Afro-Colombian Mobilization and the Aquatic Space* (Duke University Press: Durham).

Osorio Perez, Flor Edilma. (2000). 'Viejas y nuevas ruralidades a partir de la migraciones internas. Algunas reflexiones desde la realidad colombiana.' in *Una nueva ruralidad en América Latina: Pontificia Universidad Javeriana. Seminario Internacional* (Bogotá: CLASCO).

———. (2009). *Territorialidades en suspenso: Desplazamiento forzado, identidades y resistencias* (Codhes, Antropos Ltda: Bogotá).

Palacios, Marco. (2006). *Between Legitimacy and Violence: A History of Colombia, 1875–2002* (Duke University Press: Durham, NC).

Papadopoulos, Renos. (2002). 'Introduction' in Renos Papadopoulos (ed.), *Therapeutic Care for Refugees: No Place like Home* (H. Karnac: London).

Pearce, Jenny. (1990). *Colombia. Inside the Labyrinth* (Latin America Bureau Limited: London).

Pécaut, Daniel. (2001). *Guerra contra la sociedad.* (Espasa: Bogotá).

Poland, Blake and Ann Pederson. (1998). 'Reading between the lines: interpreting silences in qualitative research', *Qualitative Inquiry*, 4(2): 293–312.

Raymond, Christopher M., Gregory Brown and Delene Weber. (2010). 'The measurement of place attachment: personal, community, and environmental connections', *Journal of Environmental Psychology*, 30(4): 422–34.

Relph, Edward. (1976). *Place and Placelessness* (Pion: London).

Revill, George. (1993). 'Reading *Rosehill*: community, identity and inner-city Derby' in Michael Keith and Steve Pile (eds), *Place and the Politics of Identity* (Routledge: London).

Riaño-Alcalá, Pilar. (2008). 'Journeys and landscapes of forced migration: memorializing fear among refugees and internally displaced Colombians', *Social Anthropology*, 16(1): 1–18.

Riley, Mark and David Harvey. (2007). 'Oral histories, farm practice and uncovering meaning in the countryside', *Social & Cultural Geography*, 8(3): 391–415.

Robben, Antonius C.G.M. (2014). 'Governing the disappeared-living and the disappeared-dead: the violent pursuit of cultural sovereignty during authoritarian rule in Argentina' in Finn Stepputat (ed.), *Governing the Dead. Sovereignty and the Politics of Dead Bodies* (Manchester University Press: Manchester).

Rodman, C. Margaret. (1992). 'Empowering place: multilocality and multivocality', *American Anthropologist*, 94(3): 640–56.

Roldán, Mary. (1998). 'Violencia, colonización y la geografía de la diferencia cultural en Colombia', *Análisis Político*, 35(Sep–Dec): 3–22.

———. (2002). *Blood and Fire: La Violencia in Antioquia, Colombia, 1946–1953* (Duke University Press: Durham, London).

Rose, Mitch. (2002). 'Landscapes and labyrinths', *Geoforum*, 33(4): 455–67.

Routledge, Paul. (1993). *Terrains of Resistance. Nonviolent Social Movements and the Contestation of Place in India* (Praeger: London).

Rowles, Graham D. (1983). 'Place and personal identity in old age: observations from Appalachia', *Journal of Environmental Psychology*, 3: 299–313.

Royce, Josiah. (1968). *The Problem of Christianity* (University of Chicago Press: Chicago, IL).

Ruiz, Nubia Yaneth, A. Gonzaléz Pulido, María Aysa and John Jairo Roldán. (2006). *Desplazamiento, movilidad y retorno en Colombia. Dinámicas migratorias recientes* (Universidad Externado de Colombia: Bogotá).

Salazar, Boris, María del Pilar Castillo and Federico Pinzón. (2008). *¿A dónde ir? Un análisis sobre el desplazamiento forzado* (Universidad del Valle: Cali).

Salimovich, Sofia, Elizabeth Lira and Eugenia Weinstein. (1992). 'Victims of fear: the social psychology of repression' in Juan Corradi, Patricia Weiss Fagen and Manuel Antonio Garretón (eds), *Fear at the Edge. State Terror and Resistance in Latin America* (University of California Press: Berkeley, CA/Oxford).

Sánchez, G. Gonzalo and Donny Meertens. (2001). *Bandits, Peasants, and Politics: The Case of 'La Violencia' in Colombia* (University of Texas Press: Austin).

Savage, Mike, Gaynor Bagnall and Brian Longhurst. (2005). *Globalization and Belonging: The Suburbanization of Identity* (Sage: London).

Schein, Richard. (2009). 'Belonging through land/scape', *Environment and Planning A*, 41(4): 811–26.

Schröder, Ingo and Bettina Schmidt. (2001). 'Introduction: violent imaginaries and violent practices' in Bettina Schmidt and Ingo Schröder (eds), *Anthropology of Violence and Conflict* (Routledge: London/New York).

Schütz, Alfred. (1944). 'The stranger: an essay in social psychology', *Journal of American Sociology*, 49(6): 499–507.

Scott, Joan. (1988). *Gender and the Politics of History* (Columbia University Press: New York).

Semana. (2013a). 'Restitución de tierras: Se abrió la caja de Pandora', *Semana*, 3 April 2013.

———. (2013b). 'Restitución: el nuevo conflicto', *Semana*, 23 February 2013.

Sletto, Bjørn Ingmunn. (2009). ' "We drew what we imagined." Participatory mapping, performance, and the arts of landscape making', *Current Anthropology*, 50(4): 443–76.

Smiley, Sarah L. (2013). 'Mental maps, segregation, and everyday life in Dar es Salaam, Tanzania', *Journal of Cultural Geography*, 30(2): 215–44.

Sørensen, Birgitte Refslund. (1997). 'The experience of displacement: reconstructing places and identities in Sri Lanka' in Karen Fog Olwig and Kirsten Hastrup (eds), *Siting Culture: The Shifting Anthropological Object* (Routledge: London).

Springwood, Charles Fruehling and Richard King. (2001). 'Unsettling engagements: on the ends of rapport in critical ethnography', *Qualitative Inquiry*, 7(4): 403–17.

Starr, Paul. (1992). 'Social categories and claims in the liberal state', *Social Research*, 59(2): 263–95.

Stefansson, Anders. (2004). 'Refugee returns to Sarajevo and their challenge to contemporary narratives of mobility' in Lynellyn D. Long and Ellen Oxfeld (eds), *Coming Home? Refugees, Migrants, and Those Who Stayed Behind* (University of Pennsylvania Press: Philadelphia).

Steiner, Claudia. (1994). 'Héroes y banano en el golfo de Urabá: la construcción de una frontera conflictiva' in Silva Renán (ed.), *Territorios, regiones, sociedades* (Universidad del Valle; Cerec: Bogotá).

Suárez, Andrés Fernando. (2007). *Identidades políticas y exterminio recíproco. Masacres y guerra en Urabá 1991-2001* (La Carreta Editores; Instituto de Estudios Políticos Internacionales IEPRI: Medellín).

Tilley, Christopher. (1994). *A Phenomenology of Landscape: Places, Paths, and Monuments* (Berg: Oxford).

Tilly, Charles. (1998). *Durable Inequalities* (University of California Press: Berkeley, CA).

Todd, Molly. (2010). *Beyond Displacement: Campesinos, Refugees, and Collective Action in the Salvadoran Civil War* (Wisconsin Press: Madison, WI).

Tuan, Yi-Fu. (1977). *Space and Place: The Perspectives of Experience* (University of Minnesota Press: Minneapolis; London).

Turner, Bryan. (1987). 'A note on nostalgia', *Theory, Culture & Society*, 4(1): 147–56.

Turton, David. (2005). 'The meaning of place in a world of movement: lessons from long-term field research in Southern Ethiopia', *Journal of Refugee Studies*, 18(3): 258–80.

UNHCR. (2009). Violencia de género y mujeres desplazadas (UNHCR: Bogotá).

Uribe, María Teresa. (1992). *Urabá: ¿región o territorio?* (Corpourabá y Universidad de Antioquia: Medellín).

Valis, Noël. (2010). 'Nostalgia and exile', *Journal of Spanish Cultural Studies*, 1(2):117–33.

van Dijk, Teun A. (1998). *Ideology: A Multidisciplinary Approach* (Sage: London).

Vélez Torres, Irene, Sandra Rátiva Gaona and Daniel Varela Corredor. (2012). 'Cartografía social como metodología participativa y colaborativa de investigación en el territorio afrodescendiente de la cuenca alta del río Cauca', *Cuadernos de geografía: revista colombiana de geografía*, 21(2): 59–73.

Vidal López, Roberto Carlos, Clara Inés Atehortúa Arredondo and Jorge Salcedo. (2011). Efectos del desplazamiento interno en las comunidades de las zonas de recepción. Estudio de caso en Bogotá, DC Colombia, en las localidades de Suba y Ciudad Bolívar (Brookings Institution-London School of Economics: Bogotá).

Viveros, Mara. (2000). 'Dionisios negros: sexualidad, corporalidad y orden racial en Colombia' in Maria Bernardo Figueroa, Pío Eduardo San Miguel and Olga Restrepo (eds), *¿Mestizo yo?* (Universidad Nacional de Colombia: Bogotá).

Wade, Peter. (1995). *Blackness and Race Mixture: The Dynamics of Racial Identity in Colombia* (Johns Hopkins University Press: Baltimore).

———. (1997). *Race and Ethnicity in Latin America* (Pluto: London).

Walker, Margaret Urban. (2009). 'Gender and violence in focus: a background for gender justice in reparations' in Ruth Rubio-Marin (ed.), *The Gender of Reparations: Unsettling Sexual Hierarchies while Redressing Human Rights Violations* (Cambridge University Press: Cambridge).

Weiss Fagen, Patricia, Amelia Fernandez Juan, Finn Stepputat and Roberto Vidal López. (2003). *Internal Displacement in Colombia: National and International Responses* (Institute for International Studies: Copenhagen).

Williams, Raymond. (1976). *Keywords: A Vocabulary of Culture and Society* (Oxford University Press: New York).

Winter, Jay. (2010). 'Thinking about silence' in Efrat Ben-Ze'ev, Ruth Ginio and Jay Winter (eds), *Shadows of War: A Social History of Silence in the Twentieth Century* (Cambridge University Press: Cambridge).

Young, Iris Marion. (1995). 'Gender as seriality: thinking about women as a social collective' in Linda Nicholson and Steven Seidman (eds), *Social Postmodernism: Beyond Identity Politics* (Cambridge University Press: Cambridge).

Yuval-Davis, Nira. (2006). 'Intersectionality and feminist politics', *European Journal of Women's Studies*, 13(3): 193–210.

Zambrano, Fabio. (2001). 'El poblamiento y los límites internos de la nación' in Martha Segura Naranjo (ed.), *Éxodo, patrimonio e identidad* (Ministerio de Cultura: Bogotá).

Zetter, Roger. (1991). 'Labelling refugees: forming and transforming a bureaucratic identity', *Journal of Refugee Studies*, 4(1): 39–62.

———. (2011). 'Unlocking the protracted displacement of refugees and internally displaced persons: an overview', *Refugee Study Quarterly*, 30(4): 1–13.

Index

Note: 'n.' after a page reference indicates the number of a note on that page